AN ILLUSTRATED HISTORY OF THE

RAF

AN ILLUSTRATED HISTORY OF THE
RAF

Roy Conyers Nesbit

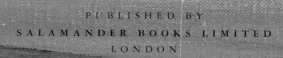

PUBLISHED BY
SALAMANDER BOOKS LIMITED
LONDON

Author's Acknowledgements

The photographs, captions and text of this book are the product of a considerable amount of detailed research, and I am extremely grateful for the assistance given to me by officials and staff of the following organisations:

Aeroplane Monthly, Cheam
Imperial War Museum, London
Ministry of Defence, Air Historical Branch, London
Royal Air Force Museum, Hendon
Public Record Office, Kew

I am also indebted to the following for supplying photographs:

Flight Officer Felicity Ashbee, WAAF; Aviation Bookshop;
Aeroplane Monthly; Ministry of Defence, Air Historical
Branch; Jeremy Flack, Aviation Photographs International;
Royal Air Force Museum, Hendon;
The late Wg Cdr Frederic E. Burton OBE, DFC, RAF;
Mr T. Malcolm English; The Keystone Collection;
Flt Lt Maurice A. Pocock, RAFVR;
The late Flt Lt Antony M. Puckle, MBE, RAFVR;
Flt Lt Ken Reeves, RAF; Herr Hans Schliephake;
The late Wg Cdr Arthur H. Simmonds, DFC, RAF;
Vintage Magazine Co., London.

My thanks are also due, for help in research and in checking captions or narrative, to:

Sqn Ldr Dudley Cowderoy, RAFVR;
Sqn Ldr Norman Hearn-Phillips, AFC, DFM, RAF;
Capt Clive Leach, RAFVR; Mr Harry M Moyle, RAFVR;
Mr Philip N Owen, RAF; Mr Roger Hayward

Designed by
Stonecastle Graphics Ltd.

Paintings by
Frank Wootton P.P.G.Av.A.

Editorial
Gill Waugh and Jane Adams

Commissioning Editor
Andrew Preston

Commissioning Assistant
Laura Potts

Production
Ruth Arthur, David Proffit,
Sally Connolly and Karen Staff

Director of Production
Gerald Hughes

A SALAMANDER BOOK
Published by Salamander Books Ltd.,
8 Blenheim Court,
Brewery Road,
London N7 9NT,
United Kingdom

© Salamander Books Ltd., 2002

A member of the Chrysalis Group plc

ISBN 1 84065 285 3

CONTENTS

FOREWORD

At the beginning of September, 1940, I joined 616 (South Yorkshire) Squadron at Coltishall in Norfolk. They had just arrived from Kenley, near Croydon, and in eight days had lost five pilots, killed or missing, with five others wounded and in hospital, and had been 'taken out of the line' to regain their strength. These were bad times for the Squadron, Fighter Command, and England, because the Germans, having conquered Europe in six weeks with *Blitzkrieg*, their new and terrifying style of air-ground warfare, were using the same strategy against these Islands – their intention being to take out Fighter Command and gain air superiority so that their *panzers* could cross the Channel unopposed; and during those fine autumn days they nearly succeeded because we were losing one hundred and twenty five experienced pilots each week who could only be replaced by sixty-five inexperienced pilots like me.

One would have thought, therefore, that with Fighter Command wasting away morale might have been a little shaken. On the contrary, it was superb, and this was well-illustrated to me when one evening all off duty ranks were recalled to the airfield.

Once there, we found Alert No 1, 'invasion imminent and probable within twelve hours', had been declared and our defences were to be brought to the highest state of readiness. The officer's mess was crowded, confused and noisy – that is until Squadron Leader Douglas Bader stumped in and demanded to know what all the flap was about. On being told, he said: 'So the bastards are coming. Bloody good show! Think of all those juicy targets on those nice flat beaches. What shooting!' And he made a rude sound with his lips which was meant to resemble a ripple of machine-gun fire. This was my first encounter with the already legendary Douglas Bader. His spirited and spontaneous riposte serves as a good example of how high morale was, even though the odds were stacked against us.

This book has been written in an easily accessible and informative style which charts the development of the Royal Air Force from the days of experimental balloons and kites, to the modern sophistication of today's advanced technology. It is superbly illustrated with photographs, diagrams and posters, many previously unpublished. These factors combine to produce what I consider to be a vivid and fascinating portrait of the Royal Air Force, surely a fitting tribute to the men and women with whom I served, and to those who today maintain its traditions of enthusiasm, high spirits and comradeship.

Johnnie Johnson.

AIR VICE-MARSHAL J. E. JOHNSON, CB, CBE, DSO, DFC, DL

CHAPTER 1

WAITING FOR WINGS

Below: *The British Army Dirigible No. 1 was named* Nulli Secundus *('Second to None') and first ascended from Farnborough on 10 September 1907. It had a length of 122 feet, a diameter of 26 feet, and a capacity of 50,000 cubic feet. The engine was French, a 50 h.p. Antoinette. The airship made only one long-distance flight in its original form, from Farnborough to London and then to Crystal Palace on 5 October 1907. It was destroyed in a storm five days later.*
Source: RAF Museum 331113

"What is the use of a balloon?" was a question put to Benjamin Franklin, when he was American plenipotentiary to France in the early 1780s. "What is the use of a new-born infant?" replied the great statesman and scientist.

For centuries, scientists and philosophers had been obsessed with the flapping of birds' wings as a means of ascending into the air but, since this method had proved disastrous for man, the balloon offered an alternative. When the first manned and free flight was made, in a hot-air balloon in Paris on 21 November 1783, the military possibilities became apparent to many observers. In 1785, a successful crossing of the Channel was made in a hydrogen balloon and in the same year two British officers travelled about twenty miles from London and landed unharmed in Essex.

The first balloon corps was formed in France in 1793, and was subsequently employed on military operations. In the early nineteenth century the British scientist Sir George Cayley set out the aerodynamic principles for heavier-than-air machines, using gliders for experiments. But in the absence of a compact means of propulsion in that period, developments continued to be concentrated on balloons. Captive observation balloons were used in the American Civil War of 1861-5, and free-flying balloons were used in the siege of Paris in 1870. In the British army, balloon sections accompanied expeditions to Bechuanaland in 1884 and to the Sudan in 1885. A permanent balloon section was formed within the Corps of Royal Engineers in 1890. This carried out reconnaissance duties during the South African War ten years later, to the fury of the Boers, who looked on such technical superiority as unfair.

After the South African War, the activities of the Balloon Factory, which had been opened at Farnborough in Hampshire in 1894, were scaled down. Meanwhile, experiments in France had resulted in the development of an electrically propelled airship in 1884. This was non-rigid, but semi-rigid airships followed in that country. In Germany, it was Graf von Zeppelin who developed the fully rigid and steerable airship powered by internal combustion engines. By 1909, Zeppelins had become established as passenger carriers and were also used in military and naval exercises.

In an attempt to keep up with the pace of developments abroad, technicians at Farnborough completed in September 1907 the army airship *Nulli Secundus,* constructed from a balloon covered with a net from which was suspended a gondola. Powered by a 40-h.p. engine, it flew on 5 October on a journey of three and a half hours to London and then landed at Crystal Palace. The flight caused much excitement, particularly since the Kaiser was staying in Buckingham Palace as a guest of King Edward VII.

In Britain, non-rigid and therefore collapsible airships were termed B-limps, giving rise to the somewhat derogatory name which then entered the English language. *Nulli Secundus* was followed by the semi-rigid *Nulli Secundus II,* and then by *Beta* and *Gamma.* Although these British airships suffered from engine troubles, they were responsible for the formation of a nucleus of aircrews and ground crews. Two more airships were ordered, a non-rigid and a semi-rigid, both from France.

However, events were taking place which overshadowed the development of airships. On 17 December 1903, near Kitty Hawk beach in North Carolina, the brothers Wilbur and Orville Wright made a powered flight in their biplane *Flyer*, after seven years of research and development. Strangely, this success met at first with indifference in the U.S., where the government dismissed the brothers as charlatans. The Wright brothers continued experimenting and offered their patents and machines to the British, but these were refused by the War Office in 1906 and by the Admiralty in 1907. A French syndicate, far less sceptical, thereupon purchased the inventions and, with the active assistance of Wilbur Wright, took the lead in aeronautical progress. In Britain, development was left to the private enterprise of such pioneers as Robert Blackburn, F. Handley Page, A.V. Roe, Horace and Oswald Short, and T.O.M. Sopwith. Military aeronautical expenditure by the British government amounted to no more than £13,750. Then, on 25 July 1909, Louis Blériot took off in his monoplane from Les Boraques near Calais and, thirty-seven minutes later, landed on a hilltop near Dover. The significance of this flight was not lost on the British government and its military authorities. At the same time, the Press also created public interest in flying.

The military airfield of Larkhill in Wiltshire was opened, while Hendon became the civilian airfield for London. In March 1910, the Royal Aero Club issued its first pilot's certificate. In April of the following year, the War Office formed an Air Battalion at Farnborough, consisting of two companies. No. 1 for balloons, kites and airships, and

Above: *The first Zeppelin, LZ-1 (Luftschiff Zeppelin Nummer 1), was assembled in a floating hangar on the Bodensee (Lake Constance) and launched on 2 July 1900.*

Source: Air Historical Branch (RAF), MoD, private collection no PRM3478

No. 2 for aeroplanes. Based largely on French designs and adapted French machines, four categories of aircraft were designated. These were the S.E. (Santos Experimental, after Santos-Dumont, the first man to fly an aeroplane in France), the B.E. (Blériot Experimental), the F.E. (Farman Experimental, after the brothers Henri and Maurice Farman), and the R.E. (Reconnaissance Experimental).

Britain still lagged well behind France. In 1911, over 200 aircraft could be seen during army manoeuvres in France, whereas the British army and navy could muster only twelve, with three airships. It was also known that Germany possessed a fleet of thirty Zeppelins. Public alarm at this state of affairs led to a consideration within the Committee of Imperial Defence, which recommended the setting up of a new service to be known as the Flying Corps, with a military wing and a naval wing, as well as a central flying school. King George V, who had succeeded King Edward VII, granted the royal warrant for the Royal Flying Corps, which came into being on 13 April 1912. A flying badge and the motto *Per Ardua ad Astra* were also approved. The factory at Farnborough became the Royal Aircraft Factory. Fortunately, Britain possessed the technical expertise and industrial strength to begin catching up with her continental rivals, following these far-seeing arrangements.

The Admiralty was determined that no independent service should have control over affairs which it considered were within its authority, and the naval wing began to operate separately from the military wing. The Central Flying School at Upavon in Wiltshire began training military crews, while the naval wing opened a school at Eastchurch in Kent. On 1 July 1914, the Royal Naval Air Service was formed, and the Royal Flying Corps continued solely as an army air force.

Flying training in the RFC took place in Farman, Avro, B.E.2 and B.E.8 biplanes, with engines ranging from 50-h.p. to 80-h.p. All the engines were French. Trainees were recruited from all branches of the army, not solely from the Royal Engineers. Aerobatics were forbidden, and a pilot usually logged about twenty-five hours before being awarded his wings.

At Farnborough, the Royal Aircraft Factory opted for stability in aircraft as its main criterion. In this period, it was envisaged that the primary military role of the aeroplane would be an extension of that of the balloon, observation of enemy dispositions and artillery spotting. Early monoplanes proved difficult to fly and crashed more frequently than biplanes, although they were faster and sometimes more agile. Thus development was concentrated on biplanes, resulting in serious disadvantages to the RFC within the next few years. The engines in these biplanes were usually of the pusher variety, and the observer sat in the nose, from where he had an excellent view. The pilot sat behind the observer and behind him was the engine. Fewer early experiments were made with tractor engines in aircraft. Little consideration was given to armament or to bombing enemy troops.

Above: *The army airship HMA Beta, 84 feet long and powered by a single 25 h.p. engine, made her first experimental flights in June 1908. In a reconstructed form with a 33 h.p. engine, she flew from Farnborough to London and back on 3 June 1910. Subsequently, she took part in army manoeuvres and became part of the RFC's Military Wing. This photograph was taken in 1914.*

Source: Air Historical Branch (RAF), MoD, private collection.

Left: *HMA Delta entered service with No. 1 (Airship) Squadron of the RFC in November 1912, joining the other two airships Beta and Gamma. The airships of the RFC were turned over to the RNAS when it was formed on 1 July 1914.*

Source: Air Historical Branch (RAF), MoD, private collection 176/5/45

The naval wing, or RNAS, did not look solely to the Royal Aircraft Factory for its aircraft. It turned instead of private industry, with the result in the early years that its aircraft were often superior to those of the RFC. Its policy tended towards aggression, in addition to employing aircraft for observation. Experiments took place with flying aircraft off ships, developing seaplanes, dropping 100-lb bombs and even torpedoes. It also set up a string of ten air bases around the British coasts, for one of the traditional roles of the Royal Navy was the defence of the British Isles.

On 1 September 1913, a separate Directorate of Military Aeronautics was established under Brigadier-General David Henderson, reporting directly to the Secretary of State instead of the War Office. The following year, £1,000,000 was allocated to the RFC, enabling orders to be placed throughout the infant aircraft industry and not solely with the Royal Aircraft Factory. By then, six RFC squadrons had been formed or were coming into being. With the approach of war, privately owned aircraft were requisitioned and lodged in the aircraft park at Farnborough, which was a maintenance and supply depot.

Seven days after the declaration of war on 4 August 1914, four squadrons of the RFC, with a collection of sixty-three aircraft which included Blériots, B.E.2s, B.E.8s, Farmans, Sopwith Tabloids and Avro 504s were either flown to France or taken by sea. Brigadier-General Henderson accompanied them as their commander. The RNAS, which mustered seventy-one aircraft and seven airships, set up a small wing at Dunkirk and also began patrolling the North Sea from British bases. These two air forces were not fully prepared for war, but they did not lack fighting spirit or enterprise.

Above: *The RFC's observation balloons were operated from winches, principally to direct artillery fire. Guide ropes were paid out as the balloon ascended.*

Air Historical Branch (RAF), MoD, private collection no 94

Above: *This tractor monoplane was a Blériot XI, similar to the machine in which Louis Blériot crossed the Channel on 25 July 1909, but fitted with a more powerful Gnome rotary engine instead of the original Anzani 35 h.p. The RFC first received deliveries of these machines in 1912. In the early months of the war, the Blériot XI was one of the most widely used reconnaissance aircraft. It was unarmed, apart from rifles and revolvers carried by the pilot. The photograph of this machine, painted with the RFC's roundels, was taken after the outbreak of the First World War.*

Source: RAF Museum P742

Left: *The Voisin pusher biplane first appeared early in 1914 and was ordered for the RFC and the RNAS. Although intended solely for reconnaissance, later versions were fitted with a machine gun in the observer's position and were also used for daylight bombing. It was from one of these machines that the first enemy aircraft was shot down from the air, by a French crew of the* Aviation Militaire *on 5 October 1914.*
Source: RAF Museum PO17685

Above: *The Royal Aircraft Factory R.E.5 was the first 'reconnaissance experimental' aircraft put into production for the RFC and RNAS. It was a large two-seater, unarmed and built for stability. Several of these machines were sent to France with the RFC soon after the outbreak of war, but their career was short-lived.*
Source: Air Historical Branch (MoD), Ref: H.429

Below: *The Royal Aircraft Factory B.E.2 was first delivered to the RFC in February 1913. It was a two-seater general-purpose aircraft, with the pilot in the rear cockpit. There was no defensive armament but it could carry up to 100lb of bombs. The type became obsolete by 1915. This photograph of B.E.2 serial 272, 3 Squadron, was taken at Larkhill in Wiltshire in 1913.*
Source: Air Historical Branch (RAF), MoD, H.1903

Above: *Pilots of B Flight, 3 Squadron, at Larkhill in Wiltshire in 1913. Their names were recorded as, from left to right, Carroll, Turner, Martin, Dibble, Newby, Aylen and Webb.*

Source: Air Historical Branch (RAF), MoD, H.1902

Right: *Three RFC squadrons were equipped with the Royal Aircraft Factory B.E.2 before the outbreak of the First World War. B.E. stood for 'Blériot Experimental', indicating a two-seat tractor biplane. It was unarmed, one of the main objectives being to design a general-purpose aircraft with very stable characteristics, primarily for reconnaissance and bombing. This photograph is of a B.E.2b, which had redesigned cockpits with better controls, produced in the early years of the war.*

Source: Air Historical Branch (RAF), MoD, 2884

Above: *The Royal Aircraft Factory B.E.2c was built for stability in the early summer of 1914, in the belief that the main use of aircraft would be reconnaissance. Although a safe aircraft to fly, it was slow and unmanoeuvrable and with a ceiling of only 10,000 feet. A few arrived in France late in the same year and in all about 1,300 were built. It was outclassed by the new Fokker monoplanes in 1915, when it earned the unhappy name of 'Fokker fodder'. After withdrawal from the Western Front, however, it did achieve some success as a night-fighter and as a trainer, remaining in service for the remainder of the war.*

Source: Air Historical Branch (MoD), Ref: H.1803

Above: *The Sopwith Tabloid was originally designed in 1913 as a two-seat biplane but during April 1914 a single-seat version was produced for the RFC and the RNAS. It was not fitted with armament when the First World War broke out, being used for scouting over the Western Front and from HMS Ark* Royal, *although it was later equipped with a Lewis gun and even carried a small bomb load. Tabloids also served in the Dardanelles, but the type was withdrawn in 1915. This photograph of serial 1207 of the RNAS was taken at Great Yarmouth.*

Source: RAF Museum P5092

CHAPTER 2

THE FIRST WAR IN THE AIR

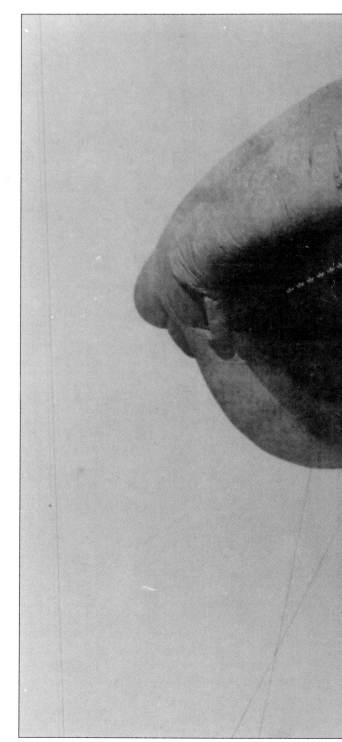

When the first motley squadrons of the RFC arrived at the Western Front, on 13 August 1914, they were stationed at Mauberge, on the river Sambre near the Belgian border. As the war progressed, the soldiers of the British Expeditionary Force were somewhat surprised to find that a different breed of men had joined them. The RFC aircrews – the officers in particular – did not conform to the general pattern of men in the old-established army regiments. Most army officers in those days were of the same type, educated at public school before passing through Sandhurst or Woolwich. But the RFC newcomers came from all parts of the British Empire and all walks of life. They wore strange badges, talked about forms of warfare which were unfamiliar to regular regimental officers, and did not treat military traditions or customs with due reverence. They were young, high-spirited and full of initiative. Doubtless some regimental officers were sceptical about the value of these RFC men but early in the war, their worth became apparent.

In spite of coming under fire from British and French as well as German lines, reconnaissance aircraft of the RFC brought back accurate information of the attacking German forces in the retreat from Mons and the battle of the Marne. After the B.E.F. succeeded in repulsing these attacks, the Germans and the British dug in and the long and terrible years of trench warfare began. The contributions being made by British aircraft to the prosecution of the war were, however, recognized by the War Office. When in early 1915 it was proposed to increase the number of RFC squadrons to fifty, with corresponding increases for the RNAS, the Secretary of State for War, Lord Kitchener, ordered the numbers to be doubled.

The first RFC aircraft to be lost was an Avro 504, brought down over enemy lines on 22 August. However, it became evident at this stage that the main danger for the RFC came from "friendly" fire, resulting from the difficulty of the troops in identifying them. The Union Jack was painted on British aircraft, and then the red, white and blue roundel was designed as an easily visible symbol which remains on RAF aircraft to this day. Aerial combats were infrequent at this stage, since no regular armanent was carried. However, to guard against the possibility, aircrews armed themselves with service revolvers, rifles and duck guns, as well as grenades to drop on enemy troops. In twin-seater aircraft, it was usually the observer who fired the gun. On 25 August, an enemy aircraft was brought down but the German crew managed to escape.

Aerial photography assumed great importance and, when the fronts stabilized, it became necessary to make longer flights over enemy territory to reconnoitre trenches, supply routes and ammunition dumps. Simple box cameras were replaced by cameras in which the plates changed automatically. Wireless telegraphy also progressed rapidly, with a more compact and lighter set developed for the observer. Before long, most squadrons were equipped with a wireless flight. Hangars with wooden frames and canvas covers became standard equipment, to protect the flimsy aircraft from the worst vagaries of the weather.

The RNAS began its policy of aggression soon after the war began. On 8 October 1914, a Sopwith Tabloid based at Dunkirk flew to Düsseldorf and dropped two 20-lb bombs on a Zeppelin shed, destroying an army Zeppelin. In November, three Avro 504s, each carrying four 20-lb bombs, took off from Belfort in southern France and bombed the Zeppelin sheds at Lake Constance. No Zeppelins were destroyed but one Avro failed to return. The RNAS also carried out long and exhausting anti-submarine patrols from its bases. Before flying boats came into service in 1916, these were accomplished partly by seaplanes and partly by airships. Coastal SS (Sea Scout) airships were introduced in the spring of 1915, capable of staying in the air for about eighteen hours. These were followed by larger C (Coastal) airships late in the same year, with an endurance of about twenty-four hours. Some seaplanes were carried by warships, being lowered into the water when the seas were too rough. Seaplanes hunted for Zeppelins as well as U-boats, and sometimes encountered enemy seaplanes. The German aircraft were faster and more agile than the British, but RNAS seaplanes were well-armed and gave good accounts of themselves. In 1916 a few twin-engined Curtiss flying boats arrived from America, and proved to have far better performances than the RNAS machines. The design was adapted by the British at Felixstowe and gave rise to the highly successful 'F' series which continued for the next ten years.

In response to the need of the RNAS for longer ranges, the more powerful engines were allocated to this branch of the services. In December 1914, the RNAS issued a specification for a 'bloody paralyser of an aeroplane' capable of carrying a minimum of six 112-lb bombs at a speed not less than 75 m.p.h, for the purpose of bombing Germany.

Below left: *A German observation balloon, numbered 371 on the wicker basket, with an officer looking through field glasses.*
Source: Air Historical Branch (RAF), MoD, private collection PRM 2841

Below: *The smoke trail from an enemy observation balloon after being hit. Since there were no parachutes in the early years of the First World War, balloons filled with hydrogen could be unpleasant death traps.*
Source: Air Historical Branch (RAF), MoD, private collection 96

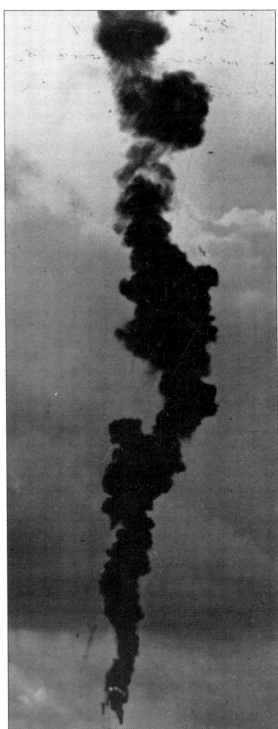

This entered service with the RNAS in France in November 1916 in the form of the Handley Page 0/100, and was followed by even heavier bombers.

One of the important arrivals on the Western Front was Lieutenant-Colonel Hugh Trenchard, who took over command of the RFC's First Wing in November 1914. Trenchard's army service had taken place mainly in Africa, but he had qualified as a pilot in 1912, when he was thirty-nine years old, by paying £75 for flying lessons at the Sopwith School at Brooklands. He had commanded the Military Wing at Farnborough after Sir David Henderson's departure for France, when he became responsible for the organization backing the expansion of the RFC for the next few months. Trenchard's progress was rapid, for when Henderson left to take up a new post in the War Office in August 1915, he was promoted to brigadier-general and given command of the RFC in France. He was the man who later became known as 'the father of the Royal Air Force'.

For the first year of the war, the RFC achieved some dominance over the Western Front. It expanded rapidly, although not as quickly as the armies it served. Squadrons were grouped into wings, and wings were formed into brigades, each supporting a British army and served by an aircraft park. Bombing attacks took place regularly over enemy territory, although only light loads were carried. Some pusher aircraft were fitted with a Lewis machine gun mounted in the front cockpit for the observer, while some scout (or fighter) tractor aircraft carried a similar gun fitted on the top plane, to be fired by the pilot over the propeller. But in June 1915 a new menace appeared in the form of the Fokker E Type monoplane, with a single Spandau machine gun synchronized to fire through the propeller arc.

It is sometimes believed that aerial combat in the First World War was a form of knightly combat, with the opposing aircraft roughly equal in armament and performance, differing mainly in the skill and determination of their pilots. Although this was partly true, a very large number of the combats took place when superior aircraft, often in packs, dived down to attack poorly defended and isolated reconnaissance aircraft. The agile fighters manoeuvred to shoot their opponents in the back or in the underbelly. Damaged aircraft often caught fire and, since there were no parachutes in the early days of the war, the occupants suffered unpleasant deaths. If a pilot succeeded in landing a damaged aircraft within his own lines, the attacking aircraft often shot it up on the ground. The chivalrous wave of the hand to an enemy did take place, but usually when a fighter had run out of ammunition and was forced to return to base. The men in the baskets of observation balloons faced similarly agonizing deaths if attacked by fighters, for they were protected by only a rifle and protective ground fire. Even here, 'dirty tricks' were practised, for decoy balloons were sometimes flown, containing explosives detonated from the ground and capable of blowing up an attacking aircraft.

The main victim of the agile Fokker monoplane was the Royal Aircraft Factory B.E.2c, which was stable and easy to fly but poorly-armed as well as slow and cumbersome. It earned the unhappy name of 'Fokker fodder', before its withdrawal from the Western Front and the beginning of a new life as a night-fighter at home. The Fokker dominated the skies soon after the battle of the Somme began on 19 August 1916. This scourge was partly ended in the spring of the following year with the introduction of the Nieuport Scout, a tractor aircraft with an overwing machine gun, and two pusher aircraft designed by Geoffrey de Havilland, the Airco D.H.2 and the Royal Aircraft Factory F.E.2b, which were sufficiently well-armed to give good accounts of themselves.

The pendulum of success over the Western Front swung to and fro for the remainder of the war. One problem for designers was speed and agility versus weight of machine guns and ammunition, but this was overcome when more powerful engines were produced. A problem for the aircrews was that of gun stoppage and engine failure, particularly at higher altitudes where icing occurred. The Germans began to regain ascendancy in September 1916 with the appearance of large formations of Halberstadt D.IIs and Albatros D.Is. The former was armed with a single gun firing through the propeller arc, but the latter aircraft was the first to be fitted with two guns. One of the pilots who began to gain a reputation at this stage was 'The Red Baron', *Rittmeister* Manfred von Richthofen. Before he was shot down and killed in a Fokker Triplane on 21 April 1918, he became the top-scoring fighter pilot of the war, with eighty victories to his credit. By April 1917, the average effective service of an RFC aircrew member was reduced to no more than two months in the front line. Losses were heavy partly because most operations took place over enemy lines, whereas the German aircraft seldom ventured over Allied territory. The aircrews also faced the problem of the prevailing westerly wind, which retarded their return journeys, especially if aircraft were damaged. RNAS squadrons were pulled in to support the RFC, while training was expanded to cater for an estimated 17,000 pilots in 1917 and 1918, together with their supporting aircrews and ground crews.

The British did not achieve final superiority against the German massed formations until the introduction of the Royal Aircraft Factory S.E.5a in March 1917 and the Sopwith Camel in the following July. These two aircraft proved more than a match for most

Above: *A section of the German line on the Western Front, showing deep trenches, mine craters and shell-pitted ground.*

Source: Air Historical Branch (RAF), MoD, private collection no 29

Above right: *The Farman MF.11 was designed by Maurice Farman in 1914 to replace his MF.7, a type which had appeared in 1913. The predecessor, which was unarmed, had long and curved outriggers with a front elevator and was nicknamed 'Longhorn' by the RFC. The MF.11, as in this photograph, had no front elevator while the observer in the rear cockpit was equipped with a machine gun; it was nicknamed 'Shorthorn' and served on the Western Front and in the Middle East until generally replaced in the autumn of 1915.*

Source: Air Historical Branch (RAF), MoD, H.1854

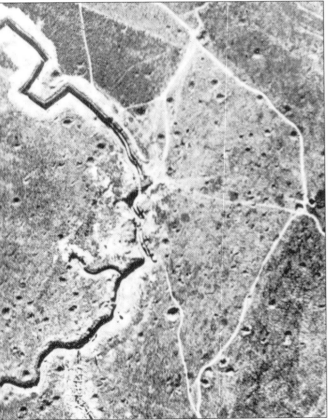

Above: *An important sector of the German Hindenburg line, showing an elaborate system of well-constructed trenches. The photograph was taken by an RAF reconnaissance aircraft from about 8,000 feet.*

Source: Air Historical Branch (RAF), MoD, private collection no 160

German aircraft and even managed to hold their own against the Fokker D.VII, which was considered to be the finest German fighter of the war after its appearance in April 1918.

While these events were taking place on the main fighting front, English civilians received their first taste of war for centuries. A minor bombing attack was made against Dover by a German seaplane in December 1914, but Zeppelin attacks began on 19 January 1915, when Folkestone was bombed. A Zeppelin attack took place against London at the end of the following May, then against Hull and the Tyneside, causing death and damage. There were more attacks against London and the Midlands. The sight of these monstrous apparitions overhead and the shattered buildings caused panic and even riots among a people who had hitherto believed that wars were fought on foreign soil. Substantial defences had to be built up, if only to restore public morale, and resources were diverted away from the Western Front with the creation of seven defensive RFC squadrons to supplement the RNAS units.

The Zeppelins were not invariably successful and several were brought down by anti-aircraft fire or fighters. The first to be destroyed by an aircraft was on 7 June 1915, when Flight Sub-Lieutenant R.A.J. Warneford of the RNAS dropped six 25-lb bombs on *LZ.37* over Belgium, an act for which he received the Victoria Cross. Zeppelins were soon compelled to switch to night bombing, a task which proved extremely difficult for them with their slow airspeeds in the uncertain British weather.

A new menace appeared over the coasts of the eastern counties in the late spring of 1917, in the shape of Gotha G.IV twin-engined bombers. Although these machines carried a much smaller load than the Zeppelins, the bombs were delivered with far greater accuracy and caused considerable damage and casualties. On 13 June 1917, fourteen of these bombers raided London in daylight, killing or injuring nearly 600 people. Further raids followed, and only one bomber was shot down. The public outrage that followed these raids led to a decision to increase the number of RFC squadrons from about 100 to 200, but this was not practicable. The anti-aircraft defences around London were strengthened, but the Germans switched to night attacks and reinforced their bombing strength with Gotha G.Vs and even a few Zeppelin (Staaken) four-engined 'Giant' aeroplanes. It was not until early 1918 that the balloons, searchlights, anti-aircraft guns and Sopwith Camel night-fighters were able to deal satisfactorily with these attacks. On 19 May 1918, the defences accounted for seven out of nineteen bombers, and the raids petered out with the pressure of events on other fronts.

There were further strains on the resources of the RFC and RNAS, in the eastern Mediterranean and the Middle East, where the forces of the British Empire were in conflict with both Bulgaria and Turkey, who had allied themselves to the Central Powers. There were basically three campaigns, in support of the armies.

When the British and ANZAC forces landed in Gallipoli, on 24 April 1915, they were accompanied by the Eastchurch Wing and the Dunkirk Wing of the RNAS. But the enterprise failed, in spite of the sacrifices and bravery of the attacking troops. Evacuations were completed by 8 January 1916, and the unhappy campaign came to an end.

Meanwhile, Serbia had been conquered by Austria and Bulgaria in November 1915. In response, British and French troops occupied Salonika the following month, where they were joined by a re-equipped Serbian army in May 1916. To provide reconnaissance for these armies, B.E.2cs and B.E.12s were sent over from Egypt but, as on the Western Front, they soon found themselves outclassed by Halberstadt D.II fighters which were escorting German bombers. Sopwith 1½-Strutters of the RNAS, together with D.H.2s of the RFC, helped to restore the situation, but the German supremacy was not broken until the arrival of S.E.5as at the end of 1917. The British aircraft made a significant contribution to the final defeat of the Bulgarian armies, which suffered the highest losses of any during the war, in terms of percentages.

The third campaign took place in Palestine and Mesopotamia against Turkish armies. In the spring of 1916 the Turks advanced along the Sinai Peninsula with the intention of occupying the Suez Canal, but their progress was faithfully reported by a handful of B.E.2cs of the RFC, and the attacks were defeated. The Turks retreated, but in early 1917 the Germans sent Halberstadt D.II and D.III fighters into the area, as well as Rumpler C.I reconnaissance aircraft. Yet again, the British were temporarily outclassed, although reconnaissance flights and map photography continued. The arrival of a number of Bristol Fighters in August 1917 helped to restore the situation, especially in destroying German reconnaissance aircraft, and complete superiority was achieved when S.E.5as arrived two months later. In September 1918, two retreating Turkish armies were caught in defiles and subjected to low-level bombing and machine gun attacks by aircraft, resulting in an appalling slaughter of the soldiers, who had little defence. The rout continued and the armies were destroyed as fighting units. Turkey had no option but to surrender at the end of the following month.

One of the consequences of the German bombing attacks against Britain was the formation of a strategic bombing force to operate over Germany, primarily against industrial targets. In October 1917, the 41st Wing was set up in France, consisting initially of Handley Page 0/100s, D.H.4s and F.E.2bs, to continue the attacks hitherto carried out mainly by RNAS aircraft. The targets included the Ruhr, Cologne, the Saar and Stuttgart. The wing increased in size and effectiveness, and in February 1918 became the VIIIth Brigade. In time, this brigade evolved into an even more important formation.

The RFC and the RNAS had grown to such an extent, with further expansion proposed, that problems developed in organization. Both the War Office and Admiralty believed that their influence should be paramount in air matters, but the prime minister, David Lloyd George, decided to invite an impartial observer to report on the matter. His choice was the eminent South African, Lieutenant-General Jan Smuts. In his report of August 1917, Smuts recommended the setting up of an independent service with an Air Ministry and an air staff. This report was approved by the War Cabinet and a bill was passed through Parliament, but the work of preparing the new organization was complex and was not until 1 April 1918 that the Royal Air Force came into being. Major-General Sir Hugh Trenchard was appointed as the first Chief of Air Staff.

Much grim fighting awaited the new RAF for the seven months that remained in the war. The Germans had opened a major offensive on the Western Front in March, following the withdrawal of armies from the Eastern Front after the armistice with Russia. Their air force was greatly outnumbered by the combined forces of the British and French, to which were added the squadrons of the American Expeditionary Force which had arrived in France during June of the previous year. Nevertheless, there were many air battles, when formations of German fighters attacked escorted reconnaissance aircraft and bombers. In June, the VIIIth Brigade was renamed the Independent Bombing Force and continued long-range strategic bombing; although these attacks were light by later standards, they set a pattern which governed much of the RAF's thinking in the future. By July, the last German offensive petered out. A few RAF squadrons were sent to Italy to support the armies which were engaged with Austrian forces.

The Allies went over to a general offensive in September on both the Western Front and the Italian Front. By now, it was apparent that the German and Austrian resources were exhausted and their defences were crumbling. Austria accepted terms on 3 November and the armistice with Germany was signed on 11 November 1918. The carnage of the war at last came to an end.

Above: *The Bristol Scout was designed before the First World War but not delivered in quantity to the RFC and the RNAS until early 1915. It was capable of the excellent speed of 95 m.p.h. but only small arms were carried. Machine guns were fitted later to a few Scout Cs while others carried darts for dropping on Zeppelins. The Scout D, delivered in November 1915, had provision for a machine gun. Almost every RFC squadron had a few Scout Ds on strength, but most of these were withdrawn by mid-1916 and continued as trainers. The Scout D in this photograph, serial 5575, was flown by James McCudden.*

Source: *Air Historical Branch (RAF), MoD, H.1910*

Above right: *The Caudron G.III was unusual in that it was a tractor and not a pusher aircraft, used widely in the early years of the First World War. The RFC used the machine, armed with a forward-firing machine gun and small bombs, for ground-strafing operations as well as for observation, while the RNAS employed it for coastal patrols. After withdrawal from front-line duties, it was very successful as a trainer. This photograph of serial 4293, still with its French serial C567, was taken at Brooklands.*

Source: *RAF Museum P9457*

Right: *The Vickers F.B.5 entered service with the RFC's 11 Squadron during February 1915. Nicknamed the 'Gunbus', it was fitted with a machine gun in the nose, operated by the observer. By the time the squadron arrived in France five months later, it was outclassed by the new Fokker E.1 monoplane with a machine gun synchronized to fire through the propeller.*

Source: *Air Historical Branch (RAF), MoD, H.1805*

Left: *The prototype of the Royal Aircraft Factory F.E.2b appeared in August 1913, but this two-seat aircraft with a pusher propeller was not produced in quantity until early 1915. The machine was equipped with two Lewis guns, one forward and one backward-firing. F.E.2bs were successful over the Western Front against Fokker monoplanes until the autumn of 1916, but were outclassed when Albatros D.1s began to appear. Many F.E.2bs were transferred to the night bombing role and continued until the end of the war.*

Source: Air Historical Branch (RAF), MoD, H.989

Above: *A faithful replica of an Airco D.H.2, registration GBH7, photographed at Mildenhall in Suffolk on 23 May 1987.*

RAF Museum colour slide PO52159

Above: *Captain Lanoe Hawker, Bristol Scout, no. 6 Squadron, 25 July 1915. The first V.C. awarded for aerial action.*

Source: courtesy of Frank Wootton, P.P.G.Av.A.

Right: *The raids by Zeppelins over south-east England in 1915 caused little damage but created such alarm among the civilian population that the sight of any aircraft overhead could cause panic. This poster was displayed to help the public recognize the difference between hostile and friendly aircraft.*

Source: RAF Museum P100174

Left: *The Morane-Saulnier Type L first appeared in 1913 and was ordered for the RFC and RNAS, with the military designation MS.3, as well as for the Aviation Militaire. Originally unarmed, it was later equipped with a forward-firing machine gun, with deflector plates fitted to the propeller blades. On 7 June 1915, Flt Sub-Lt R.A.J. Warneford of 1 Squadron RNAS, based at Dunkirk, destroyed the first Zeppelin from the air in one of these machines. He dropped six 20 lb Hale bombs on the army Zeppelin LZ.37, which fell in flames on a convent in Belgium.*
Source: RAF Museum P4988

Right: *The Nieuport 11 was ordered at the outbreak of war by the Aviation Militaire and entered service with the French in the summer of 1915, who referred to it as the Bébé. It was also ordered by the RNAS and was employed both in France and the Dardanelles, being known as the Nieuport Scout. The RFC received deliveries in France during March 1916; armed with a Lewis gun on the upper wing, it helped to overcome the menace of the Fokker monoplanes. The Nieuport Scout in the photograph was serial 3993 of the RNAS.*
Source: RAF Museum PO18140

Left: *The Airco D.H.1, designed by Geoffrey de Havilland, was a two-seat fighter and reconnaissance aircraft with a pusher propeller and dual controls. The observer sat in the front seat and was equipped with a forward-firing machine gun. D.H.1s began to appear in 1915, being employed by the RFC, mainly for home defence and later for training. This photograph is of a D.H.1A.*
Source: Air Historical Branch (RAF), MoD, H.1787

Right: *The* SS.40 *was one of a series of non-rigid airships supplied to the RNAS from May 1915 onwards. It carried a crew of two in a gondola consisting of a fuselage from an Armstrong Whitworth F.K.3 and had an endurance of about sixteen hours at an airspeed of 40 m.p.h. The main function of these 'Sea Scouts' was to carry out anti-submarine patrols in the English Channel and the Irish Sea. This photograph was taken at Kingsnorth in Kent.*

Source: Air Historical Branch (RAF), MoD, private collection 1802K

Above: *A Short 184 seaplane was the first aircraft to sink a ship by torpedo, a Turkish merchant vessel near the Dardanelles on 12 August 1915. However, the Short 184 was used primarily on more routine but vital work by the RNAS from the summer of 1915 onwards, anti-submarine patrols and reconnaissance, in home waters, the Mediterranean and the Far East. A land-based version was also employed for bombing. Short 184s continued in front-line service until April 1917.*

Source: Air Historical Branch (RAF), MoD, H.1022

Left: *Franco-British Aviation was a company which built a series of small flying boats with pusher engines, for training and for patrol purposes. This photograph shows a Type B two-seater, serial N2737, on a beaching trolley. It was built at Gosport and supplied to the RNAS in 1915.*

Source: RAF Museum P4995

Right: *The Airco D.H.2 was a single-seat fighter with a pusher propeller, designed by Geoffrey de Havilland and first delivered in quantity to 24 Squadron in January 1916. When this squadron went to France a month later, it was the first to be equipped entirely with single-seat fighters. The machine was fitted with a Lewis gun and met with some success the threat of the Fokker fighters which were appearing over the Western Front. D.H.2s also served in Palestine and Macedonia, but most were withdrawn in 1917 and continued as trainers.*

Source: Air Historical Branch (RAF), MoD, H.88

Left: *The Voisin L.A. Type 5 appeared late in 1915, a derivation of the earlier Types 3 and 4, both of which were supplied to the RFC and the RNAS. It was a two-seater light bomber with a pusher engine, with provision for a 37mm cannon in the nose for ground strafing, known by the French as the Avion Canon. This photograph of a Voisin L.A. Type 5 of 2 Wing, RNAS, was taken on the island of Imbroz, near the Dardanelles, in 1915.*

Source: RAF Museum P532

Above: *The C (Coastal) Type airship entered service with the RNAS in late 1915. Powered by two engines, usually amounting to 300 h.p., it carried a crew of five, one of whom manned a machine gun, and had an endurance of about twenty-four hours. This photograph of C.2 was taken at RNAS Mullion, in Cornwall.*

Source: RAF Museum P3149

Right: *The Vickers F.B.5 first appeared with the RFC's 11 Squadron on the Western Front in February 1915, where it was dubbed the 'Gunbus'. The observer sat in the nose, equipped with a .303 inch Lewis gun, while the machine was powered with a 'pusher' engine.*

Source: Keystone Collection

Right: *A painting used as a crewroom poster showing the unpleasant fate of the crew of an R.E.7, who were so intent on pursuing an Albatross D.III that they failed to spot two Fokker monoplanes swooping down on them. These German monoplanes, fitted with machine guns synchronized to fire through the propellers, accounted for numerous British aircraft when they first appeared over the Western Front in the autumn of 1915.*
Source: RAF Museum

Above: *The Royal Aircraft Factory R.E.7 was designed specifically to carry the new 336 lb bomb developed by the same factory. The first machines, armed with a single machine gun in the front cockpit, first entered service with the RFC's 21 Squadron in France during January 1916.*

Source: Air Historical Branch (RAF), MoD, H.992

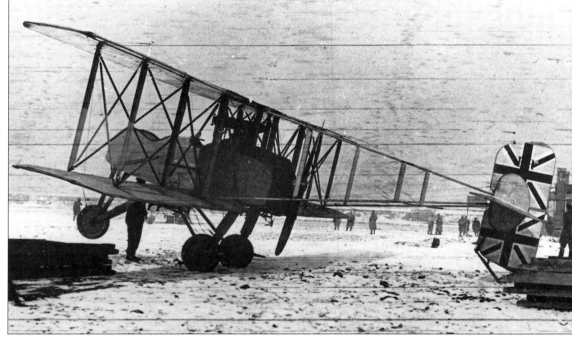

Right: *The two-seater Breguet Type 5 was ordered from France by the RNAS while others were built in Britain. Entering service in early 1916, it could carry 661 lb of bombs for a distance of about 375 miles, and was employed in the Aegean as well as France. In late 1916, it was transferred to night bombing operations.*

Source: RAF Museum PO13635

Left: *The Martinsyde G.100 Elephant performed the role of escort to bombers, although it was capable of carrying up to 224 lb of bombs itself. It was a single-seater, with a forward-firing gun mounted over the propeller and provision for a second gun on a bracket over the pilot's left shoulder. In practice, it performed best as a ground attack aircraft, serving from early 1916 on the Western Front and in Mesopotamia and Palestine. This photograph shows the prototype, serial 4735.*

Source: Air Historical Branch (MoD), Ref: H.247

Left: *The Royal Aircraft Factory B.E.2 series ended with the B.E.2e, which entered service in July 1916. Unfortunately, the insistence on a general-purpose aircraft with stable flying characteristics produced a succession of slow and unwieldy machines which were easy prey for the agile German fighters. Hundreds of these aircraft were shot down over the Western Front, even when machine guns were introduced into the observer's cockpit. They were also employed in the Middle East and Macedonia, but most survivors ended the war as trainers. An F.E.2b, serial A836, can be seen in the background of this photograph of a B.E.2e.*
Source: Air Historical Branch (RAF), MoD, H.979

Below: *The Sopwith 1½-Strutter was designed as a multi-purpose two-seat aircraft and first entered service with the RNAS in France during April 1916. It was employed by both the RNAS and RFC, and performed the roles of bomber, reconnaissance, fighter, anti-shipping and carrier aircraft. It was the first British aircraft equipped with a Vickers machine gun which was efficiently synchronised to fire through the propeller. The 1½-Strutter in this photograph, serial A6901, was converted to a single-seater. In the summer of 1917, 1½-Strutters were replaced on the Western Front, and employed at home as trainers or as single-seat night-fighters.*
Source: Air Historical Branch (RAF), MoD, H.1802

Above: *On 31 March 1916, Zeppelin L.15 of the German navy was damaged by anti-aircraft fire and by aerial darts dropped from a B.E.2c flown by a New Zealander, Second Lieutenant Alfred de B. Brandon, who took off from Hainault in Essex. She came down in the Thames Estuary. One of her crew was killed and seventeen were taken prisoner.*
Source: Air Historical Branch (RAF), MoD, private collection no 834

Right: *The Royal Aircraft Factory B.E.12 was intended to combat the Fokker monoplanes which were destroying the B.E.2 series over the Western Front. It was provided with a more powerful engine than its predecessors and was converted into a single-seater with a single forward-firing machine gun. It remained unmanoeuvrable, however, and was withdrawn as a fighter soon after its appearance in France during August 1916. Some B.E.12s were converted into light bombers while others served in home defence and in the Middle East.*

Source: Air Historical Branch (RAF), MoD, H.987

Right below: *The Armstrong Whitworth F.K.3, a two-seater bomber and reconnaissance aircraft known as the 'Little Ack' served only with 47 Squadron, in Macedonia, from April 1916 to March 1918. Its successor, the more powerful F.K.8 known as the 'Big Ack', arrived in the Western Front during January 1917; it was more widely used and operated with some success as a light bomber. This photograph is of an F.K.3.*

Source: Air Historical Branch (RAF), MoD, H.761

Above: *An observation balloon ascending with the aid of guide ropes and a motor winch, in order to spot the positions of the Turks.*

Source: Air Historical Branch (RAF), MoD, private collection no 114

Right: *The Nieuport 17 was a more powerful version of the earlier Nieuport 11, with a larger wing span. It entered service with the RNAS and RFC in the summer of 1916 and proved extremely popular among fighter pilots, who praised its agility and rate of climb. At first armed with an overwing Lewis gun, a synchronized Vickers was fitted to later machines. The machine in this photograph was serial A6648 of the RFC's 29 Squadron.*

Source: RAF Museum PO19392

Above: *The Royal Aircraft Factory F.E.8, equipped with a single machine gun in the front cockpit, arrived at the Western Front in August 1916, at a time when pusher aircraft were out-classed by German fighters. On one occasion, 9 March 1917, five of a formation of nine were destroyed by Albatros D.IIIs. Shortly afterwards, F.E.8s were withdrawn and replaced by tractor aircraft.*

Source: Air Historical Branch (MoD), Ref: H.1801

Above: *The Spad Type VII was built mainly in France, although about 100 were also manufactured in Britain. It entered service with the RFC in France in October 1916, at a time when German machines had gained superiority over the British pusher types. With a synchronized forward-firing gun and a fast turn of speed, it helped swing the balance back in favour of the Allies. In this photograph of Spad VII serial A9132, a Royal Aircraft Factory R.E.8 serial A4537 can be seen in the background.*

Source: RAF Museum P33525

Right: *On the night of 22/23 September 1916, twelve German naval Zeppelins attacked targets in London and the Midlands. Two were shot down. L.32 crashed in flames near Billericay in Essex and the crew was killed. L.33 was damaged by anti-aircraft fire and by Lieutenant Alfred de B. Brandon. It landed in a field near West Mersea in Essex and was set on fire by its crew of twenty-two, all of whom were taken prisoner. The remains of the frame of L.33 are shown in this photograph.*

Source: Air Historical Branch (RAF), private collection No 88

Above: *The Sopwith Pup was supplied at first to the RNAS in the autumn of 1916 and towards the end of the same year, in greater quantity, to the RFC. It was a very manoeuvrable and rugged single-seat fighter, normally fitted with a synchronized Vickers machine gun. The performance on the Western Front proved successful, while other Pups flew from aircraft carriers and cruisers. It was withdrawn from front-line service in early 1918 and became very popular as a trainer.*

Source: Air Historical Branch (RAF), MoD, H.296

Left: *The remains of the gondola of the Zeppelin L.33. This crash-landing provided useful technical information for the British. This class of Zeppelin had a length of about 650 feet and, powered by six engines, could reach a height of 17,000 feet at an airspeed of 62 m.p.h. The design of the rigid airships R.33 and R.34, which entered service with the RAF in 1919, was based on L.33.*

Source: Air Historical Branch (RAF), private collection No 89

Above: *The Armstrong Whitworth F.K.8 was a scaled-up version of the F.K.3, employed as a day and night bomber as well as on ground attack and reconnaissance. First delivered to the RFC towards the end of 1916, it arrived in France the following January and also saw service in Palestine and Macedonia. After the First World War, it served with 47 Squadron in support of the White Russian forces.*

Source: RAF Museum P922

Above: *A replica of a Sopwith Pup*

Source: T. Malcolm English colour slide

Left: *The Royal Aircraft Factory R.E.8 was intended to provide a better-armed alternative to the B.E.2 series, being equipped with a Lewis gun firing through the propeller as well as a Lewis gun mounted in the rear cockpit. However, R.E.8s were almost as slow and unmanoeuvrable as their predecessors, and proved no match for agile German fighters. First delivered to the Western Front in November 1916 and known as 'Harry Tates' after the music hall comedian, they plodded through anti-aircraft fire on army co-operation work and were also employed as night bombers. More R.E.8s served in France than any other British two-seater.*

Source: Air Historical Branch (RAF), MoD, H.1855

Above: *A replica of a Bristol F.2B Fighter, serial D8096.*

Source: T. Malcolm English colour slide

Below: *The Handley Page 0/100, a four-seater heavy bomber with folding wings, was designed specifically for the long-range bombing of Germany. It first went into service with the RNAS in France during November*

1916. Carrying up to 2,000 lb of bombs, the machine was used at first for daylight sea patrols and then for night bombing. An S.E.5 also appears in this photograph.

Source: Air Historical Branch (RAF), MoD, H.1455

Left: *The Vickers F.B.19 Mark II, a single seater scout fitted with a single machine gun synchronized with the propeller, appeared in France at the end of 1916 but was not accepted by the RFC. A few were sent to the Middle East and others served on home defence or as trainers.*

Source: RAF Museum PO14079

Right: *The Bristol F.2A Fighter first arrived in France in December 1916 and, although losses were heavy initially, began to achieve considerable success with improvements in tactics. The F.2B, a modified version, was produced in far greater numbers and eventually served with many squadrons on the Western Front as well as with home defence squadrons and two more in Palestine. A tough and reliable reconnaissance fighter, it was known by RAF crews as the 'Biff' and acquired a fearsome reputation with German pilots, who were sometimes reluctant to tackle the machine. Before the end of the First World War, 3,100 Bristol Fighters had been accepted by the RFC and RAF. It then continued in service with the post-war RAF, at home until 1926 and overseas until 1932, being known as the 'Brisfit'. This photograph shows a Bristol F.2B of 208 Squadron in 1925, based at Ismailia in 1925.*

Source: RAF Museum P1414

Left: *Aircrews of the RFC photographed in France, in front of a Bristol Fighter.*

Source: Keystone Collection

Right: *The Airco D.H.4 was designed by Geoffrey de Havilland as a fast day bomber, but it was also employed on many other tasks. It was armed with a forward-firing gun, as well as a single gun on a ring in the observer's position, and could carry about 450 lb of bombs. D.H.4s were delivered to the RNAS and the RFC in France in March 1917, and were also employed in the Mediterranean and the Middle East. Over 1,400 D.H.4s were built in Britain, but in addition nearly 4,900 were manufactured in the United States, where it was named the 'Liberty Plane'. This photograph of D.H.4 serial B9480 was taken at Manston in Kent in September 1917.*

Source: RAF Museum P735

Right: *One objective of every fighter pilot was to fire at the vulnerable under-belly of an enemy aircraft. A crewroom poster showed this desirable state of affairs, with the pilot of a Nieuport 11 scoring hits with his Lewis gun on an unlucky German two-seater of an indeterminate type.*

Source: RAF Museum

Below: *This crewroom poster showed the folly of a pilot of what appeared to be an S.E.5a, who attempted an exuberant loop after shooting down an Albatros D.III. He was evidently unaware that there was structural damage to his tail, presumably caused by enemy fire.*

Source: RAF Museum

Above: *The Royal Aircraft Factory S.E.5 appeared on the Western Front in March 1917 and rapidly established a reputation as a fast and tough single-engined fighter, with good altitude performance. It was also heavily armed for its day, with a synchronized Vickers gun on the port side and a Lewis gun mounted on the upper wing. It remained in service until the end of the war, in the Middle East as well as in France. This photograph of an S.E.5a of 111 Squadron, based at Ramleh in Palestine, was taken in 1918.*

Source: Air Historical Branch (RAF), MoD, H.1875

Below: *The Airco D.H.6 was designed solely as a primary trainer for the RFC and began to appear in early 1917. It proved safe and reliable, remaining as the standard trainer until the arrival of the Avro 504 late in the same year. Some D.H.6s were employed on anti-submarine work around coastal waters by the RNAS, carrying a bomb load of up to 100 lb, while others served on home defence.*

Source: Air Historical Branch (RAF), MoD, H.982

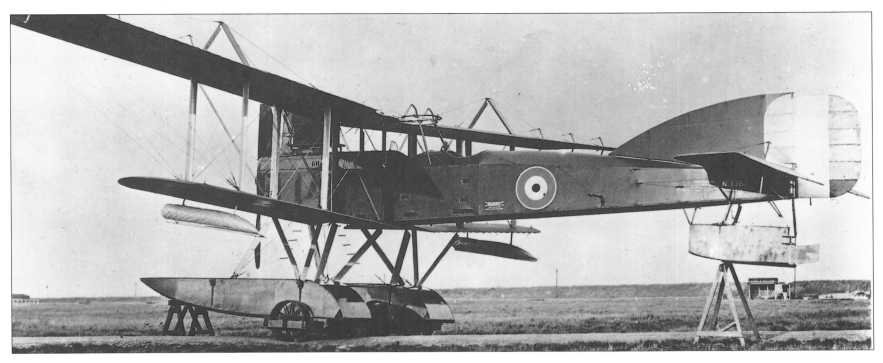

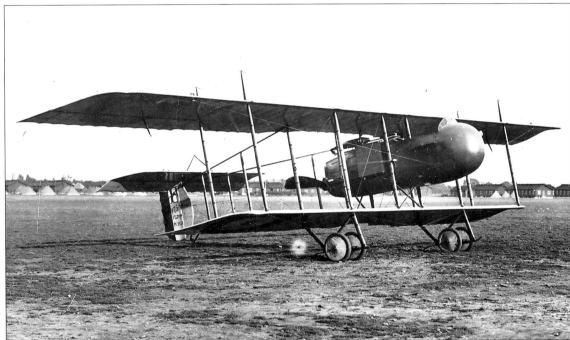

Above: *The Short 320 was the last of seaplanes used for anti-submarine and reconnaissance work in the First World War. As with similar aircraft, it could also be used for torpedo bombing. Short 320s came into service from August 1918 onwards and equipped four RAF squadrons, continuing until October 1919. This photograph is of serial N1361, on a beaching trolley.*

Source: Air Historical Branch (RAF), MoD, H.1024

Left: *The Farman F.40 was designed jointly by the brothers Maurice and Henri, and entered service early in 1916. It was used for reconnaissance and bombing but, armed only with a single machine gun, was found to be too vulnerable for daylight work and was switched to night bombing before withdrawal from front-line squadrons in 1917. This photograph of an RNAS Farman F.40 was taken in 1917.*

Source: RAF Museum PO12317

Left: *The drum-fed machine gun and sight on the centre-section of a Royal Aircraft Factory S.E.5a.*

Source: T. Malcolm English colour slide

Right: *The Curtiss JN, or 'Jenny', was a tractor trainer manufactured in the United States and Canada, employed by both the RNAS and the RFC from 1917 onwards. After the war, many of these aircraft were sold on the civil market and used in 'flying circuses'. This photograph shows a Curtiss JN-4A, serial B1926, delivered from America for the RNAS.*

Source: RAF Museum P7289

Above: *The Handley Page 0/400 followed the 0/100 as the standard heavy bomber of the First World War. It was fitted with fuel tanks in the fuselage instead of the engine nacelles and with successively more powerful engines. Over 650 were built, the first becoming operational as day bombers in France during April 1917. By the following October, the squadrons were switched to night bombing over Germany. The 0/400 continued in service until 1920.*

Source: RAF Museum P4840

Below: *The Sopwith Triplane was developed from the earlier Sopwith Pup, deliveries beginning to squadrons on the Western Front towards the end of 1916. Like the Pup, it was fitted with a synchronized machine gun, although a few are known to have been fitted with two. With its extraordinary agility and rate of climb, the Triplane fighter caused some alarm among German pilots. It continued in front-line service until the summer of 1917, when replaced by the Sopwith Camel.*

Source: Air Historical Branch (RAF), MoD, H.1950

Above: *The largest bomb manufactured by the Royal Aircraft Factory by 1918 was this formidable 1,650 pounder.*

Source: Air Historical Branch (MoD), Ref: H.504

Above: *Perhaps the best-known of British fighters in the First World War, the Sopwith Camel was first delivered to the Western Front in July 1917. It was not an easy aircraft to fly but, once mastered, RAF pilots found that they could out-turn most German fighters. The Camel was credited with destroying more enemy aircraft than any other Allied fighter. It is estimated that, by the end of the war, over 2,500 Camels were on charge with RAF squadrons, but these did not remain long in service after the war, being replaced by the Sopwith Snipe.*

Source: Keystone Collection

Right: *Another view of the Sopwith Camel.*

Source: Air Historical Branch (MoD), Ref: H.1806

Above: *A replica of a Sopwith Triplane.*

Source: T. Malcolm English colour slide

Left: *The Airco D.H.5, a single-seat fighter with the upper wing staggered backwards to give the pilot a better view and a Vickers machine gun synchronized with the propeller, first entered service in France during May 1917. Its performance proved inadequate at higher altitudes, however, and it was employed mainly for strafing until withdrawn in January 1918.*

Source: Air Historical Branch (RAF), MoD, H.91

Above: *The Airco D.H.9A was a refined version of the D.H.9, with a more reliable engine and a larger wing area. It was delivered to RAF squadrons in France from June 1918 onwards, where it served in the Independent Bombing Force in raids over Germany. It also served with the Allied forces which landed in Murmansk in the same summer. Known as the 'Ninak', it had a remarkably long and successful career in the RAF, until 1931. The photograph shows serial J7013.*

Source: Air Historical Branch, private collection John Stroud: Ref: H.806

Below: *The Airco D.H.9, designed as a two-seat aircraft intended to replace the D.H.4 and undertake day bombing over Germany, began to appear in December 1917. It was armed with a forward-firing Vickers gun and a Lewis gun in the rear cockpit, and could carry up to 500 lb of bombs. The machine suffered from frequent engine failures, but served in France and the Middle East, as well as the Russian theatre, until the end of the war. This photograph was taken at a training unit.*

Source: Air Historical Branch (RAF), MoD, H.1856

Right: *The Fairey Campania seaplane was the first aircraft to be designed for flying off an aircraft carrier, being named after the liner* HMS Campania, *which was refitted as a warship. Take-off from the deck was achieved by using a trolley gear, which was then jettisoned. Campanias were delivered to the RNAS from November 1917 and eventually equipped three RAF squadrons. They were withdrawn in the summer of 1919.*
Source: Air Historical Branch (RAF), MoD, H.43

Below: *The Felixstowe F.2A was first delivered to RNAS squadrons in November 1917. Known as the 'F-boat', it was the first of a series of large and highly successful flying boats. During the remainder of the First World War, 'F-boats' were employed on anti-submarine patrols and escort duties. They could carry up to 460 lb of bombs and had an endurance of about six hours. With a crew of four and an armament of up to seven machine guns, they gave good accounts of themselves in encounters with German seaplanes. They were also credited with shooting down at least two Zeppelins. This photograph of an F.2A named 'Saturn', serial N4438 of 267 Squadron, was taken in Malta in 1922.*
Source: Air Historical Branch (RAF), MoD, H.1336

Above right: *Kite balloons were used by both the RNAS and the RFC. At sea, they were operated from special tenders and used for naval gun spotting. The four or five drogue parachutes steadied the balloon but increased drag on the vessel. Over land, they were operated from winches and used mainly for artillery spotting.*

Source: Air Historical Branch (RAF), private collection no 813

Right: *Pilots of 80 Squadron, photographed in January 1918, when the squadron was equipped with Sopwith Camels and setting off for the Western Front.*

Source: Air Historical Branch (RAF), MoD, H.1857

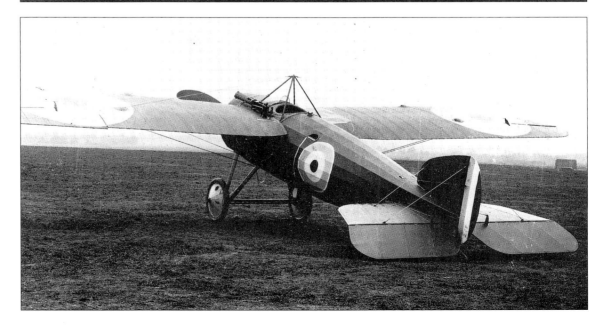

Right: *Monoplanes of the RFC suffered so many crashes before the First World War that there was much prejudice against the prototype Bristol M.1A monoplane when it first flew, even though it reached 132 m.p.h. Only a handful of M.1Bs were built, one of which is shown in this photograph. One hundred and twenty-five M.1Cs were ordered; none of these flew on the Western Front but a few reached the Middle East and Macedonia, while others were used as trainers at home.*

Source: Air Historical Branch (RAF), MoD, H.999

Above: *Captain James T.B. McCudden of 56 Squadron earned the first Victoria Cross awarded to the RAF, gazetted on 2 April 1918. He was also one of the most famous and highly decorated pilots of the First World War, being additionally awarded the DSO and bar, the MC and bar, the MM and the Croix de Guerre. When he lost his life in a flying accident, in July 1918, he had been credited with the destruction of fifty-seven enemy aircraft.*

Source: Air Historical Branch (RAF), MoD, H.1874.

Right: *"Knights of the Air" – Captain James T.B. McCudden, V.C. in aerial battle with the Red Baron, 1918.*

Source: courtesy of Frank Wootton, P.P.G.Av.A.

Left: *The Avro 504 served with both the RFC and the RNAS in the early months of the war, but is best remembered for its remarkable success as a trainer. The first variation for this purpose was the 504J which first appeared in the autumn of 1916. It proved highly reliable as well as fully aerobatic. This 504J was photographed at Abu Sueir in Egypt in 1918.*
Source: RAF Museum PO22214

Below: *The Blackburn Kangaroo was delivered to 246 Squadron at Seaton Carew in Durham during May 1918. This was the only squadron to fly the new four-man bomber which, with an endurance of about eight hours, was engaged on anti-submarine patrols in the North Sea. Before the Armistice, Kangaroos sank one U-boat and damaged several more. The squadron was disbanded in April 1919.*
Source: Air Historical Branch (RAF), MoD, H.1852

Right: *The Sopwith T.1 Cuckoo was the first of the RAF's landplane torpedo bombers, first delivered in June 1918. It had fold-back wings and served on board carriers, but was too late for active service. Cuckoos remained in service until April 1932 with 210 Squadron at Gosport.*

Source: Air Historical Branch (RAF), MoD, H.966

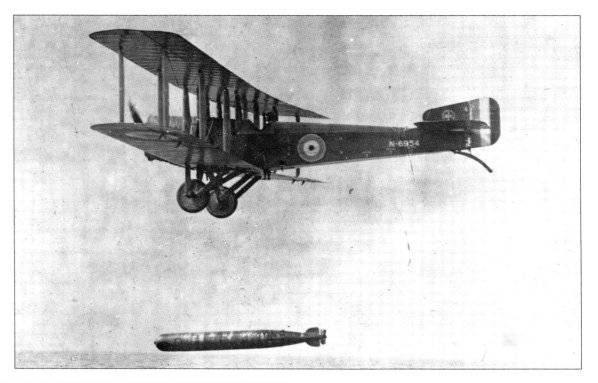

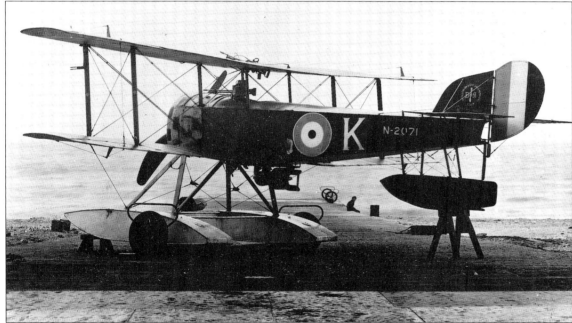

Left: *The Sopwith Baby floatplane served with the RNAS from early 1917 onwards, from bases round the British coast and from seaplane carriers in home waters and in the Mediterranean. Armed with a single machine gun on the upper wing, or a synchronized gun firing through the propeller, they operated on fighter patrols or carried a bomb load of up to 130 lb. Some were converted to landplanes. Most were withdrawn in the summer of 1918.*

Source: Air Historical Branch (RAF), MoD, H.993

Below: *In the summer of 1918 the Felixstowe F.3 followed the F.2A. It was a slightly larger flying boat and was employed in the Mediterranean as well as in home waters. The performance proved less satisfactory than that of the F.2A, however, and it was withdrawn in 1921 whereas its predecessor continued until August 1923.*

Source: Air Historical Branch (RAF), MoD, H.1029

Below: *The formation of the Royal Air Force on 1 April 1918, from the amalgamation of the Royal Flying Corps and the Royal Naval Air Service, offered future recruits an attractive alternative to life in the trenches or at sea.*
Source: RAF Museum POO205

Right: *A Sopwith F.5.1 Dolphin, serial D5261, of the RFC, photographed in 1918.*
The first of these single-engined fighters were delivered to 19 Squadron at Sainte Marie Cappel in France in January 1918. Later, three more squadrons were equipped with Dolphins which, equipped with two Lewis guns and four 25 lb bombs, were often used for ground attack. They remained in service until 1919, when most remaining aircraft were scrapped.
Source: Air Historical Branch (RAF), MoD, H.1874

Above: *A replica of an Avro 504K, serial 3404.*

Source: T. Malcolm English colour slide

Left: *The Sopwith Snipe was designed to succeed the Sopwith Camel as Britain's premier single-engined fighter, with improved performance and better vision. The first deliveries were made to 43 Squadron in September 1918, and several squadrons flew Snipes before the Armistice on 11 November. This photograph of Sopwith 7F.1 Snipe, serial E8179, was taken in 1918.*

Source: Air Historical Branch (RAF), MoD, H.1945

Left: *The Handley Page V/1500 was the first four-engined bomber in the RAF as well as the largest British aircraft to be produced in the First World War. It was also the first of the RAF's strategic bombers, having a radius of action of 600 miles and being capable of bombing Berlin from bases in England.*
It arrived too late to fly operationally and was considered too expensive for peacetime service, preference being given to the smaller Vickers Vimy. However, between December 1918 and January 1919 a V/1500 made the first successful flight from England to India, even though the final landing at Karachi was made on only two engines.
Source: RAF Museum P4842

Right: *The Sopwith TF.2 Salamander was developed as a ground attack aircraft towards the end of the war, TF standing for 'trench fighter'. It carried two Vickers machine guns synchronized to fire through the propeller, while armour-plating protected the pilot. Only thirty-seven aircraft were delivered to the RAF by the time of the Armistice, the majority of those on order being cancelled.*
Source: Air Historical Branch (RAF), MoD, H.1012

Left: *After the war, the Sopwith Snipe served with thirteen home-based squadron as well as four overseas squadrons, continuing in service until August 1926.*
Source: Aviation Bookshop

Right: *The Martinsyde Buzzard F.4 was first delivered to the RAF towards the end of the First World War, too late to fly operationally. It was a fast fighter with two Vickers machine guns synchronized to fire through the propeller, but further production was cancelled with the Sopwith Snipe as the RAF's standard fighter after the war. This photograph is of serial D4261.*

Source: RAF Museum P4914

Below: *The British Aerial Transport Bantam, nicknamed the 'Bat', was a fast and highly manoeuvrable fighter armed with twin Vickers machine guns, but by the time various problems with engines were overcome, the First World War was over. The machine in this photograph, serial B9945, was one of three prototypes.*

Source: Air Historical Branch (RAF), MoD, H.814

Below: *The Vickers Cow-gun fighter was designed to a specification for an all-metal monoplane capable of firing a quick-firing 37 mm gun manufactured by the Coventry Ordnance Works, in order to fire shells into the underbellies of enemy aircraft. Although this prototype, serial J9566, proved stable, interest was not sustained and the aircraft did not go into production.*

Source: Air Historical Branch (RAF), MoD, H.1819

CHAPTER 3

TRENCHARD IN THE TWENTIES

Below: *The Felixstowe F.5 flying boat followed the F.3 in 1919, having a slightly larger wing span and a longer range. It continued in service until 1925. This photograph is of serial N4838, believed to have been on the strength of 230 Squadron at Calshot.*

Source: Air Historical Branch (RAF), MoD, H.1780

Right: *The de Havilland 10 Amiens, a four-seat day bomber capable of carrying 900 lb of bombs, entered squadron service slightly too late to see action in the First World War and did not remain in the RAF beyond 1919. This machine was photographed while serving with 216 Squadron in Egypt.*

Source: Air Historical Branch (RAF), MoD, H.749

In November 1918, the strength of the RAF amounted to about 27,500 officers and 264,000 other ranks. There were also about 25,000 women of the Women's Royal Air Force, which had been formed on 1 April 1918 from volunteers who had served with the air units of the Women's Royal Naval Service and the Women's Auxiliary Army Corps. There were over 22,500 aircraft, including 3,300 in the front lines, and about 100 airships.

This enormous force could not be sustained and most squadrons were rapidly wound down and disbanded. Men and women were demobilized, and even Sir Hugh Trenchard lost his job. Thousands of aircraft were scrapped or, if possible, sold and converted to civilian roles. The Independent Bombing Force was disbanded. Outstanding contracts with manufacturers were cancelled, and many companies in the aero industry faced closure or liquidation. The portion of the RAF which remained in Britain was divided into a Southern Area, a Northern Area and a Coastal Area, the last corresponding to the old RNAS.

There is little doubt that, with hindsight, these measures were far too drastic. On the other hand, the participants in the holocaust of the previous four years were sickened with their experiences, together with the appalling loss of life and the maiming of an even greater number of men. It was genuinely believed that it had been a 'war to end wars'. There seemed little point in maintaining a third armed service, and for a while there existed the strong possibility of breaking up the RAF and bringing some of its units back into the control of the army and navy. Only one matter raised the RAF in public esteem, the setting up of an air mail service from Hendon to the British soldiers in the Army of Occupation in Germany.

After the Armistice, some units of the RAF remained in North Russia, having been despatched to Murmansk in the summer of 1918 together with the Allied forces which had landed there after the collapse of the Russian forces, to prevent the use of the base by German U-boats. When the White Russians began their attemps to wrest control of the country from the communists, these Allied forces were reinforced and began a drive towards Moscow in their support. But, under pressure of public opinion, the Allied troops and aircraft were withdrawn and the White Russians were defeated by the Red Army.

It was Winston Churchill who was largely responsible for the salvation of the RAF, after his appointment as Secretary of State for War and Air in January 1919. Although Churchill detested air warfare and particularly the bombing of civilians, he was far-seeing enough to invite Trenchard back to his old position as Chief of Air Staff.

Trenchard was a single-minded commander, highly determined and with a strong sense of purpose. Although he knew that the RAF was in danger of being broken up, or at least losing some of its squadrons to the army and the navy, he led a devoted team which set about putting the whole structure on a permanent basis. In April 1920 he opened the RAF College at Cranwell in Lincolnshire, where suitable cadets underwent a highly professional training before qualifying as officers. Two months later, in a measure designed both to improve morale within the service and to impress civilians, he set up

the RAF Central Band at Uxbridge in Middlesex. This band soon established a high reputation for the quality of its performances. Trenchard realized that public interest and approval was essential to the survival of the RAF and, in a remarkably astute exercise in public relations, opened the first RAF Pageant at Hendon on 3 July 1920.

This opening was well-timed, for interest in flying had been re-awakened by the achievement of Alcock and Brown, who had made the first direct crossing of the Atlantic from west to east on 14-15 June of the previous year, in a modified Vickers Vimy bomber. This was followed a few weeks later by the RAF airship *R.34*, which crossed the Atlantic from east to west and then back again. In November, a four-man team flew from England in another Vimy and arrived in Australia less than thirty days later. Thousands flocked to the first RAF pageant and were duly impressed and thrilled by the displays of aerobatics, mock bombing and formation flying. This pageant became a popular annual event and served the additional purpose of attracting youngsters into the flying and technical branches of the RAF.

However, it was the events overseas which finally established the RAF in its permanent form as a third branch of the armed forces. For some years, RAF squadrons had been active on the North West Frontier of India and in Egypt. During this period a dissident known as 'The Mad Mullah' had been so active that some areas of Somaliland had passed to his control. All the efforts by the army to dislodge him and his followers had proved both expensive and unsuccessful. In January 1920 Trenchard sent out a squadron of D.H.9s which promptly bombed the Mullah's forts and camps, putting the tribesmen to flight. A small force of the Camel Corps then occupied the positions and peace was established throughout Somaliland, for a relatively trifling expenditure.

The lesson of this short campaign was not lost on the British government. In February 1921, Churchill took over as Secretary of State for Air and the Colonies, an apparently strange combination. He authorised Trenchard's scheme for the 'air control' of Iraq, a country previously under the control of Turkey but mandated to Britain, which had set up an Arab government preparatory to complete independence. Some powerful tribes disputed the authority of this new government, but they were duly suppressed by the RAF's bombing of villages, after preliminary warnings had been given. Troops were flown in by the RAF to support threatened British garrisons, while columns of armoured cars worked in co-operation with these tactics. An uneasy peace was established in the country, once again at a fraction of the cost of normal army operations. The results were considered so satisfactory that, shortly afterwards, Palestine also came under the control of the RAF. The squadrons in Iraq added to their laurels in 1928 when the Vickers Victorias based at Habbaniya evacuated over 500 British civilians who were threatened

Above: *In 1919 the Australian government offered £A10,000 for the first Australian airmen to fly within thirty days in a British aircraft to Australia. The brothers Lt Keith M. Smith and Capt Ross Smith, together with two mechanics, took off in a Vimy bomber on 12 November 1919 from Hounslow in Middlesex and arrived at Port Darwin on 10 December. Both the Smith brothers were knighted. Left to right: Sgt W.H. Spiers, Lt K.M. Smith, Capt R. Smith, Sgt J.M. Bennett.*
Source: Keystone Collection

Left: *The R.34 was one of two RAF airships, each with a length of 643 feet and powered by five engines, which entered service in 1919. She was based at Pulham in Norfolk, as shown in this photograph, and became notable for the first transatlantic flight made by a lighter-than-air craft. She left East Fortune in East Lothian in the early morning of 2 July 1919 and arrived over Mineola airfield, near New York, four days later. On 10 July, she took off again and arrived at Pulham after a flight of 75 hours. Unfortunately she was damaged beyond repair after hitting a hill on 28 January 1921, although there were no casualties.*

Source: Keystone Collection

Above: *The Vickers Vimy came into service in 1919, too late to see service in the First World War. It was a heavy bomber which could carry nearly 2,500 lb of bombs and was originally intended to attack targets in Germany. However, eight RAF squadrons were equipped with the machine, which remained on squadron strength until 1926. It was in a Vimy, but not a standard RAF machine, that Captain John Alcock and Lieutenant Arthur Whitten Brown made the first direct flight across the Atlantic, from St John's in Newfoundland to Clifton in Ireland, on 14-15 June 1919. This photograph shows the take-off from St John's.*

Source: Keystone Collection

Right: *The Vickers Vimy which made the record flight to Australia in 1919.*

Source: Keystone Collection

by rebel tribesman in Kabul in Afghanistan. In a period of two months, the civilians were successfully flown over mountains 10,000 feet high, without casualties. In the same year, the RAF's Aden Command was set up, controlling a vast area of southern Arabia.

At home, Trenchard was not successful in retaining full control of naval aviation. Squadrons had been allocated to army and naval co-operation, but a hybrid arrangement had developed between the crews of the naval squadrons, whereby the air observers were naval officers but the pilots remained in the RAF. Such a situation could not continue when the first flush-deck carrier, HMS *Eagle*, was commissioned in 1923. On 1 April 1924, the Fleet Air Arm of the RAF was formed. In spite of this title, control passed partially to the Admiralty.

On the other hand, an expansion of RAF squadrons took place. Trenchard did nothing to calm the fears of a public which remembered with dismay the series of German bombing attacks of a few years before. In fact, he coined the grim phrase "the bomber will always get through", a prediction which became deeply impressed in the public consciousness. In March 1922 *The Times* reported that the French Air Force possessed a front-line force of about 600 aircraft, whereas the RAF's defences amounted to less than forty aircraft. In those days, France was considered a potential enemy and there was considerable public alarm. In June of the following year, the Cabinet authorised the creation of an Air Defence of Great Britain, consisting of fifty-two squadrons, although several years were to pass before this force was completed. It was divided into four sections. There were the Fighting Areas and the Bombing Areas. There were the Special Reserve squadrons, composed of a mixture of regular airmen and local volunteers. Lastly, there was the Auxiliary Air Force, consisting of squadrons which depended on 'weekend fliers' in local areas, such as 600 (City of London) Squadron, 601 (County of London) Squadron, 602 (City of Glasgow) Squadron and 603 (City of Edinburgh) Squadron. These four auxiliary squadrons were formed in 1925 and were followed by others.

Another measure put into force by Trenchard in 1924 was the creation of the short-service commission, a system by which suitable applicants were trained and then commissioned for a limited number of years, with the possibility of a permanent commission at the end of that period. Another scheme was the establishment of an apprentice scheme at Halton in Buckinghamshire, where youngsters underwent a rigorous technical training. These became known as 'Trenchard's Brats', a term which the entrants adopted with pride. Some graduated into the flying branch and achieved great distinction in later years. Even nowadays, a 'Halton Brat' is highly regarded in the RAF. In 1925, Trenchard began to form the University Air Squadrons, initially at Oxford and Cambridge, but eventually almost every university boasted its own Air Squadron. Another measure was the creation of the Aeroplane and Armament Experimental Establishment at Martlesham Heath in Suffolk, later to move to Boscombe Down in Wiltshire. The RAF Benevolent Fund also had its origins in the Trenchard era.

On the other hand, financial stringency prevented the design and manufacture of RAF aircraft from progressing at the same rate as during the First World War. At the end of the twenties, many aircraft were little more than improved versions of wartime

Above: *The Avro 504K served for many years after the war as the RAF's standard trainer. Over 10,000 Avro 504s of various marks were built, a few carrying on until the beginning of the Second World War. This photograph of a 504K was taken in 1920.*

Source: Air Historical Branch (RAF), MoD, H.1444

Right: *In 1921, Queen Alexandra, the widow of King Edward VII, attended the RAF pageant at Hendon. The eldest daughter of King Christian IX of Denmark, Queen Alexandra died in 1925 at the age of 80.*

Source: Keystone Collection

Above: *A recruitment poster for the WRAF, which was formed at the same time as the RAF, on 1 April 1918.*

Source: Vintage Magazine Co. colour slide

Right: *The Fairey IIID entered service in late 1920 and could be used as either a floatplane or a landplane, being easily convertible from one configuration to the other. It could be used as a bomber or for reconnaissance. The floatplane version was employed by the Fleet Air Arm as well as by the RAF. Four landplane Fairey IIIDs made the RAF's first formation flight from Egypt to Capetown, in March/April 1926, and then flew back to England.*

Source: Aviation Bookshop

aircraft – wooden and fabric biplanes. Exceptions were, however, the sleek and fast monoplane seaplanes designed by Reginald J. Mitchell, with which the RAF began to win the Schneider Trophies in 1927. These were the forerunners of the splendid Spitfire of a decade later. The same period saw the end of the RAF's ventures with airships, with the tragic destruction of *R. 101* in France on 5 October 1930.

In 1927, Trenchard became the first Marshal of the Royal Air Force. Two years later, it was time for him to retire. But the RAF could not bear to part with him, and decreed that holders of their highest rank should *never* retire but stay on the active list for the rest of their lives. Thus Trenchard remained nominally in this position until he died on 10 February 1956, even though he became commissioner for the Metropolitan Police and served as a director of various companies.

The author was one of a handful of bomber crew members who were addressed by Marshal of the Royal Air Force Lord Trenchard at an RAF station in the spring of 1941. It was not a good period of the war for Britain, which was still fighting without allies other than the Commonwealth. Trenchard was sixty-eight years of age, dressed in his uniform and wearing his cap. He looked very old to his young listeners, with an iron-grey moustache and a tired face. His words of encouragement fell somewhat flat for, although his reports and memoranda were models of clarity and incisiveness, his voice was so gruff and inarticulate that he was known as 'Boom' Trenchard. But there was an air of fatherliness and kindness about him. He probably knew, better than anyone, that many of the young men in front of him would not survive the war.

Left: *A mock bombing attack by Bristol Fighters on an 'enemy village' during the Hendon Air Display of 1921.*

Source: Keystone Collection

Below: *The Vickers Vernon was the first of the RAF's troop carriers. It entered service with 45 Squadron in March 1922 and with 70 Squadron the following November, both based at Hinaidi in Iraq. These two squadrons employed their Vernons with great effect in that country, carrying troops to trouble spots, evacuating sick and wounded, and carrying mail to and from Baghdad. Vernons were replaced by Vickers Victorias in 1927.*

Source: Air Historical Branch (MoD), Ref: H-337

Left: *Hendon aerodrome photographed from 800 feet on 20 March 1932.*
Source: RAF Museum P7578

Below: *Troops with a Vickers Victoria or Valentia transport aircraft, on manoeuvres in Egypt. Two squadrons were equipped with these machines, both based at Hinaidi in Iraq.*
Source: Keystone Collection

Bottom: *One of the first replacements for the First World War fighters was the Armstrong Whitworth Siskin III, which came into service in 1924. Only two squadrons were equipped with the machine, which was replaced with the Siskin IIIA in 1927.*
Source: RAF Museum PO12151

Above left: *The Hawker Woodcock was delivered to the RAF in May 1925, being allocated the role of a night-fighter. It was fitted with lights under the wings. Only two squadrons were equipped with the machine, which continued in service until 1928.*
Source: Aviation Bookshop

Above: *In 1924, during a period of acute financial difficulties, the Fairey Fawn was the first of the post-war generation of light day-bombers to enter service in the RAF. It replaced the de Havilland 9A, the standard bomber which dated from the last few months of the war, and continued in service until 1929.*
Source: Aviation Bookshop

Left: *The Supermarine Southampton was one of the longest-serving flying boats in the RAF. It first entered service in August 1925 and continued until 1936. Designed by Reginald J. Mitchell, it set the pattern for flying boats until the introduction of the Short Sunderland. In October 1927 four Southamptons of the Far East Flight set off for Singapore, Australia and the China Sea, returning to Singapore without serious problems. This was a remarkable technical achievement for the era. This photograph is of a Southampton of 201 Squadron, based at Calshot, flying over The Needles, Isle of Wight.*
Source; RAF Museum P1010 25

Right: *The Gloster Grebe was one of the first of the post-war generation of RAF fighters, first coming into service in October 1923. In 1926 two Grebes were launched from the airship R33, as an experiment. The machine continued in first-line service until 1929.*
Source: RAF Museum P4493

Above: *The Handley Page Hyderabad, a heavy night-bomber, entered service with 99 Squadron at Bircham Newton in Norfolk during December 1925, and eventually equipped three other RAF squadrons. It was the RAF's last heavy bomber of wooden construction, and was withdrawn from front-line service at the end of 1930. This photograph shows a formation of Hyderabads of 99 Squadron.*
Source: Air Historical Branch (RAF), MoD, H.1198

Left: *The Gloster Gamecock was a highly aerobatic fighter, introduced into the RAF in March 1926, although only production for the RAF numbered only 91. One of these machines was flown by Pilot Officer Douglas Bader at the RAF air display at Hendon in 1931. The machine went out of service in 1933.*
Source: Aviation Bookshop

Right: *Together with the Gloster Grebe, the Armstrong Whitworth Siskin III began to replace the wartime generation of fighters which had remained as standard equipment for five years. It came into service in May 1924 and, in a time of financial stringency, equipped only two squadrons. Siskins were finally withdrawn in November 1931.*

Source: Air Historical Branch (MoD), Ref: H.12

Right: *The Armstrong Whitworth Atlas was the first RAF aircraft designed specifically for the role of army co-operation. It first entered service in October 1927, replacing the adapted Bristol Fighter which had been employed on this capacity hitherto. Fitted with dual controls, it was also employed as an advanced trainer. The machines in this photograph, dated 1932, were on the strength of the Oxford University Air Squadron.*

Source: RAF Museum P101666

Left: *The Fairey Fox day-bomber was first delivered to 12 Squadron in June 1926 and proved over 50 m.p.h. faster than the Fairey Fawn which it superseded. It was also faster than any RAF fighter at the time. However, owing to national financial constraints, no other squadron was supplied with the machine, which remained in service with 12 Squadron until 1931.*

Source: Aviation Bookshop

Right: *The Vickers Virginia, known with affection as the 'Ginny', saw service as a heavy night-bomber in the RAF with a series of marks from 1924 to 1937. Even after withdrawal from front-line service, some machines continued as parachute trainers, and a few carried on in varied capacities right up to 1941. Although the four-man crew were accommodated in open cockpits and the machine trundled along at less than 100 m.p.h., the Virginia was well-liked for its dependable and robust qualities. This photograph is of a Mark X, the last of the series, part of the Parachute Test Section at Henlow in Bedfordshire.*

Source: RAF Museum P101427

Above: *The Avro 504N, or 'Lynx-Avro' was the post-war version of the Avro 504K trainer, fitted with a Lynx radial in 1927. Fully aerobatic, it was used with great success in flying schools until 1933, when replaced with Avro Tutors. This photograph shows an Avro 504N of the Cambridge University Air Squadron.*

Source: RAF Museum P100773

Right: *The Fairey IIIF entered service in late 1927 and proved a reliable day-bomber at home and a general-purpose aircraft in the Middle East. There was also a seaplane version, which continued at Malta until August 1935.*

Source: Aviation Bookshop

Left: *Manston aerodrome photographed from 3,000 feet, showing Vickers Virginias in the foreground.*

Source: RAF Museum P4331

Right: *The eleventh Schneider Trophy was held in the Solent in September 1929, following the RAF's win at Venice two years before. In preparation the RAF formed a High Speed Flight and entered two Supermarine S.6 seaplanes as well as two Gloster VI Seaplanes. Fl Off H.R.D. Waghorn came in first place in Supermarine N247 (pictured here) at an average speed of 328.63 m.p.h.*

Source: Keystone Collection

Below: *An airman adjusting the fusing mechanism of a Royal Aircraft Factory 520 lb bomb beneath a Vickers Virginia, photographed in 1928 when the RAF was engaged in air raid manoeuvres over London.*

Source: Keystone Collection

Below: *In 1927, the RAF entered a team for the first time in the Schneider Trophy. This contest was an international event, first held in 1913 by Jacques Schneider, a patron of French aviation. The three machines entered by the RAF were Supermarine S.5 seaplanes, designed by Reginald J. Mitchell, who later designed the Spitfire. The contest was held in Venice and was won on 27 September 1927 by Flt Lt N. Webster in N220 at an average speed of 281.65 m.p.h. Second place was won by N219 (photographed here at Calshot in Hampshire after a test flight) flown by Flt Lt O.E. Worsley at an average speed of 273.07 m.p.h.*

Source: Keystone Collection

Left: *The RAF team for the eleventh Schneider Trophy in 1929 consisted of (left to right) Fl Off H.R.D. Waghorn, Fl Off T.H. Moon, Flt Lt D'Arcy Greig, Sqdn Ldr A.H. Orlebar, Flt Lt G.H. Stainforth and Fl Off R.L.R. Atcherley.*

Source: Keystone Collection

Below: *The* R.101, *777 feet long, over the town of Bedford in October 1929, after leaving Cardington on one of her test flights. She suffered from several technical problems, including engine defects.*

Source: Keystone Collection

Left: *From 1928 most Vimys were refitted with radial engines and employed at Flying Training Schools. Some were used for training parachutists, at Henlow in Bedfordshire. This photograph was taken at the Henlow Air Pageant in June 1931.*
Source: Keystone Collection

Below: *The twelfth Schneider Trophy was held in the Solent in September 1931. The two main entries by the RAF were Supermarine S.6B seaplanes. First place went to Flt Lt J.N. Boothman in S1595 (pictured here after a test flight, with Fl Lt F.W. Long being carried ashore) who achieved an average speed of 340.08 m.p.h. This gave the RAF its third successive win in the Schneider Trophy, and thus, they retained the trophy in perpetuity.*
Source: Keystone Collection

Bottom: *The pilot being brought ashore.*
Source: Keystone Collection

Left: *The remains of the R.101 after her crash at 02.08 hours on 5 October 1930, near Beauvais in France, while on her journey from Cardington to India. The airship burnt out and there were only six survivors from the fifty-four on board. Among those who lost their lives were the Air Minister, Lord Thompson, and the Director of Civil Aviation, Sir Sefton Brancker. In this photograph, the French firemen are holding up the Royal Air Force ensign.*

Source: Keystone Collection

Above: *The Handley Page Hinaidi was a heavy night-bomber, the successor to the Handley-Page Hyderabad. It first came into service in October 1929, and four RAF squadrons were equipped with the Hinaidi before the Handley Page Heyford arrived in 1933.*

Source: RAF Museum PO15337

Left: *The Westland Wapiti is best remembered for its active service on the North-West Frontier of India and in Iraq, where it was employed as a day-bomber on army co-operation. First delivered in July 1928, it remained in service until 1939. Several Auxiliary Air Force squadrons at home were also equipped with the machine. It proved to be strong and reliable, as well as fully aerobatic. This photograph shows Wapiti IIAs of 604 Squadron in 1931, when the squadron was based at Hendon.*

Source: RAF Museum P101174

Above: *Lord Trenchard, Marshal of the Royal Air Force, speaking after he had opened the town headquarters of 604 (County of Middlesex) Squadron at Hampstead on 7 April 1934. The squadron was part of the Auxiliary Air Force, based at Hendon and equipped with Westland Wapiti IIA day bombers.*

Source: Keystone Collection

Right: *The Hawker Horsley was employed both as a day-bomber and as a torpedo-bomber. Although only 128 Horsleys were manufactured for the RAF, they began as all-wooden construction, then of wood and metal, and finally as all-metal. The machine entered service in 1927 and continued to 1935.*

Source: Aviation Bookshop

CHAPTER 4

PRELUDE TO WAR

Trenchard's place as Chief of Staff was taken over by one of his lieutenants, Sir John Salmond, but this period of tenure was quite short and uneventful. In 1933, Sir Edward Ellington was appointed to the position. Although Ellington was a self-effacing commander who was not considered to have the charisma of Trenchard, he proved to be a first-class staff officer who presided over a technical revolution which shaped the RAF of the Second World War.

These were the years which saw the rise of dictatorships and international aggression, in which air forces played prominent and unpleasant roles. In 1932, the Japanese began the bombing of China from the air, and the world saw films of the horrifying effect on a defenceless civilian population, especially in Shanghai. Mussolini had assumed the Fascist dictatorship of Italy in 1922, after his 'march on Rome', but this caused little public disquiet in Britain until it was realized that Germany was developing its own version of this political philosophy with the rise of the National Socialist Party. In 1933, when Adolf Hitler was appointed Chancellor, the industrial strength and military prowess of Germany were feared far more than any threat from Italy.

The conditions of the Treaty of Peace with Germany, signed at Versailles in June 1919, had reduced that country's military forces to an army of 100,000 with a small navy, for defensive purposes, and completely prohibited any air force. However, in the post-war years it became apparent that aircrews in Germany were receiving military training under the guise of civilians, allegedly for sporting purposes, while others were being trained in other countries, including Russia. Moreover, German aircraft designers were able to exercise their skills in Sweden, Switzerland and Italy, while their home industry had produced civil aircraft for the German airline *Lufthansa* which were readily adaptable to military use. The Junkers Ju52 and the Heinkel He111 became examples of such conversions.

Although the danger of a resurgent Germany with a National Socialist philosophy, which included the dangerously explosive concept of the right to territorial expansion in Europe under the name of *Lebensraum*, was startlingly apparent to some observers in Britain, the overwhelming mass of people still refused to believe that another European war was possible. Improved standards of living and the conquest of unemployment, together with a widespread belief in pacifism, dominated the thoughts of many British people. Advocates of re-armament and a stronger air force were not popular, although at the same time there was a fascination with flying. The long-distance records established by such pilots as Charles A. Lindbergh, Amelia Earhart, Amy Johnson and Charles Kingsford Smith were headline news and greeted with wild acclaim bordering on worship of the achievers.

In 1934, only forty-two of the fifty-two RAF squadrons ordered in 1923 had been established, with a first-line strength of 488 aircraft. However, in that year the government decided to embark on another expansion programme, against opposition in Parliament and some censure in the Press. The RAF was to increase as rapidly as possible to seventy-five squadrons, and to a hundred and twenty-eight squadrons within five years. This programme was dominated by the theory of the 'knock-out

Below: *The Bristol Bulldog was one of the most successful RAF fighters in the inter-war period, first entering service in May 1929. It was fast, extremely strong, fully aerobatic and, by comparison with its predecessors, took off quickly and had a high rate of climb. Over 300 aircraft were eventually supplied until, in 1937, the fighter was replaced with Gloster Gauntlets and Gladiators or Hawker Demons.*
Source: RAF Museum P3599

Right: *A restored Hawker Hart, registration G-ABMR, repainted as J9941 of 57 Squadron, which was equipped with Harts from October 1931 to May 1936.*

Source: RAF Museum colour slide P36021

Left: *The air displays at Hendon had become popular events by the 1930s, and most of the RAF's aircraft could be seen at these. This poster, representing a Hawker Hart, appeared in 1931.*

Source: RAF Museum (Crown copyright) P00512

Below: *The Hawker Hart, a light day-bomber, was the progenitor of a series of derivatives which served in the RAF in the inter-war period. First delivered in January 1930, it outpaced every RAF fighter in its day. It had a tendency to swing to the left on take-off but this was followed by a steep rate of climb and an excellent performance in aerobatics. The streamlined and elegant shape included a tapered nose which gave the pilot a splendid view. It was still in service in 1939 and continued on active operations in India until 1942. Other Harts continued as trainers in the early war years.*

Source: Keystone Collection

blow', for it was believed that air bombardment alone could win a war and that Britain should be equipped with a force capable of getting in the first major attacks. Additional fighter squadrons were to be formed, but primarily as a defensive force to appease a population which feared the type of air attacks they saw in cinemas and newspaper photographs.

At this stage, the RAF was still equipped mainly with biplanes in its bomber, fighter and coastal squadrons, mostly of wood or metal frames covered with fabric, resulting from the continuation of the belief that these were safer to fly than monoplanes. This thinking had not prevailed among civilian airliner companies, with the incongruous situation that some civil aircraft were faster than those of the RAF. However, the situation was changing, with the development of military monoplanes such as the Avro Anson reconnaissance aircraft, the Vickers Wellesley and Wellington bombers, the Armstrong Whitworth Whitley heavy bomber, the Handley Page Hampden medium bomber, the army co-operation Westland Lysander, and the Short Sunderland flying boat. In addition, the team headed by Sir Edward Ellington put out three far-seeing specifications which heralded further technical advances.

The first was Air Ministry Spec. F.5/34, issued in November 1934 but revised the following year after a design conference. This called for a fighter to replace the four-gun Gloster Gauntlet and Gladiator biplanes which were in production. It was to have a much better speed, rate of climb and ceiling, as well as the ability to carry eight machine guns. Two private companies responded to this specification. These were Hawker, with Sydney Camm as chief engineer, and Supermarine, with Reginald J. Mitchell as chief designer. Both design teams worked in close collaboration with RAF officers, fortunately at a time when two other technical developments came to fruition. These were the Merlin engine designed by Rolls Royce and the .303 inch Browning machine gun perfected by the Armament Research Department of the Air Ministry. The various strands came together in the prototypes of the Hawker Hurricane, which eventually entered service in December 1937, and the Supermarine Spitfire, which was delivered to RAF squadrons from June of the following year.

The second specification was B.12/36 of July 1936, which resulted in the Short Stirling, the first four-engined bomber to serve in the RAF, from August 1940 onwards. The third specification was P.13/36 of September 1936, which called for an all-metal medium/heavy bomber with a mid-wing and twin engines. This resulted in the Avro Manchester, a bomber which entered service in November 1940 and proved unsuccessful but earned its place in RAF history as the progenitor of the famous four-engined Lancaster. The other bomber which resulted from this specification was the very successful Handley Page Halifax, originally designed as a twin-engined aircraft but modified to take four engines, which also entered squadron service in November 1940. Another important development took place in this period, almost by accident. The

belief that 'the bomber will always get through' had led to the setting up in January 1935 of a Aeronautical Research Committee consisting of a number of eminent scientists, charged with the function of finding ways to repel an air attack. One of the possibilities examined was the notion of a 'death ray' which would destroy approaching aircraft. The scientists consulted R.A. Watson-Watt of the Radio Department of the National Physical Laboratory, who pointed out that, although the death ray idea was nonsense, approaching aircraft re-radiated radio signals. From this, the concept of Radio Direction Finding (RDF) was born, later to be shortened to 'radar'. The instruments led eventually to the setting up of twenty 'Chain Home' (CH) radar stations around the coasts of Britain, and to the invention of the 'Identification Friend or Foe' (IFF) equipment carried in all operational RAF aircraft. By the time war broke out, it was possible to detect approaching enemy aircraft from distances up to 100 miles from British shores, with considerable accuracy.

Meanwhile, the march of the dictators continued. Hitler assumed complete power in Germany in 1934 and in February of the following year the *Luftwaffe* was reborn, in defiance of the Treaty of Versailles. With Hermann Goering, a renowned pilot of the First World War, as its commander-in-chief, it possessed over 1,800 aircraft (of which about 580 were first-line) and 20,000 personnel. Moreover, it was set on an accelerated pace of expansion. Factories which had hitherto manufactured products which were apparently unwarlike were suddenly able to make machine guns, while other companies such as Henschel and Blohm und Voss found that they were capable of manufacturing military aircraft, especially trainers.

Italy attacked Abyssinia on 3 October 1935, bombing villages and eventually even using poison gas, a weapon banned by the League of Nations. The world was shocked by films and photographs showing these attacks against villagers. Economic sanctions were instigated against Italy as an alternative to military intervention, but these proved ineffectual. The RAF moved squadrons to Egypt, Somaliland and Malta, while Ellington even offered to bomb northern Italy from bases in southern France, but no military action was taken.

In the same year, the Saar was returned to Germany, following a plebiscite. In March 1936, Hitler began the remilitarisation of the Rhineland, and made no secret of his territorial ambitions in Europe. In July of that year, General Francisco Franco brought troops from Morocco to Spain in an attempt to overturn the government and impose a Fascist dictatorship on the country. He achieved this objective after almost three years of cruel civil war, assisted by contingents of aircraft from Italy and Germany. Once again, films of attacks against civilian populations were shown around the world. For the first time, the effectiveness of German aircraft such as the Heinkel He111, the Dornier Do17, the Junkers Ju52 and the Messerschmitt Bf109, became apparent to the RAF.

In 1936, the RAF at home was divided into five sections: the Western Area, consisting of heavy bombers; the Central Area, with light bombers and general-purpose aircraft; the Fighting Area, with single-engined fighters; the Inland Area, with army co-operation squadrons; and the Coastal Area, with flying boats and a squadron of torpedo bombers. Overseas, there were five commands: the Middle East, the Mediterranean, India, Aden and the Far East. In May of that year, important structural alterations began at home, dividing the RAF according to function. A Training Command was set up, while the operational sections were grouped into Bomber Command, Fighter Command and Coastal Command, each responsible to the Chief of Air Staff via the Air Council. These Commands controlled regional Groups, which administered their own stations, which in turn administered squadrons. This was the structure of the RAF which fought the Second World War.

At the same time as the expansion programme got under way, the RAF was authorised to increase the number of its aerodromes from fifty-two to a hundred and thirty-eight. Many of these new aerodromes were built in East Anglia, Lincolnshire and Yorkshire, facing Germany. Bomber squadrons which had formed the Western Area, with France as a potential enemy, were transferred to these new aerodromes.

Another measure organized in 1936 was the creation of the Royal Air Force Volunteer Reserve, a form of 'Citizen Air Force' which was the RAF's equivalent of the Territorial Army. Young men were invited from April 1937 onwards to learn to train as pilots, observers or wireless operators in their spare time. The scheme proved extremely popular, so much so that by the time war broke out the RAFVR stood at over 10,000 men in these three aircrew categories, the majority being pilots.

On 1 September 1937, Sir Cyril Newhall took over from Sir Edward Ellington as Chief of Air Staff. In that year, the Air Estimates rose to £137.6 million, compared with only £16.8 million in 1933. The new Chief of Air Staff presided over the continued expansion, at a time when the international situation became even more threatening.

In July 1937 the Japanese had begun their attempted conquest of the whole of China, causing appalling casualties with a series of bombing attacks designed to spread terror among civilians. This war was still continuing when the Japanese attacked Pearl Harbour on 7 December 1941. In February 1938 Germany annexed Austria, with the apparent enthusiasm of the majority of the Austrian population. Neville Chamberlain, the prime minister of a coalition government, flew out to Munich and returned with a piece of paper signed by Hitler, Mussolini, Daladier and himself, purporting to

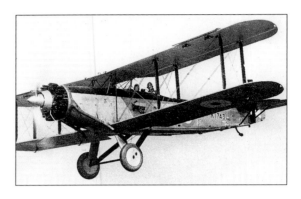

Above: *The Fairey Gordon entered service in the RAF in England in April 1931, and was employed as a light day-bomber. It remained in front-line service, both at home and in the Middle East until 1938. Several aircraft were lost on operations during the insurrections in Palestine. The machine continued as a drogue-tower and armament trainer in the early months of the Second World War.*

Source: Aviation Bookshop

Below left: *The Hawker Fury I became one of the most admired of the RAF's standard fighters after it entered service in May 1931. It was the first RAF fighter to attain a maximum speed of over 200 m.p.h. with a full warload. The sleek and elegant lines exemplified its high manoeuvrability and instant response at the controls, which were demonstrated by formation flying at air shows. An improved version, the Fury II, was introduced in December 1936, but by the Second World War the Fury was rendered obsolete with the arrival of the monoplane Hurricane.*

Source: Aviation Bookshop

Below: *The cockpit of a Hawker Fury. Within a few years, the flying panels of most operational aircraft in the RAF were standardised to present six instruments in a set pattern: airspeed indicator, artificial horizon, rate of climb, altimeter, gyroscope, and turn and bank.*

Source: Air Historical Branch (RAF), MoD, H.1985

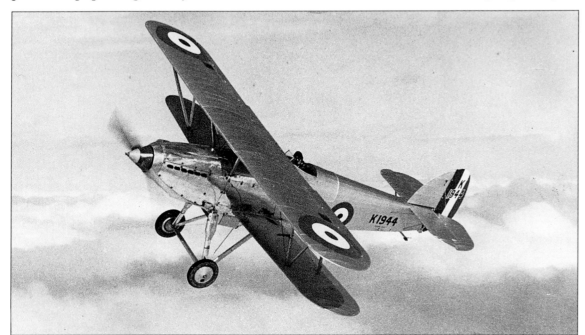

Right: *The Hawker Demon was a two-seat fighter, a variant of the Hawker Hart day-bomber, originally called the Hart Fighter. It began service in March 1931 and eleven home-based squadrons were eventually equipped with the machine, as well as seven overseas. Later Demons were fitted with a Fraser-Nash folding metal cupola, to protect the gunner from the slip-stream. The machine was taken out of service in 1939.*

Source: Aviation Bookshop

Right: *Yet another variation of the Hawker Hart was the Hawker Audax. It first went into service from February 1932 with army co-operation squadrons but perhaps became better known as an advanced trainer with Service Flying Training Schools. As a front-line aircraft at home, it was replaced in 1938 but it continued as a trainer until the early years of the Second World War. Overseas, it saw action with 237 (Rhodesian) Squadron in East Africa and also during the investment of RAF Habbaniya in Iraq in May 1941.*

Source: Aviation Bookshop

guarantee 'peace for our time'. Very few people were convinced, but the RAF breathed a sigh of relief, for its expansion programme had not yet reached fulfilment.

The worst fears were realized when Hitler annexed Bohemia and Moravia from Czechoslovakia in March 1939, and forced Lithuania to cede the region of Memel in the same month. Italy occupied Albania in April, and entered into the 'Axis' pact with Germany. Germany began a propaganda campaign against Poland. Not even the most blinkered observer could have any doubts about the approach of war when Britain and France 'guaranteed' the Polish frontiers. Then Germany signed a non-aggression pact with Russia, giving Germany a free hand on Poland's western frontier.

The expansion of the RAF continued apace. In November 1938, a Balloon Command was formed, with barrages around most major cities, and its own squadrons. On 24 May 1939, the future of the Fleet Air Arm was settled when this air arm, which had been somewhat neglected in the programme, was returned in its entirety to the Admiralty. A week later, the Women's Royal Air Force was established, and those volunteers who had trained in the Auxiliary Territorial Service for service with the RAF were transferred to this new body.

The German invasion of Poland began on 1 September and, when Hitler failed to respond to the British and French ultimatum, war was declared two days later.

Left: *Over 1,000 de Havilland Tiger Moths were delivered to the RAF before the Second World War, the first consignments arriving in February 1932. The Tiger was the last biplane* ab initio *trainer employed by the RAF in the UK and continued until 1947, by which time about 8,800 had been built. Although the open cockpits could be cold and draughty, the trainer was robust and easy to fly. It was regarded with great affection by most RAF pilots of the era. This photograph was taken at 32 Elementary Flying Training School at Swift Current, Bowden, Alberta. In Canada, many Tigers were fitted with canopies as protection against the bitterly cold winters.*
Source: RAF Museum PO16608

Right: *The Avro Tutor succeeded the Avro 504N and was first delivered to the Central Flying School in 1932, becoming standard as an* ab initio *trainer in RAF flying schools until 1939. This photograph shows an Avro Tutor of the Cambridge University Air Squadron.*
Source: RAF Museum P3773

Left: *The Vickers Vildebeest was first delivered to the RAF in 1932 and continued in service until 1942. On the outbreak of the Second World War, it was the only torpedo bomber available to Coastal Command and the maritime squadrons overseas. The home-based squadrons were re-equipped with the Bristol Beaufort in 1940. This photograph shows Vildebeest IVs, from the last batch of seventeen delivered to the RAF in 1937. Torpedoes were suspended in a nose-down attitude, so that they would enter the sea at the correct angle when dropped from the operating height of eighty feet.*
Source: Keystone Collection

Above: *The Westland Wallace was similar to the Westland Wapiti, but fitted with a more powerful engine and a lengthened fuselage. It first entered service in January 1933 and eventually four squadrons were equipped with this general-purpose aircraft. The Westland Wallace II, as in this photograph of serial K6085, was fitted with an even more powerful engine and an enclosed canopy for both seats. After withdrawal from front-line service, Wallaces continued as target-towers until final retirement in 1943.*

Source: Air Historical Branch (MoD), Ref: H.1989

Above: *'Stunt flying' was of great interest to the air-minded public of the 1930s, with perhaps the opportunity to go up in an aircraft for a short flight at 5/- a time. Many young men who joined the RAF in the Second World War had their first taste of flying at Hendon.*

Source: RAF Museum (Crown copyright) P00404

Left: *The Handley Page Heyford, with its fuselage attached to the upper wing and its equally distinctive 'dustbin' ventral turret, was the last of the RAF's biplane heavy bombers. The first Heyfords were delivered to the RAF in late 1933, and the aircraft continued in front-line service until 1937, when most gave way to the Vickers Wellington. Some machines then continued as trainers and test vehicles, the last being withdrawn in July 1941. In this photograph, a Heyford I with its dustbin retracted is being 'attacked' by a Hawker Demon.*

Source: RAF Museum P105338

Left: *The World's Long-distance Record for Aviation was a prize which the Air Ministry wished to gain for Great Britain in the late 1920s, and two long-range monoplanes were specially designed by Fairey for this purpose. They could carry up to 1,000 gallons of fuel, giving them a range of over 5,000 miles. Unfortunately the first, serial J9479, crashed in 1929 in Tunisia, killing the crew of two. The second, serial K1991, flew on 27-28 October 1931 from Cranwell to Abu Sueir in Egypt; this photograph was taken in Heliopolis. On 6 February 1933, it took off from Cranwell and reached Walvis Bay in S.W. Africa after 57 hours 25 minutes, a distance of 5,309 miles, thus gaining the record for Great Britain.*

Source: RAF Museum P1540

Right: *A view of the amphibian Walrus, flying low over Southampton Water in May 1936. The wheels are folded up into the wings.*

Source: Keystone Collection

Above: *Only 209 Squadron, based at Mount Batten in Devonshire, was equipped with the Blackburn Iris, from February 1930 to June 1934. In this period, the Iris was the largest aircraft in service in the RAF and flew on a number of V.I.P. flights, to Iceland, Gibraltar and Egypt. The last Iris to be manufactured was fitted with a 37 mm C.O.W. gun in an enlarged front cockpit. The Iris flying boats were eventually replaced with Blackburn Perths.*

Source: Air Historical Branch (MoD), Ref: H.2056

Left: *The Blackburn Perth entered service in January 1934, as the fastest RAF flying boat of its period. Only four were built, serving with 209 Squadron at Mount Batten in Devon until January 1936.*

Source: RAF Museum P101403

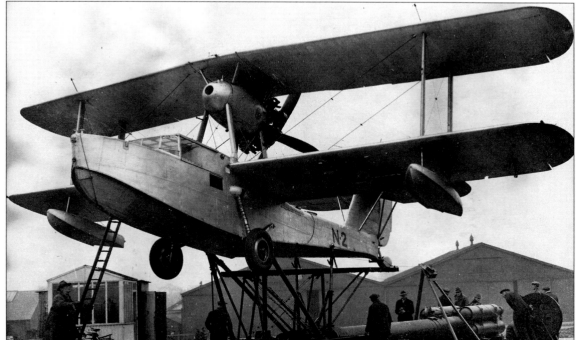

Left: *The Supermarine Walrus, originally known as the Seagull V, came into RAF service in 1934. It was an amphibian aircraft with a pusher engine, used by both the Fleet Air Arm and the RAF. Although it had an ungainly appearance and only a slow cruising speed, it was regarded with enormous affection by RAF airmen, who referred to it somewhat disrespectfully as the 'Shagbat'; according to RAF legend, this was a mythical Egyptian bird which could fly in ever-decreasing circles until it finally disappeared. The Walrus achieved renown during World War Two as an air-sea rescue aircraft at home, in the Mediterranean and the Indian Ocean. Many heroic and life-saving deeds were performed by the aircrews who flew this machine, which remained in service until the end of the war, being built by Saro as well as Supermarine.*

Source: Keystone Collection

Left: *The Short Singapore III first entered service in January 1935. The four engines of the flying boat were of the 'push-pull' variety, in tandem. Thirty-seven were built for the RAF, equipping six squadrons at home and two overseas. Some Singapores remained with the RAF at the outbreak of the Second World War, both at home and abroad, but these were soon replaced by Sunderlands.*

Source: Keystone Collection

Below: *The Supermarine Scapa was a development on the highly reliable Southampton flying boat, first entering service in May 1935 with 202 Squadron at Kalafrana in Malta. Scapas were employed on anti-submarine patrols during the Spanish Civil War, to protect shipping. Only fourteen were built for the RAF, continuing in service until December 1938. This photograph is of serial K4191 of 204 Squadron, refuelling from a depot ship.*

Source: Air Historical Branch (MoD), Ref: H.332

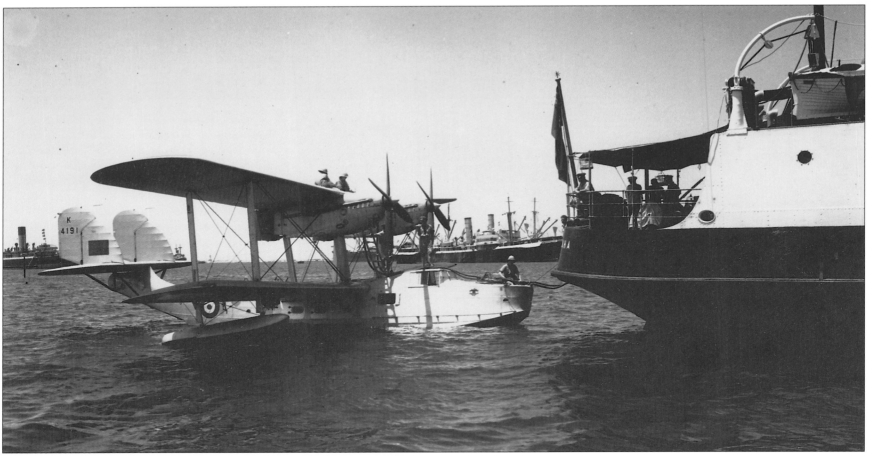

Above: *The Boulton Paul Overstrand, a medium bomber which was delivered to 101 Squadron in 1935 and remained in front-line service until 1938. It was the first RAF bomber to be fitted with the new power-operated turret, in the nose, with a single Lewis gun. In the Second World War, it saw active service for a few months as a gunnery trainer.*

Source: Keystone Collection

Below: *The Vickers Valentia was developed from the Vickers Victoria troop carrier. It first entered service in September 1935, with 216 Squadron at Heliopolis in Egypt. Most Valentias flew in the Middle East and India, until phased out in 1941. This photograph was taken in Egypt, with the pyramids in the background.*

Source: Keystone Collection

Above: *The first power-operated turret in the RAF, in the nose of the Boulton Paul Overstrand, fitted with a single .303 inch Lewis gun.*

Source: Keystone Collection

Above: *The Gloster Gauntlet was the fastest fighter in the RAF from 1935 to 1937, fourteen squadrons being equipped with the machine. Unlike the Gladiator which followed it, the cockpit was open. The machine was obsolescent at the outbreak of the Second World War but four Gauntlets operated against the Italians in the autumn of 1940.*

Source: Aviation Bookshop

Right: *A Hawker Audax flying over the Pyramids of Giza. The aircraft was probably from 208 Squadron, which was based nearby at Heliopolis from April to December 1936.*

Source: Keystone Collection

Above: *A Lewis Mark III .303 inch machine gun with a ring sight, in the gunner's cockpit of a Hawker Audax. The foresight was a Norman Vane Sight, which turned with the slipstream and compensated for the motion of the gunner's aircraft, although it was still necessary to make allowances for deflection caused by the manoeuvres of the enemy aircraft.*

Source: Keystone Collection

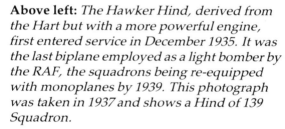

Above left: *The Hawker Hind, derived from the Hart but with a more powerful engine, first entered service in December 1935. It was the last biplane employed as a light bomber by the RAF, the squadrons being re-equipped with monoplanes by 1939. This photograph was taken in 1937 and shows a Hind of 139 Squadron.*

Source: Keystone Collection

Above: *A Hawker Hart of 603 (City of Edinburgh) Squadron, which was equipped with the machine from February 1934 to February 1938.*

Source: RAF Museum P101457

Below: *A flight sergeant holding a gun camera above the Scarff ring in the rear fuselage of an aircraft. The badge on the fuselage is similar to that of 603 (City of Edinburgh) Squadron.*

Source: Keystone Collection

On 16 January 1936, a standard frame for unit badges for the RAF was devised, with the King's Crown above and a scroll beneath. Squadrons and other units were able to submit specimens to an Inspector of Royal Air Force Badges. Several were approved within the next few months, and these were published in 1936 and 1937.

No. 2 (Army Co-operation) Squadron, equipped with Hawker Audaxes and based at Hawkinge in Kent.

RAF Museum colour slide PO30006

No. 4 (Army Co-operation) Squadron, equipped with Hawker Audaxes and based at Farnborough in Hampshire. Motto: To see into the Future.

RAF Museum colour slide PO30011

No. 12 (Bomber) Squadron, equipped with Hawker Hinds and based at Andover in Hampshire.

RAF Museum colour slide PO30028

No. 15 (Bomber) Squadron, equipped with Hawker Hinds and based at Abingdon in Berkshire.

RAF Museum colour slide PO30033

No. 18 (Bomber) Squadron, equipped with Hawker Hinds and based at Upper Heyford in Oxfordshire. Motto: With Courage and Faith.

RAF Museum colour slide PO30039

No. 22 (Torpedo Bomber) Squadron, equipped with Vickers Vildebeests and based at Hal Far in Malta. Motto: Valiant and Brave.

RAF Museum colour slide PO30044

No. 33 (Bomber) Squadron, equipped with Hawker Harts and based at Mersa Matruh in Egypt.

RAF Museum colour slide PO30056

No. 40 (Bomber) Squadron, equipped with
Hawker Hinds and based at Abingdon in
Berkshire. Motto: To Drive the Enemy from
the Sky.

RAF Museum colour slide PO30067

No. 41 (Fighter) Squadron, equipped with
Hawker Demons and based at Catterick in
Yorkshire.

RAF Museum colour slide PO30070

No. 74 (Fighter) Squadron, equipped with
Hawker Demons and based at Hornchurch in
Essex.

RAF Museum colour slide PO30104

No. 201 (Flying Boat) Squadron, equipped
with Short Southamptons and Saro Londons,
and based at Calshot in Hampshire. Motto:
Here and Everywhere.

RAF Museum colour slide PO30173

No. 203 (Flying Boat) Squadron, equipped
with Short Singapores and based at Basra in
Iraq. Motto: West and East.

RAF Museum colour slide PO30175

No. 207 (Bomber) Squadron, equipped with
Fairey Gordons and based at Gebeit in the
Sudan. Motto: Always Prepared

RAF Museum colour slide PO30179

No. 230 (Flying Boat) Squadron, equipped
with Short Singapores and based at Seletar in
Singapore. Motto: (Malay)
We Seek Far.

RAF Museum colour slide PO30198

No. 604 (County of Middlesex) Squadron,
equipped with Hawker Demons and based at
Hendon in Middlesex. Motto: If You Want
Peace, Prepare For War.

RAF Museum colour slide PO30245

Right: *The Avro Anson was originally ordered by the RAF for coastal reconnaissance duties and came into service in March 1936. It was one of the first aircraft in the RAF with a retractable undercarriage, although this was wound up with a handle which required 122 turns. The Anson entered the war with twelve squadrons of Coastal Command, engaged mainly on reconnaissance and convoy escort duties, but was gradually replaced with more modern machines such as the Hudson and the Beaufort. However, the Anson continued as a standard twin-engined trainer for pilots, navigators, wireless operators and air gunners, remaining in service until 1968. A highly reliable and well-liked machine, it deserved its nickname of 'Faithful Annie'.*

Source: Keystone Collection

Above: *Wheeling in an Avro Anson after a flight.*

Source: Keystone Collection

Left: *The Saro London entered service with the RAF in April 1936 and flew operationally until mid 1941. At the end of 1937, five Londons of 204 Squadron, fitted with long-range tanks, cruised from England to New South Wales and returned the following May.*

Source: RAF Museum P101501

Below: *The RAF gained the World's Altitude Record on two occasions with the Bristol Type138A, serial K4879, constructed of wood to meet an Air Ministry specification. In September 1936 it flew from Farnborough to reach the record height of 49,967 feet. This record was beaten by Italy the following May, but regained for the RAF on 30 June 1937 when the Type 138A reached 53,937 feet.*

Source: RAF Museum PO12644

Above: *The Fairey Hendon in this photograph entered service with 38 Squadron in November 1936. It was a heavy night-bomber, but only fourteen machines were built. The machine was replaced by the new Wellington bomber in July 1939.*

Source: Aviation Bookshop

Below: *The Saro Cloud was an amphibian flying boat, used for training pilots and navigators. It entered service in August 1933 at Calshot in Hampshire and was retired in 1936. Only sixteen of this aircraft were produced.*

Source: Keystone Collection

Right: *The Handley Page Harrow came into service in January 1937 as one of the first monoplane heavy bombers to replace the RAF's biplanes. It could carry 3,000 lb of bombs but was already out-dated by the outbreak of the Second World War, by which time the squadrons had converted to Wellingtons. Apart from some work in aerial minelaying and as a troop transport, the Harrow did not see operational service. This photograph was taken in November 1936 and shows the first Harrow, at Radlett aerodrome in Hertfordshire on the occasion of its christening by the Mayoress of Harrow.*

Source: Keystone Collection

Left: *The last of the RAF's biplane fighters was the Gloster Gladiator, which first entered service in February 1937 and equipped more than thirty squadrons. It proved easy to fly and was highly manoeuvrable, being quite formidable with four Browning guns. Most Gladiators were superseded by monoplane fighters by the outbreak of the Second World War, but some went to France as part of the Advanced Air Striking Force, while others operated in Norway during the German invasion of that country. The Gladiator is perhaps best remembered for the heroic defence of Malta and for operations in Africa against the Regia Aeronautica, before being outclassed by German fighters. This photograph of serial L7619 of 33 Squadron was taken in Ismailia in Egypt.*

Source: RAF Museum P8548

Right: *The Armstrong Whitworth Whitley, first delivered to the RAF in March 1937, formed part of the heavy bomber force in the early years of the Second World War. Its appearance was rather ungainly and it required firm handling, but the construction was rugged enough to absorb a lot of punishment. It was the first bomber to be equipped with a power-operated turret containing four Browning machine guns, as well as the first to fly over Berlin, on a leaflet raid of 1/2 October 1939. The last operational flight was on the night of 29/30 April 1942. These three Whitleys of 102 Squadron were photographed in 1940.*

Source: Keystone Collection

Above: *The Supermarine Stranraer entered service with 228 Squadron in April 1937, four Coastal Command squadrons being eventually equipped with this flying boat. Stranraers were steadily replaced with Sunderlands and Catalinas, being finally withdrawn from squadron service in April 1941, although some continued as trainers. This photograph shows serial K7295 of 240 Squadron, taking off.*

Source: RAF Museum P7375

Right: *When the Fairey Battle monoplane entered service with the RAF in May 1937, it was hailed a worthy successor to biplane light bombers. In the event, it proved seriously under-powered and under-armed. Although obsolescent by the outbreak of the Second World War, several squadrons equipped with the machine were sent to France in 1939. When the Wehrmacht attacked through the Low Countries in May 1940, these Battles went into action, unescorted and in daylight; in spite of the astonishing bravery of the crews, they suffered very heavy losses. Most Fairey Battles were retired from front-line service by the end of 1940 and were used as trainers for bomb aimers and air gunners.*

Source: Keystone Collection

Left: *The Hawker Hector entered service in May 1937 as a replacement for the Hawker Audax, in the role of army co-operation. Most Hectors were replaced by Westland Lysanders by the outbreak of the Second World War, but several went into action during the German invasion of France in May 1940. Thereafter, the remaining aircraft were used primarily as glider towers.*

Source: Aviation Bookshop

Right: *The Blemheim I first appeared in RAF squadrons in 1937, as a fast monoplane bomber. However, by the outbreak of the Second World War, the home bomber force of Blenheim Is had been largely replaced by Blenheim IVs, and many aircraft had been converted into night-fighters. Overseas, the Blenheim I saw operational service in Greece and the Western Desert. This photograph shows a Blenheim I of 90 Squadron, which was a training squadron for Bomber Command from May 1937 to April 1940.*

Source: RAF Museum P1680

Right: *In September 1937 the first monoplane trainer entered service with the RAF. This was the Miles Magister, made of wood and fully aerobatic. Known inevitably as the 'Maggie', it was a successful* ab initio *trainer which equipped Elementary Flying Training Schools until the end of the war.*

Source: RAF Museum PO14437

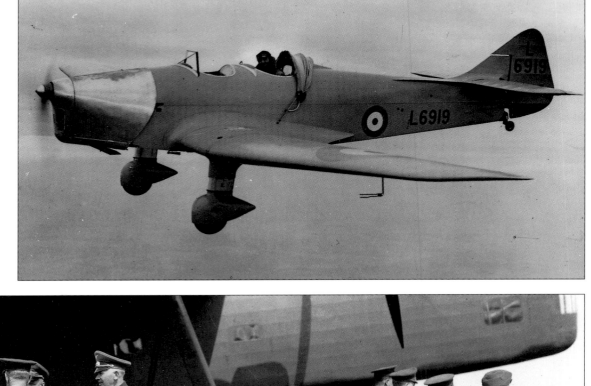

Below: Feldmarshall *von Blomberg visiting RAF Andover in Hampshire, in 1937. The aircraft is a Harrow Mark I.*

Source: Keystone Collection

Right: *The Airspeed Oxford, first introduced in November 1937, was the first twin-engined monoplane to be used as an advanced trainer by the RAF. The Oxford I was fitted with a dorsal turret, since the aircraft was designed as a trainer for pilots, navigators, wireless operators and air gunners. In the event, however, the machine was employed primarily for training pilots at Service Flying Training Schools, and the Oxford II was built without a turret. A later version, with Wasp engines instead of Cheetah's, was the Oxford V. By the end of the Second World War, over 8,500 Oxfords had been produced, these being employed in Britain, Canada, Australia, New Zealand, Southern Rhodesia and Egypt. After the war, the Oxford continued in service until 1954.*

Source: RAF Museum PO16741

Above: *The guns of a Hawker Hurricane in action at night, against the butts.*

Source: Keystone Collection

Above right: *The prototype Hawker Hurricane, serial K5083, designed by Sydney Camm. It was ordered on 21 February 1935 and made its first flight on 6 November 1935.*

Source: Air Historical Branch, MoD. Ref: H.1848

Left: *The possibility of air attacks against British cities necessitated a rapid expansion of Balloon Command. A recruiting drive was begun with the aid of posters.*

Source: RAF Museum (Crown copyright)

Left: *In December 1937 the new Hawker Hurricane I entered service with 111 Squadron at Northolt, inaugurating a new era of eight-gun monoplane fighters which could fly faster than 300 m.p.h. The following May, a Hurricane of this squadron flew from Edinburgh to Northolt at an average speed of 408 m.p.h. This was a remarkable achievement at the time, although the aircraft was helped by a strong tail wind. Hurricanes bore the brunt of the war in France and, during the Battle of Britain, shot down eighty per cent of all aircraft claimed by the RAF. Although less elegant than the Spitfire, it was a tough and reliable aircraft which gave splendid service in all the RAF's theatres of war.*

Source: Keystone Collection

Right: *One of the most remarkable aircraft to enter RAF service before the Second World War was the Vickers Wellington. The first production model flew in December 1937, and Wellingtons then formed the mainstay of Bomber Command's force until the arrival of four-engined bombers. The metal lattice work of the airframe gave the aircraft the ability to withstand considerable punishment from enemy fire. Wellingtons continued in service throughout the war, being employed not only with Bomber Command but on weather reconnaissance, on anti-submarine patrols, as transport aircraft and even as torpedo bombers. Well-liked by RAF crews, it was nicknamed the 'Wimpy' after the character J. Wellington Wimpy in the Popeye cartoons. The aircraft in this photograph is a Wellington I, crossing the toll bridge over the river Wey, in Surrey, between the Weybridge factory and Brooklands aerodrome.*

Source: Keystone Collection

Left: *The Westland Lysander, nicknamed 'The Lizzie', entered service in the RAF in May 1938. It was the first high-wing monoplane specially designed for army co-operation. Four Lysander squadrons were sent to France in 1939, where they fought gallantly and also helped cover the evacuation from Dunkirk. The aircraft also gave excellent service in the Western Desert, Greece, Palestine and India. After retirement from army co-operation in 1941, Lysanders continued in roles such as air-sea rescue, target tugs, liaison as well as landing and retrieving Allied secret agents in Occupied Europe. It had an excellent downward field of vision together with the ability to land on strips of no more than 150 yards in length. This photograph shows the prototype Lysander, serial K6127, which made its first flight on 15 June 1936.*

Source: Keystone Collection

Above: *The prototype Supermarine Spitfire, serial K5054, which made its maiden flight in March 1936, probably on the 6th, at Eastleigh in Hampshire. It was fitted with a fine pitch propeller for the first flight and the undercarriage was locked down.*

Source: Air Historical Branch, MoD. Ref: H.1835

Left: *In June 1938, the Short Sunderland I was the first monoplane to replace the biplane flying boats with which the RAF had been equipped since the First World War. It was derived from the Imperial Airways flying boat and, equipped with nose and tail turrets as well as beam guns, became known to German airmen as 'the flying porcupine'. This splendid aircraft gave noble service in Coastal Command as well as in maritime squadrons abroad. Sunderlands of various marks continued in RAF service for twenty years.*

Source: Keystone Collection

Left: *Two volunteers, from British Columbia and Vancouver Island in Canada, en route to the RAF Reception Depot at West Drayton in Middlesex, photographed on 24 August 1938.*

Source: Keystone Collection

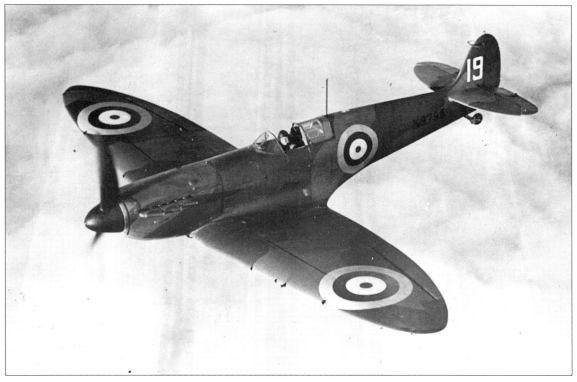

Left: *The legendary Spitfire, designed by R.J.Mitchell, entered service with the RAF in June 1938. Its performance, ease of handling, and elegant appearance delighted those pilots who were fortunate enough to fly the splendid machine. This photograph shows a Spitfire I, serial K9759, of 19 Squadron at Duxford in Cambridgeshire. This was the first squadron to be supplied with the new machine. By September 1939, nine RAF squadrons were fully equipped with Spitfire Is.*

Source: Keystone Collection

Right: *The Handley Page Hampden I was first delivered to 49 Squadron in September 1938 and became one of Bomber Command's premier trio of aircraft on the outbreak of the Second World War, the others being the Armstrong Whitworth Whitley and the Vickers Wellington. In spite of poor armament and cramped crew accommodation, the Hampden was not unpopular with aircrews, who named it the 'Flying Suitcase'. Its merits were a good field of vision, ease of handling, excellent manoeuvrability and long range. The Hampden was the last of the twin-engined monoplane bombers in Bomber Command, and continued on night operations until September 1942. This photograph of Serial L4033 was taken in 1939.*
Source: RAF Museum P5628

Left: *A Vickers Wellesley, flying over Eritrea. This was the first RAF aircraft to introduce the geodetic 'basket-weave' construction, in advance of the Vickers Wellington. The machine became well-known for its long-distance performance; in November 1938, three Wellesleys flew non-stop from Egypt to Australia. After the outbreak of war, it was employed as a light bomber or on reconnaissance work in the Middle East, becoming obsolete in August 1943.*
Source: Keystone Collection

Right: *The de Havilland Dominie was the military version of the civilian Rapide and first entered service with the RAF in September 1939 as a trainer for wireless operators. Also used for communication duties, it continued in service throughout the war.*
Source: RAF Museum PO15259

Left: *The North American Harvard proved one of the most successful trainer aircraft in the RAF. After the first deliveries from the US in December 1938, Harvards remained in service for sixteen years, mainly in RAF Service Flying Training Schools throughout the Commonwealth. It was nick-named 'the yellow peril', since the first aircraft were painted in that colour and the Pratt & Whitney Wasp engine gave out a rasping sound. However, the machine performed well in aerobatics while the array of instruments in the front cockpit provided excellent instruction for the pupil pilot before graduating on to operational machines. This photograph shows one of the earliest machines, a Harvard I.*
Source: Keystone Collection

Right: *Vickers Wellesley Is of 45 Squadron, at Helwan in Egypt in November 1938.*
Source: Keystone Collection

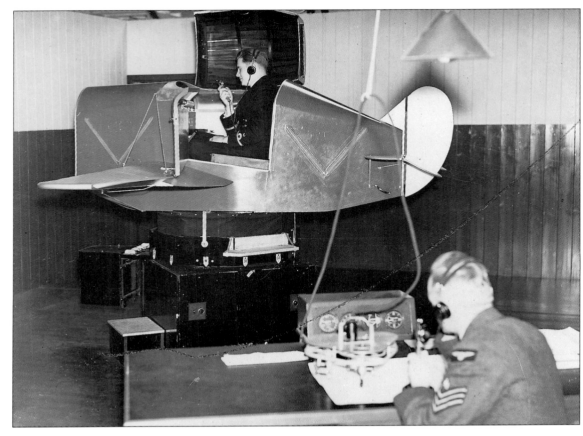

Right: *Soldiers of the Royal Ulster Rifles disembarking on 14 August 1939 from a Bristol Bombay at RAF Yatesbury, for manoeuvres on Salisbury Plain, after transport from the Isle of Wight.*

Source: Keystone Collection

Above: *The defence of RAF aerodromes against air attack was practised by the army, with temporary machine gun posts dotted around the perimeters during exercises.*

Source: Keystone Collection

Above: *Introduced shortly before the Second World War, the Link Trainer proved an effective and inexpensive means of teaching instrument flying to pilots, even after they had earned their wings. The hood could be closed, so that the trainee flew 'blind'. This photograph, taken on 31 October 1938 at No 1 Flying Training School, Netheravon, Wiltshire, shows a Fleet Air Arm pilot receiving instruction from an RAF flight sergeant.*

Source: Keystone Collection

Right: *On 16 April 1939 the Rt Hon Winston Churchill, who had been gazetted as an air commodore, arrived by air on a visit to 615 Squadron at Kenley in Surrey. At the time, the squadron was part of the Auxiliary Air Force, equipped with Gloster Gauntlet IIs; these were replaced with Gloster Gladiator Is the following month.*

Source: Keystone Collection

Far right: *The Hawker Demon, which entered service at the end of 1931, was the first two-seat fighter in the RAF since the First World War, serving at home and in the Middle East. Demons continued as trainers after 1939. In this photograph, which was taken in August 1940, the trainee is holding his parachute pack above what appears to be a Vickers K machine gun, apparently fitted with a camera gun. On foot, a wireless operator is carrying an amunition drum.*

Source: Keystone Collection

CHAPTER 5

THE PHONEY WAR

The first eight months of the Second World War were so inactive on the Western Front that they earned the name of 'The Phoney War' in America and *la drôle de guerre* in France. However, these terms did not apply to the operations of every squadron in the RAF, nor to the activities of the Royal Navy's warships or Britain's merchant vessels.

In September 1939, the first-line strength of the home (or Metropolitan) RAF was 1,476 aircraft, while there were 435 more aircraft overseas. The total strength of the RAF's regular personnel was 118,000, with 68,000 reservists. Britain's intelligence concerning the strength of the Luftwaffe was accurate. Germany possessed about 3,600 first-line aircraft, with 500,000 personnel. In addition there were 500,000 personnel in Germany's anti-aircraft defences, which came under the control of the *Luftwaffe*.

Although Germany was temporarily occupied with her drive through Poland, and was joined on 17 September by Russian troops attacking from the east, it became obvious to Britain's War Cabinet that the RAF was not capable of executing the 'knock-out blow' so favoured by strategists. The French Air Force possessed only a negligible number of heavy bombers. Any air attack by the Allies on German soil would invite a massive retaliation from the *Luftwaffe*, which became fully available when Poland capitulated on 27 September. That unfortunate country was partitioned and occupied by her two giant invaders.

Bomber Command, commanded by Air Chief Marshal Sir Ludlow Hewitt, mustered only thirty-three squadrons at the outbreak of war, the aircraft consisting of Armstrong Whitworth Whitleys, Vickers Wellingtons, Handley Page Hampdens, Bristol Blenheim Is and IVs, and Fairey Battles. Of these, ten squadrons of Battles of 1 Group had flown out to France on 2 September as part of the Advanced Air Striking Force, commanded from January 1940 by Air Marshal Sir Arthur Barratt. They were joined by five squadrons of Blenheims, four of Hurricanes, and five of Westland Lysanders for army co-operation.

Of the Bomber Command aircraft remaining in Britain, the seven squadrons of Blenheims in 2 Group had too short a range to bomb deep into Germany from Britain. Only the squadrons of 3, 4 and 5 Groups possessed medium or heavy bombers capable of such a bombing offensive. The War Cabinet came to the conclusion that the only military attacks to be made by Bomber Command should be against naval warships at sea. Over land, orders were given to confine flights to leaflet-dropping. The Whitley squadrons were chosen for this task, supported occasionally by Wellington squadrons. These began immediately, operating at night. The leaflets told the German people the truth, although this was not apparent at the time: the war could only end in disaster for them and would cost the lives of many of their citizens and the ruination of their country. But this propaganda had little, if any, effect on people who had been thoroughly indoctrinated with the Nazi philosophy and who knew that the *Wehrmacht* was sweeping victoriously across Poland. In any event, the punishments which awaited those who dared to challenge the state were so hideous that those who agreed with the propaganda were forced to keep their thoughts to themselves.

However, the leaflet flights, known as 'Nickel', did demonstrate to the Germans that

the RAF was capable of flying over their territory, even as far as Berlin, Prague and Vienna. The operations were also beneficial to the RAF in terms of reconnaissance, intelligence and experience, but one enemy proved to be the winter weather. Losses were heavy, about six per cent on average per numbers of sorties, a level which later in the war was considered unacceptable for any sustained period.

Towards the end of the Phoney War, the efforts of these heavy bomber squadrons were directed towards minelaying at night. The magnetic mine, code-named 'cucumber' weighed about 2,000-lb and lay on the sea-bed, waiting to be activated by the steel hull of a vessel passing over it. The results of these rather undramatic operations were shown, both during and after the war, to have been very effective.

The attacks against warships began the day after war was declared, with a daylight strike by ten Blenheim IVs against the German pocket battleship *Admiral von Scheer* and the cruiser *Emden* off Wilhelmshaven. It was an extremely gallant attack, but fruitless. Two 500-lb bombs bounced off the armoured deck of the battleship and did not explode. Five Blenheims failed to return, one of which crashed on the fo'c'sle of *Emden* and caused some damage. At almost the same time, fourteen Wellingtons attacked naval vessels off Brunsbüttel. No damage was caused and two aircraft were lost.

At the beginning of the war, the RAF set great store by its power-operated turrets, which were fitted with twin Browning guns in many bombers. It was believed that if squadrons of bombers such as Wellingtons flew in close formation in daylight,

Below: *There was never any shortage of volunteers for RAF aircrew in the Second World War, as can be seen from this photograph of men waiting in the early morning of 17 June 1940 for the opening of a recruiting bureau in Cannon Street, City of London. All RAF aircrew were volunteers, none being conscripted into this branch of the armed services.*

Source: Keystone Collection

Above left: *Three volunteers signing up as RAF aircrew, in December 1941.*

Source: Keystone Collection

combined fire from the front and rear turrets would render them almost invulnerable from enemy fighter attack, although anti-aircraft fire could cause casualties. This belief was proved incorrect during a series of further attacks. On 26 September, a sortie by eleven Hampdens resulted in the loss of five aircraft. On 13 December, twelve Wellingtons took off on an attack against warships and five were shot down, while another crashed near home. It was still believed that most of the losses resulted from anti-aircraft fire. However, five days later, twenty-two Wellingtons took off on an attack against warships, which were found so close to the shore that bombing was not possible, for fear of causing civilian casualties. The Germans could not understand the tactics of the RAF, which appeared suicidal. Their fighters brought down ten Wellingtons, for the loss of four of their number. Two more Wellingtons 'ditched' nearer home and three crash-landed in England. After this tragedy, Bomber Command recognized that long-distance fighter escorts were essential for daylight bombing against German targets, but these were not available at this stage of the war.

Another bombing operation, which was proposed but not carried out, was an air attack against the Russian oil wells and refineries in the Caucasus. This was the period when Germany and Russia were in an uneasy alliance. Germany, which had almost no natural supplies of oil and depended largely on synthetic production, had access to these Russian deposits with which to wage war. The Supreme War Council, consisting of the Prime Ministers of Britain and France, together with senior members of their Cabinets, ordered an examination of the possibility of destroying the Russian installations at Batum, Grozny and Baku. It was intended to use a combined force from the RAF and the French Air Force, from bases in Syria and Iraq. Two reconnaissance and photographic flights were made over Russia, on 30 March and 5 April 1940, by an RAF

Above: *Civilian and RAF volunteers for pilot and navigator training reporting for duty on 6 October 1939. The next move was then to Initial Training Wing for drill and ground instruction.*

Source: Keystone Collection

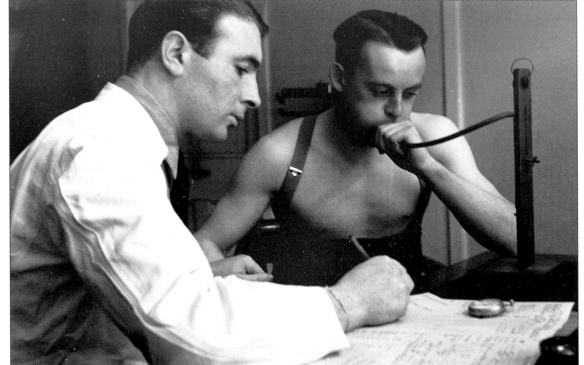

Right: *A volunteer for pilot or observer under medical examination, blowing into a 'U-tube manometer' while his pulse rate is monitored. Medical requirements were stringent and many applicants were rejected for quite minor physical defects, to their dismay.*

Source: Keystone Collection

Left: *One of the proudest occasions for trainees was the issue of their full flying kit. This was photographed in July 1940.*
Source: Keystone Collection

crew in a 'civilian' Lockheed 14 airliner, from Habbaniya in Iraq. Although dressed in civilian clothes, the men were serving officers and airmen of the RAF's Photographic Development Unit at Heston. It was estimated that the bombing attacks would begin at the end of the following June, the force consisting of four squadrons of Bomber Command's Blenheim IVs and one squadron of Wellesleys already based in the Middle East, together with five squadrons of Marylands of the French Air Force. Both the British and the French were highly optimistic about the results which these attacks would achieve. This plan, which is likely to have brought Russia into military alliance with Germany against Britain and France, was shelved following the attack of the *Wehrmacht* in the west in May 1940.

Coastal Command entered the war with three groups, in the west and east of England, and in Scotland, under the command of Air Chief Marshal Sir Frederick Bowhill. Its collection of aircraft consisted of Avro Ansons, Lockheed Hudsons from America, antiquated Vickers Vildebeest torpedo bombers, together with the flying boat squadrons of Short Sunderlands, Saro Londons and Supermarine Stranraers. Their main duty was reconnaissance over the North Sea, a task which had been begun on 24 August 1939. In addition, the aircraft performed the role of escorts for Atlantic convoys, when within range of the British coast. U-boats were sometimes found and attacked, but the bombs carried at the time proved of little use. Depth charges were rapidly developed for use by aircraft.

Another function was to explode the magnetic mines laid by the Germans around the British coasts, which began to account for many ships in home waters. This was accomplished by fitting Wellingtons with enormous rings containing a magnetic coil operated by an engine within the fuselage, and then flying low over the sea. This process, known as 'degaussing', soon achieved remarkable results.

Although Coastal Command was known as 'the Cinderella of the RAF', since it received lower priority than the other two operational Commands, it carried out its work with considerable efficiency. It was a Hudson which scored the RAF's first aerial victory of the war, by shooting down a Do18 flying boat over Jutland on 8 October 1939. Together with the Royal Navy, the aircraft of Coastal Command established an effective economic blockade of Germany's North Sea coastline in the first eight months of the war.

The work of Fighter Command, commanded by Air Chief Marshal Sir Hugh Dowding, was largely confined to building up its strength in the early months of the war. It was estimated that fifty-three squadrons were needed for the air defence of Great

Above: *New RAF cadets marching to a Receiving Centre in London to collect their kit, on 15 September 1942, before undergoing training as either pilots or navigators.*

Source: Keystone Collection

Right: *Men in reserved occupations could obtain release by volunteering for RAF aircrew, as can be seen from this poster. All aircrew members were volunteers, even if they had been first conscripted into the armed forces.*

Source: RAF Museum (Crown copyright) P00774

Left: *Before the U.S.A. entered the war, General Henry H. 'Hap' Arnold devised a scheme whereby his country undertook to train 8,000 RAF pilots each year. The first group of 550 cadets set sail for the U.S.A. in June 1941, and were divided among six civilian training schools in the Southern States. This photograph of one of the first groups of British cadets, wearing the olive-green overalls of the U.S. Army Air Corps, was taken at the Southern Aviation School at Camden, South Carolina.*

Source: Keystone Collection

Left: *A pupil pilot entering a Harvard trainer, in September 1940.*

Source: Keystone Collection

Left: *Volunteers to fly with the RAF arrived from all parts of the Commonwealth. These two pilots were part of a batch from the Indian Air Force which arrived in England during October 1940.*

Source: Keystone Collection

Right: *All aircrew were expected to understand the mechanism of RAF machine guns, such as the standard Browning .303 inch being shown here to a group of trainee air gunners. Air gunners, as well as pilots and navigators in 1940, were taught how to strip down and reassemble the gun, as well as how to identify and clear stoppages.*

Source: Keystone Collection

Above: *The Miles Master II, which came into service in November 1939. This high-speed trainer, in which the pupil pilot could also practice low-level bombing and forward-firing gunnery, saw service mainly in Advanced Flying Units.*

Source: Keystone Collection

Britain, but only thirty-five had been formed in September 1939, within three Groups. These were equipped with Hawker Hurricanes, Supermarine Spitfires, and Gloster Gladiator biplanes. Dowding was the most vociferous as well as the most successful of the commanders in demanding new squadrons and aircraft, although some of these new squadrons were equipped temporarily with Blenheims and Battles, since the output of Hurricans and Spitfires could not meet the demand.

In one major respect, the RAF had reason to be thankful for the Phoney War, for it provided a breathing space in which training could be accelerated. The number of technical schools was doubled. Operational Training Units were created, even at the expense of pulling experienced aircrews away from operational squadrons to act as instructors. Above all, the Empire Air Training Scheme was formed, with Canada, Australia and New Zealand agreeing in December 1939 to set up Elementary Flying Training Schools, Service Flying Training Schools, Air Observer Schools, Bombing and Gunnery Schools and Air Navigation Schools, partly staffed with RAF instructors. Southern Rhodesia set up a training group, largely staffed and run by the RAF, while South Africa also provided facilities. By mid 1942, when this scheme was at full flow, it was producing as many as 11,000 pilots and 17,000 other aircrew each year. The first school was opened in Canada on 29 April 1940, but by then the *Wehrmacht* had attacked Norway.

Left: *Air gunnery involved hitting a flying object from a moving platform. One method of training in the ground was the 'hareplane', which trundled electrically round a track. This gave the trainees some experience of handling a power-operated turret on the move while twisting the handlebar grips up and down and from side to side. Aircrew cadets wore white flashes in their forage caps to indicate their trainee status.*

Source: Keystone Collection

Below: *Air gunners received training in power-operated turrets, such as that fitted to the Avro Anson. This photograph shows the men carrying their parachute packs while one trainee has a Browning .303 inch machine gun over his shoulder. This gun had a rate of fire of 1,150 rounds per minute. Training took place against drogues towed by other aircraft, the numbers of holes being counted later for assessment purposes.*

Source: Keystone Collection

Right: *Another method of training air gunners consisted of aiming at a low-flying aircraft from turrets mounted on the ground. The aircraft acting as 'target practice' was a Miles Martinet.*

Source: Keystone Collection

Below: *The Miles Martinet T.T.1 was designed as a target-tug and served in the RAF from 1942 to 1948. It was an adaptation of the Miles Master, with a longer nose to compensate for shift to aft of the centre of gravity. After the war, some Martinets were built as pilotless and radio-controlled targets.*

Source: RAF Museum colour slide P100482

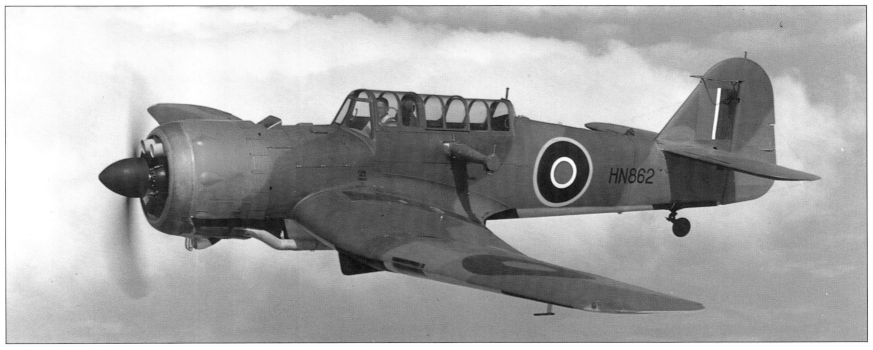

Right: *On the ground, trainee air gunners practised range and 'deflection firing' with the reflector sight against scale models of German aircraft such as the Bf110 and Bf109. The models were manoeuvred by other trainees. This photograph shows a group of Lysander airmen of the RCAF training with a Vickers gun.*

Source: Keystone Collection

Above: *In July 1940, King George VI made a tour of the Operational Training Units of Bomber Command. In this photograph, he is looking through the reflector sight, an example of those fitted in power-operated turrets. Two of the airmen are wearing one-piece Sidcot suits, designed by Sidney F. Cotton, who became the first commanding officer of the RAF's Photographic Development Unit, later the Photographic Reconnaissance Unit.*
Source: Keystone Collection

Top right: *When this photograph was taken, on 13 December 1941, air navigators were called air observers. They were trained in navigation, bombing and gunnery, being expected to perform all these functions on sorties. At Operational Training Units such as this, navigation exercises were carried out on the ground as well as in the air. The instrument by the right hand of the officer instructor is a 'course and speed calculator' for solving the 'triangle of velocities' caused by wind speed and direction. On the other side of the screen, another instructor is giving imaginary tracks and other information to the trainee, who is making calculations and entering them in his log.*
Source: Keystone Collection

Right: *The RAF trained its own despatch riders, drawn from volunteers among the ground personnel. After passing their course, the despatch riders were posted to RAF units at home and abroad.*
Source: Keystone Collection

Left: *These practice bombs weighed 11½ lb and exploded with a small puff of smoke, enabling the results to be plotted by observers on the ground. The bomb aimer was then assessed at the end of his training. The photograph was taken on 13 March 1940.*
Source: Keystone Collection

Above: *The RAF School of Cookery trained cooks, butchers, messing advisers and caterers. Six leading civilian chefs were on the training staff in 1941, and the dishes were specified in an Air Ministry diet sheet. Morning parade included an inspection of hands and nails.*

Source: Keystone Collection

Top left: *By 1942, the RAF had set up its own pig farm in central London and, in addition to the meat, was able to turn out 6,000 lb of pork sausages per week.*

Source: Keystone Collection

Above: *There was a school for RAF firemen, who were then posted to all aerodromes. This fire tender was capable of 65 m.p.h. and carried a 300 gallon tank which produced 3,000 gallons of air foam per minute. There were four air foam projectors and two gas jets.*

Source: Keystone Collection

Right: *The crew of six in the fire tender included one man in an asbestos suit.*

Source: Keystone Collection

Above: *The Percival Proctor I, a military version of the Vega Gull, entered service with the RAF in 1939 as a three-seat communications aircraft. Later marks were also employed as radio trainers. This photograph is of a Proctor Mark IV, serial LA589, a prototype of the last mark which saw service in the RAF; it was taken on 10 August 1943.*

Source: RAF Museum colour slide P100507

Right: *Boy entrants were admitted into the RAF, principally as trainee fitters and riggers. They were known as 'brats', a term which carried high status when they progressed in their career.*

Source: Keystone Collection

Left: The WAAF formed its own band in 1939.

Source: Keystone Collection

Below: WAAF armourers under training, practising the installation of Browning .303 inch machine guns in a Spitfire.

Source: Keystone Collection

Right: *Another trade in which airwomen were engaged was that of radio operator.*

Source: Keystone Collection

Right: *WAAF parachute packers were often responsible for the highly-important task of ensuring that the packs and harnesses of aircrew were in good order. Each aircrew member collected his own pack and usually kept it in a locker in the crew room, but it was checked from time to time. The straps on the harnesses were adjustable.*

Source: Keystone Collection

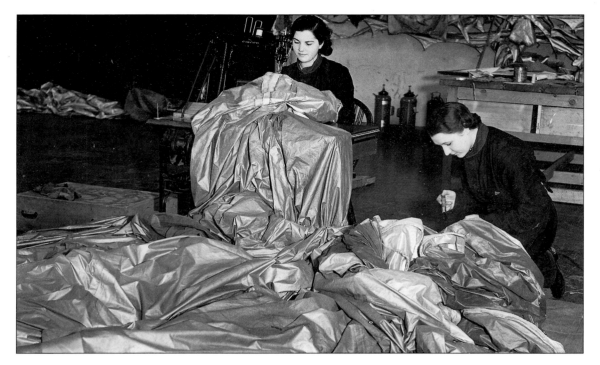

Left: *Another trade which was fulfilled by the WAAF was that of 'fabric worker, balloon'. Balloons were subject to considerable wear and tear from the weather, particularly from electrical storms.*
Source: Keystone Collection

Right: *These standard 'low zone' balloons protected cities and towns, usually flown at an altitude of about 5,000 feet.*
Source: Keystone Collection

Below: *WAAF balloon operators studying the construction of balloons from a model.*
Source: Keystone Collection

Left: *A WAAF instrument mechanic working on the automatic pilot, called 'George', in a Lancaster bomber.*
Source: Keystone Collection

Right: *Three volunteers for the WAAF signing up at Kingsway in London as motor transport drivers, in January 1941. This was one of the most popular trades open to women.*
Source: Keystone Collection

Left: *One of the positions open to the WAAF was flight mechanic (airframe), which involved the skills of acetylene welding and paint-spraying.*
Source: Keystone Collection

Above: *A WAAF motor transport mechanic greasing the wheels of a lorry.*
Source: Keystone Collection

Right: *Selected WAAF underwent training as flight mechanics, for both engineering and airframes.*
Source: Keystone Collection

Right: *Two WAAF flight mechanics working on an aircraft.*

Source: Keystone Collection

Below: *Some of the ladies of No 5 Ferry Pilots Pool Women's Section, in full flying kit.*

Source: Keystone Collection

Right: *Although not part of the RAF, the men and women of the Air Transport Auxiliary provided invaluable and sometimes dangerous help by delivering new aircraft to aerodromes. The officer commanding No 5 Ferry Pilots Pool Women's Section, based at Hatfield in Berkshire, was Miss Pauline Gower (centre), the 27 year old daughter of Sir Robert Gower, M.P.*

Source: Keystone Collection

Below: *Two fighter pilots on standby during the Phoney War while away the time in the crew room by playing chess, while another is dozing with a bull terrier. Black appears to be winning on the chess board, which is placed on two parachute boxes.*

Source: Keystone Collection

Left: *A Whitley bomber crew reporting to the intelligence officer in the operations room after an operational flight. In the early part of the Second World War, RAFVR officers were allowed to wear VR insignia on their uniforms, but this privilege was later withdrawn, to their indignation.*

Source: Keystone Collection

Below: *The wireless operator in a Wellington Mark I passes a message to the second pilot. This photograph is dated May 1940 and the wireless operator has the rank of leading aircraftman. In autumn of that year, all airmen who had qualified as aircrew were upgraded to the minimum rank of sergeant.*

Source: Keystone Collection

CHAPTER 6

THE BATTLES OF NORWAY, FRANCE AND BRITAIN

When Russia attacked Finland in November 1939, the assault was resisted with extraordinary valour by the forces of that small country, until she was finally forced to agree to terms of surrender on 13 March 1940. At the time, the Supreme War Cabinet gave serious thoughts to backing the Finns by occupying part of northern Norway and Sweden, to allow the passage of 'volunteer brigades' to come to their aid. There was an additional purpose in such a project. Some two-thirds of Germany's consumption of iron ore was mined in Sweden, and much of this passed through the Norwegian port of Narvik before being shipped to Germany. When the Baltic was frozen over, this was the only route. Denial of this source would limit severely Germany's capacity for waging war, and would also pre-empt any plans which the Russians might have for occupying the region.

It is known that these considerations weighed heavily on Hitler's mind when, in December 1939, he ordered his forces to make plans to secure control of Denmark and Norway. The operation, code-named *Weserübung*, began on 9 April 1940, although the expedition set sail for Norway three days earlier. Some naval units were spotted by the RAF and attacked by a squadron of Blenheims on 7 April. By this time, the British government had warned Norway and Sweden that it intended to lay mines off their coasts. Bomber Command began these operations on the night of 7/8 April, while the Royal Navy also laid mines off Norway.

The German naval forces were favoured by low cloud and poor visibility, escaping further detection from the air. However, the Norwegian government was sufficiently alerted to order general mobilisation. The German vessels entering Oslo fjord and Kristiansand met stiff opposition, although there was less resistance elsewhere. On 9 April, 600 German bombers and 600 air transports appeared in the skies over Norway. Paratroops and ground forces seized control of almost every airfield and port in the country. At the same time, the *Wehrmacht* entered Denmark, shortening the German lines of communication, while the British were faced with the problem of operating over a distance of 600 miles or more.

Some German warships were spotted on their return journeys, and twelve Wellingtons attacked two cruisers off Bergen, inflicting minor damage. One of these vessels, the *Königsberg*, was sunk by a dive-bombing attack by Blackburn Skuas of the Fleet Air Arm on 10 April, operating from the Orkneys. A further attack on warships, by twelve Hampdens of Bomber Command, resulted in the loss of half this number by German fighters. Thereafter, the efforts of Bomber Command were concentrated on night attacks against Norwegian airfields, particularly Stavanger/Sola, which was within easy range.

One of the responses of the Supreme War Cabinet to the German invasion was the

Below: *Bristol Blenheims in low level flight over Holland.*

Source: courtesy of Frank Wootton, P.P.G.Av.A.

Left: *The aircrew and ground crew of a Bristol Blenheim IV of 21 Squadron, which was equipped with these machines from September 1939 to July 1942.*

Source: Keystone Collection

Left: *The Blenheim IV began to replace the Blenheim I in RAF service during 1938, the main difference being a longer nose to accommodate the navigator/bomb aimer. Later modifications were armour-plating, an extra gun in the dorsal turret and armour plating. Blenheim IVs were employed on daylight attacks, usually without fighter escort, and suffered very heavy casualties. They continued with Bomber Command until August 1942, and served overseas in Singapore and the Western Desert. This photograph shows a Blenheim IV of 53 Squadron which, after heavy losses in the German invasion of France, was transferred to Coastal Command in July 1940. It was then engaged on equally dangerous sorties, against shipping and ports.*

Source: RAF Museum PO19544

despatch of a combined force to northern Norway. The first contingent put ashore at Namsos on 14 April, with the intention of recapturing Trondheim. This was followed by a landing at Aandalsnes, with a third in the north near Narvik. Although these troops linked up with Norwegians who were putting up a desperate defence, they were harried from the air by German aircraft. There was a severe shortage of anti-aircraft guns, and the Germans inflicted considerable damage, particularly at Namsos.

Meanwhile, the RAF continued to bomb airfields and to lay mines in the approaches to German ports. The Allied expeditionary force received continued support from FAA aircraft but, in the absence of landing grounds from which to operate, the RAF was unable to provide direct assistance. A single squadron of Gladiators left on 23 April on board the carrier HMS *Glorious* and attempted to operate from the frozen waters of Lake Lesjaskog, inland from Aandalsnes. Most of the engines refused to start and, when the *Luftwaffe* attacked, the machines were soon destroyed. Most of the pilots were transported safely back to Britain.

More German troops were transported northwards, and the Allied military situation in the two southerly areas of Aandalsnes and Namsos became hopeless. Evacuation began on 2 May, leaving the contingent near Narvik. An RAF survey team was sent out to this remaining area and chose a landing ground at Bardufoss, north of Narvik, as a suitable spot for aircraft. The two short landing strips were extended by Trojan efforts, including assistance from about 1,000 Norwegian volunteers. The re-equipped Gladiator squadron returned to Norway on the carrier HMS *Furious*, arriving on 21 May. Two days later, a Hurricane squadron arrived on HMS *Glorious*.

By then, the *Wehrmacht* had attacked through the Low Countries, and the Allied effort in Norway could not be sustained. The pilots of both squadrons fought effectively against continual *Luftwaffe* attacks. Narvik was captured by the Allied troops and the port installations were destroyed, before the final evacuation from Norway. The airfield at Bardufoss was demolished and the RAF aircraft made successful landings on HMS *Glorious*. Tragically, this carrier was sunk on the return journey, together with her two destroyer escorts, by the battleships *Scharnhorst* and *Gneisenau*. Only a handful of men survived.

On 10 May 1940 the German assault in the west began with *Panzer* divisions crossing the frontiers of the Low Countries, with the support of dive-bombing attacks by Ju87s. Bombers attacked airfields and transports dropped paratroops in key positions, while other troops landed in gliders.

The direction of these attacks, out-flanking the defensive Maginot line along France's border with Germany, had been anticipated by the Anglo-French forces, who immediately advanced into Belgium. At the same time, the RAF's Advanced Air Striking Force in France went into action. Five squadrons of Lysanders and four of Hurricanes supported the British troops. Ten squadrons of Battles and Blenheims bombed the advancing Germany columns in Belgium, escorted by two squadrons of Hurricanes. In the northern sector, seven squadrons of Blenheims of Bomber Command attacked in daylight, while two squadrons of Whitleys delivered night attacks. The RAF had intended to bomb marshalling yards and oil refineries in the Ruhr, but the French insisted that all attacks should be made in the vicinity of the front line.

Above: *Soon after the evacuation from Dunkirk, Queen Elizabeth visited Wellhouse Hospital at Barnet in London, to talk to some of the wounded.*

Source: Keystone Collection

Three more Hurricane squadrons were sent to France, bringing the total number of fighter squadrons up to ten. Other squadrons operated from England, including mixed formations of Spitfires and Boulton Paul Defiants. An enormous toll was taken of the *Luftwaffe*, particularly Bf110s and He111s, although the RAF was heavily outnumbered. Even a few Gladiators, which remained with some of the Hurricane squadrons in France, acquitted themselves well in combats.

The employment of medium bombers proved disastrous, however. The new chief of Bomber Command, Air Chief Marshal Sir Charles Portal, voiced strong objections to sending out his Blenheims in daylight, and events soon proved that he was correct. The squadrons of Battles and Blenheims in France fared even worse than Bomber Command. Their targets were bridges and armoured spearheads, and they were met with hails of gunfire and swarms of fighters. Hurricanes could provide only partial support. Within three days, the number of RAF bombers in France was reduced from 135 to 72, while some of the surviving aircraft were damaged. In spite of the heroism of the crews, the results achieved were small.

The *Panzers* broke through the French lines and, on 14 May, were attacked once more by the remaining Battles and Blenheims. Seventy-one took off and forty did not return. Twenty-eight Blenheims of Bomber Command lost seven of their number on the same day. This further sacrifice was not entirely in vain, for there is evidence that the attacks contributed to a slowing down of the German advance.

In Holland, the Dutch forces put up a fierce resistance, but their air force was destroyed within three days. Rotterdam was subjected to an intense bombardment by Ju87s, which destroyed 20,000 buildings and killed almost 1,000 civilians. On 14 May, the Dutch capitulated. At last, the British War Cabinet, with Winston Churchill at the head of a new coalition government, gave permission for the RAF to bomb the Ruhr, and the first attacks began on the night of 15/16 May.

Meanwhile, four more Hurricane squadrons flew out to France, and six more operated alternatively from the congested French airfields, while continuing to be based in England. These were all that could be spared, with the need to protect Britain from air attack. The squadrons fought well and inflicted losses, but they were hampered by the lack of an effective radar system in France. The losses of medium bombers continued. On 17 May a squadron of twelve Blenheims from England was caught by Bf109s and all save one were shot down.

It seemed that nothing could stop the remorseless advance of the *Panzers*. As the Allied troops fell back, the RAF aircraft flew back to prepared grass airstrips, their equipment being transported in lorries. On 19 May, almost all the serviceable aircraft flew to England, from where they could operate equally effectively with the shortened lines of communication. The Hurricane squadrons, originally amounting to 261 aircraft, left behind 195 of their number, either destroyed in combat or too badly damaged to be flown home. About a quarter of the RAF's modern fighters had been lost, but operations over northern France continued at the rate of about 200 sorties a day.

The Germans entered Boulogne on 24 May, and Belgium capitulated three days later. By then, the remaining British Expeditionary Force and some French contingents were hemmed in at Dunkirk, and the Royal Navy began its miraculous evacuation. Heavily out-numbered, RAF fighters covered the beaches from first to last light, although resources were so short that only up to four squadrons could be present at any one time. Meanwhile, RAF bombers pounded enemy batteries and troops. Inevitably, most of these encounters took place out of sight of the troops, resulting in bitterness among soldiers who believed that the RAF was doing little to protect them from the Ju87 dive-bombers. In fact, if the RAF aircraft flew too close to the beaches and naval vessels, they were almost invariably fired on by their own side. The flotilla of 'little ships' began to arrive at Dunkirk on 30 May. French as well as British troops were taken off, and by 4 June the evacuation was as complete as human endeavour could achieve. Over 335,000 men reached England.

The remaining French troops to the south faced an impossible task. The Germans broke through their lines at will, and on 10 June Italy invaded Southern France through the Alps. Thereupon, Whitleys of Bomber Command gave Turin and Genoa a small taste of things to come, after refuelling in the Channel Islands. Some elements of the British forces remained in France and evacuations were arranged from ports on the north and west coasts, protected by detachments of RAF fighters. A major disaster took place on 17 June when German bombers sank the liner *Lancastria* in the port of St Nazaire, with the loss of over 3,000 lives.

On 22 June, France accepted terms for an armistice, and hostilities ceased three days later. During May and June, the RAF had lost 959 aircraft, but had played a major part in the destruction of 1,284 enemy aircraft.

The defeats in Norway and France did not create a feeling of hopelessness in Britain, even though the country was fighting alone against a military giant. Instead, its people

Above: *After the fall of France in June 1940, merchant convoys sailing around the British coasts came under intense attacks from German aircraft. To help protect the convoys, the RAF's Balloon Command formed the Mobile Balloon Barrage Flotilla. RAF personnel served on the balloon barrage vessels, often in conditions of great danger. In this photograph, a vessel is leaving Southampton, bound for the Thames Estuary. It is flying a 'low zone' balloon, which would be raised to about 2,000 feet during an attack. The balloon is painted with an anti-dazzle band, with chevrons on the nose representing each convoy successfully completed.*

Source: the late Flight Lieutenant A. Puckle, MBE

were imbued with a sense of resolve and even cheerfulness, later known as the 'Dunkirk spirit'. Political and social differences were forgotten as everyone bent themselves to the task of increasing military strength and effectiveness. It was obvious that the might of the *Wehrmacht* would shortly fall on Britain, and that somehow the country must be prepared for an onslaught, at first from the air. The prospect of ultimate defeat was barely considered.

It was fortunate that the RAF's radar system was already largely established and that Fighter Command still retained much of its strength. The radar system was rapidly extended to the west and north, to cover the whole of Britain's southern and eastern coastlines, while the efficient network of Observer Corps posts covering the entire country was similarly expanded. Aircraft production remained a major priority, under the direction of Lord Beaverbrook of the Ministry of Aircraft Production, and this was already rising. At the expense of other military production, Beaverbrook continued the expansion, from 256 fighters in April 1940 to 476 the following August.

Meanwhile, the Germans consolidated their gains in Europe and Hitler looked for signs that Britain was prepared to reach a settlement with Germany, for his immediate military ambitions lay to the east rather than to the west. It was not until mid July when he decided that, if Britain wished to remain obstinate, plans must be prepared for her invasion. The prelude would be a massive air attack, to begin on 10 August, under the code-name of *Unternehmen Adlerangriff* (Operation 'Attack of the Eagles'). The code-name for the eventual invasion of Britain was *Seelöwe* (Sealion).

These few weeks of respite proved a godsend to the RAF, which was able to make good the losses suffered in the Battle of France and indeed to increase the number of its fighter squadrons. The fighter groups were increased from three to four. When the Battle of Britain opened, Dowding had over 700 operational aircraft at his disposal. Although these faced some 1,000 fighters, 1,000 long-range bombers and 250 dive-bombers, within three German air fleets, the situation was a great deal better than had been feared.

After France fell, German aircraft were active over England, although not in any great strength, bombing airfields and coastal convoys in daylight, and laying mines at night. In general, the losses were roughly equal on both sides when they encountered Hurricanes or Spitfires. However, Bf109s proved their superiority over Defiants when not accompanied by single-seat fighters; in a short encounter on 19 July, nine of the RAF turret fighters lost six of their number.

In this period, the RAF was able to improve its system of air-sea rescue, forming the squadrons of reconnaissance aircraft and high-speed launches which were to prove so efficient in the coming months. At the same time, both Bomber Command and Coastal Command were active, bombing airfields and shipping, and causing extensive fires in enemy ports. Heavy bombers raided German aircraft manufacturing industries at night, but these attacks achieved little, other than demonstrating to the Germans that the RAF was still a potent force.

Unfavourable weather prevented *Reichsmarschall* Hermann Goering from opening his main offensive until 12 August. It began with a series of attacks against radar stations and airfields. Damage was inflicted, although almost all stations were quickly back in action. On the next day, the attacks were directed solely at airfields. During the same night, German bombers raided aircraft factories, without much result. It was evident that the initial purpose of the *Luftwaffe* was to knock out the RAF, and indeed the German high command believed that they were doing this, for their crews brought back grossly exaggerated reports of the number of fighters they had shot down, roughly treble the true figures. At the same time, German propaganda announced only about half the true losses of the *Luftwaffe* to the public. The British government gave out figures of German losses which, after the war, were shown to be over twice the true numbers, although the announcements of RAF losses were accurate.

The next couple of days were much quieter, both by day and night, for Goering was waiting for clearer weather before launching a massive attack by all three of his air fleets, *Luftflotte 3* in Western France, *Luftflotte 2* in Northern France, Belgium and Holland, and *Luftflotte 5* in Norway and Denmark, thus spreading the RAF's defences as thinly as possible. The day of 15 August proved suitable, and again the main targets were airfields. In north-east England, formations of He111s and Bf110s attacked outside the range of escorting Bf109s, and their losses were so severe that they never attempted further daylight attacks in that area; the RAF suffered no losses at all. In the south and south-east of England, the air combats were less one-sided, but overall on the day the enemy lost fifty-five aircraft while the RAF lost thirty-four. Damage to installations was negligible.

The battles continued with over 1,700 German aircraft over England on 16 August. There was a respite during the next day, but the *Luftwaffe* achieved some success on 18 August, when they caused damage to airfields and radar stations; but they lost forty-nine aircraft against the RAF's twenty-seven. Since 8 August, Fighter Command had

Above: *The RAF held out great hopes for the Boulton Paul Defiant when it entered service with 264 Squadron in December 1939. It was believed that the turret, with four machine guns and rotating through 360 degrees, would account for many enemy aircraft. These hopes seemed to be justified when the Defiant proved quite successful during the German invasion of the Low Countries, but the German pilots soon realized that the Defiant was not very fast or manoeuvrable and that the turret cut out automatically in the forward position. Two Defiants squadrons were almost wiped out by Bf109s during the Battle of Britain and the survivors were withdrawn for duties as nightfighters. This photograph is of Defiant Mark I, serial N3313, of 264 Squadron.*

Source: RAF Museum PO17822

Above: *The Observer Corps was formed in 1924 and the resulting groups became an integral part of the defence of Great Britain during the Second World War. RAF radar located enemy aircraft approaching British shores, but thereafter the aircraft were tracked by the Observer Corps (later the Royal Observer Corps), working in close liaison with the RAF. This photograph shows one of the group headquarters and the plotting table.*

Source: Keystone Collection

Left: *After the failure of Fairey Battles during the German attack through the Low Countries, many remaining machines were turned over to training. Some became target-towers while others were used for pilot training in dive bombing. This photograph shows a Battle being bombed up with 250 lb general-purpose bombs on 13 September 1940.*

Source: Keystone Collection

Below: *The Filter Room of Fighter Command's headquarters at Bentley Priory in Middlesex, after underground building had been completed on 9 March 1940. WAAF 'plotters' moved arrow-topped counters on the table in response to information about enemy aircraft fed in from the Chain Home (CH) and Chain Home Low (CHL) radar stations sited around the coasts. In the balconies above, RAF and WAAF 'tellers' interpreted these movements, which were then "filtered" and passed on via a controller to operations rooms in sectors and stations of Fighter Command. This Filter Room was known as 'The Hole' to those who worked in it.*

Source: Flight Officer Felicity Ashbee

lost 183 aircraft in combat and thirty on the ground, together with 154 pilots. Of course, some pilots were able to bale out while others were picked up by air-sea rescue. But the losses of Spitfires and Hurricanes exceeded the rate of replacement, and it seemed that the *Luftwaffe* might win the war of attrition unless there was some respite.

There was heavy cloud in the next five days, with only desultory attacks. The mass assaults began again on 24 August and continued until 6 September, normally with over 1,000 sorties per day. The damage to the buildings on some airfields was considerable, but somehow the stations continued to function. This period saw the final withdrawal of the Defiants, however, which lost heavily in every combat. The whittling down of Hurricanes and Spitfires continued to be serious. It is estimated that if the attacks against airfields and the RAF had continued at the same scale, the reserves of fighters would have been exhausted within three weeks. Fortunately for Britain the Germans changed their tactics at a critical time.

Infuriated by Bomber Command raids over Germany and perplexed by the capacity of Fighter Command to put up so many aircraft, Goering ordered his bombers to strike at the British civilian population. Hitler decided that London was to be the main target. On 7 September a great air battle took place when about 300 RAF fighters engaged formations of about 900 German bombers and fighters near the capital, with heavy losses on both sides. Large areas of London's East End were set ablaze.

These attacks continued over the next few days, but the *Luftwaffe* was not able to penetrate to the capital in any great strength and lost heavily. The climax came on 15 September when they lost about fifty aircraft. The RAF claimed to have shot down 187, their greatest exaggeration of the whole campaign. This is the day now commemorated as the Battle of Britain Day, and although it is now widely recognized that double or treble counting of downed German aircraft must have occurred, it was nevertheless a great victory. The *Luftwaffe* continued to attack in daylight until the end of September, when Goering decided to change tactics to night bombing.

Post-war German figures show that the *Luftwaffe* lost over 1,400 aircraft over Britain from 10 July to the end of September, together with many of its best pilots and crews. Although there were greater air battles later in the war, these were losses which could not be sustained at the time. They effectively ended any German invasion plans, which were shelved on 12 October. Morale in Britain rose even higher among the civilian population, and the myth of German invincibility was shattered around the world. In particular, the victory demonstrated to America that Britain was unbowed and, moreover, could provide a platform from which to win the final victory.

Left: *A further photograph of the pilots of 32 Squadron at Biggin Hill. It is dated July 1940.*

Source: Keystone Collection

Right: *Pilots scramble to their Hurricane Mark Is. These aircraft are part of 111 Squadron, which was the first to receive the new fighter, in December 1937 when at Northolt.*

Source: Keystone Collection

Below: *Hurricanes of 501 Squadron taking off from Gravesend on 14 September 1940, at the height of the Battle of Britain. They had been refuelled and re-armed.*

Source: Keystone Collection

Left: *The front gunner in a Heinkel 111 tries to bring his single 7.92 machine gun to bear on a Spitfire Mark I which has probably made an attack on the rear of the German bomber and is breaking away for another pass.*
Source: Keystone Collection

Above: *An He111H of* Kampfgeschwader 1 *on a bombing attack over Biggin Hill on 18 August 1940, sometimes known as 'the hardest day' for the RAF. This German bomber carried war correspondent Bankhardt, who later included in his caption for this photograph: '"Further to the left!" cried the observer'.*
Source: RAF Museum P7002

Left: *On the night of 25/26 August 1940, the RAF made a bombing attack against Berlin, in retaliation for German attacks against London. This was the first occasion the German capital had been bombed since the First World War. Eighty-one heavy bombers of the RAF took part in the attack, which was repeated over the next few nights. This photograph, taken on 31 August 1940, shows some of the crews who participated.*
Source: Keystone Collection

Right: *The Spitfire Fighter Fund raised considerable sums of money during and after the Battle of Britain, from collection centres and boxes. In this poster, the serial number K9795 was taken from the first production batch of Spitfire Is.*
Source: RAF Museum (Crown copyright) P00548

ASKING FOR IT

DO NOT LET YOURSELF BE SURPRISED BY THE ENEMY. KEEP A GOOD LOOK-OUT ALL ROUND AT ALL TIMES.

Drawing by *Flight*

H.R. MILLAR

MAY, 1940	AIR DIAGRAM 1305
ISSUE NO.	1
DATE	MAY, 1940

FOR OFFICIAL USE ONLY

Left: *One piece of advice given to fighter pilots did not alter in either of the two world wars – keep a good look-out at all times. This crewroom poster showed Bf110s diving down on unwary Hurricane pilots.*
Source: RAF Museum AD1305

Right: *A Messerschmitt Bf109E of 7/Jagdgeschwader 27, flown by Oberleutnant Karl Fischer, was damaged on 30 September 1940 and the pilot attempted to crash-land in Windsor Great Park. The machine turned on its back, but was later righted, as shown here. Fischer, who was taken prisoner, was lucky to be uninjured.*
Source: Keystone Collection

Above: *A fine photograph of a Hurricane I of 32 Squadron at Biggin Hill, after landing.*
Source: Keystone Collection

Right: *The Hurricane was refuelled immediately, while the pilot left the cockpit to report to the squadron intelligence officer.*
Source: Keystone Collection

Above: *An armourer loading magazines with .303 inch rounds during the Battle of Britain. Both the main fighters, the Hurricane and the Spitfire, carried eight guns firing simultaneously. Each magazine held 300 rounds, enough for bursts of fire of up to four seconds.*

Source: Keystone Collection

Right: *Supermarine Spitfire II, serial P7350, in 266 Squadron markings. Hawker Hurricane IIC, serial LF363, in 242 Squadron markings, banking in the background. These two aircraft form part of the Battle of Britain Memorial Flight.*

Source: Keystone Collection

Above left: *This crewroom poster reminded Spitfire pilots that their machine guns would not fire unless their radiator (which was ducted to the guns to prevent freezing) was between 80 and 90 degrees Centigrade, or their pneumatic pressure (which operated the firing mechanism) was between 280 to 300 lb per square inch. The poster showed the fate of an unwise pilot, who had failed to check his instrument dials and was duly shot down by the front gunner of an He111.*
Source: RAF Museum AD1303

Above right: *Two German airmen being escorted from their burning aircraft by British soldiers. The airman on the left is a Feldwebel, or sergeant. The airman on the right, smoking a cigarette which might have been given to him by a soldier, is an Unteroffizier, or corporal.*
Source: Keystone Collection

Left: *A Dornier Do17 bomber burning out after a crash-landing.*
Source: Keystone Collection

Above left: *On 24 November 1940, Air Marshal Sir W. Sholto Douglas took over Fighter Command from Air Marshal Sir Hugh C.T. Dowding.*

Source: Keystone Collection

Left: *From left to right, Mrs Gabrielle Patterson and Mrs Grace Brown, pilots of the Air Transport Auxiliary, with a Tiger Moth. Mrs Patterson was a qualified instructor. Mrs Brown astonished RAF pilots when she landed at an advanced airfield in France during the German attack, carrying consignments of blood for the wounded. This photograph was taken on 7 October 1940.*

Source: Keystone Collection

Above: *On 14 September 1942, this photograph was taken at the Air Ministry to commemorate some of the pilots who were part of the 'Few' in the Battle of Britain two years before.*

Left to right: Sqdn Ldr A.C. Bartley, DFC, (England)
Wg Cdr D.F.B. Sheen, DFC and bar, (Australia),
Wg Cdr I.R. Gleed, DSO, DFC, (England),
Wg Cdr M. Aitken, DSO, DFC, (Canada),
Wg Cdr A.G. Malan, DSO, DFC, (South Africa),
Sqdn Ldr A.C. Deere, DFC, (New Zealand),
Air Chief Marshal Sir Hugh Dowding, GCB, GCVO, CMG,
Flt Off E.C. Henderson, MM, (Scotland),
Flt Lt R.H. Hillary, (England),
Wg Cdr J.A. Kent, DFC, AFC, (Canada),
Wg Cdr C.F.B. Kingcombe, DFC, (England),
Sqdn Ldr D.H. Watkins, DFC (England), and
Warr Off R.H. Gretton (England).

Source: Keystone Collection

CHAPTER 7

THE TURN
OF THE TIDE

The price that had to be paid for the success of the RAF in the Battle of Britain was the nightly bombardment of cities and towns. It was known by British scientists that the Germans possessed a system of identifying targets by flying along a beam, which they called *Knickebein*, and then releasing the bombs when the beam intersected another. The system was sufficiently accurate for the "area bombing" of large towns, but fortunately by the time the *Blitz* on London began, British scientists had found a way of 'bending' the beams so that the bombs would be likely to fall wide of the target.

However, Fighter Command, by then commanded by Air Marshal Sir W. Sholto Douglas, did not at this time possess any specialized night-fighters, but depended instead on Blenheims and obsolescent Defiants. The air interception radar fitted to the Blenheim had a limited range, while the aircraft was slower than many of the attacking bombers. Hurricane and Spitfire squadrons were pressed into service but the usual method of attack was visual, often carried out in the middle of anti-aircraft fire and searchlights. Ground control of night-fighters was inadequate, partly because the 'Chain Home' radar system was directed only towards the sea. Inland tracking depended on the Observer Corps who, although extremely accurate during the day, experienced more difficulties at night. Balloon barrages usually flew at 5,000 feet, while searchlights were ineffective above 12,000 feet and there were insufficient heavy anti-aircraft guns for the upper altitudes.

Thus the early attacks by the *Luftwaffe* over London met with little effective opposition. However, the anti-aircraft defences were soon strengthened and the barrage became tremendous. The racket of the guns was music to the ears of Londoners while the intensity of fire forced the bombers to fly higher, but few bombers were shot down. Great fires were started in the capital, mainly from incendiaries, during the 12,000 sorties which the *Luftwaffe* flew between the nights of 7/8 September and 12/13 November. Over 13,000 civilians were killed, with 20,000 injured. Yet morale held up surprisingly well, and Londoners became proud of their demonstration to the world that they could 'take it'.

The ordeal of London was lessened when Goering decided to switch some of the attacks to other industrial centres. These opened with a raid on Coventry on the night of 14/15 November, intended to demolish aircraft plants and other industrial works. The attack was led by the 'Pathfinder' unit *Kampfgruppe 100*, which used an advanced form of beam known as '*X*' Gerät. Many of the bombs and parachute mines fell on the city centre, killing 380 civilians, injuring 800 others, and destroying numerous buildings and public works. From this beginning, which created a wave of fury in Britain, attacks were launched against other towns and ports, some of which were severely hit. They continued until February 1941, but during this period there was improved jamming of the enemy's navigation system coupled with the use of decoy fires to divert the main bomber streams. The German high command then decided that ports must be given top priority, since Britain's capacity to wage war depended largely on imports reaching the country by sea. At the same time, the U-boat war was intensified.

Up to 12 May 1941, the weight of the onslaught fell on English, Welsh, Scottish and Northern Irish ports, which were badly damaged. But by now the raiders themselves were under attack, for a new Mark IV air interception radar was fitted to the cannon-firing Beaufighter, while the ground control stations directing the aircraft were improved and expanded. Suddenly the bombers began to lose a significant proportion of their number. British propaganda spread 'disinformation' which asserted that RAF pilots had improved their night vision by the diligent eating of carrots, a belief that gained widespread credence.

The bombing attacks began to diminish in June. Although the British public was unaware of the reason at the time, the *Luftwaffe* was withdrawing its units to join in the invasion of Soviet-occupied territory. This was operation 'Barbarossa', Hitler's plan for conquering Russia, which began on 22 June 1941 and led to the greatest series of land battles in history. For nearly four years, Germany's strength bled away in a war against a country which the world believed possessed such a rickety military structure that it would soon collapse.

The British War Cabinet realized that this was the time to turn to the offensive, if only to draw some of the resources of the *Wehrmacht* away from Britain's new military ally. It was obvious that an invasion of German-occupied Europe (the Second Front) was beyond Britain's capacity for the present, but at least Britain possessed a strategic strike force in the form of the RAF's Bomber Command.

Below: *The P-38 Lockheed Lightning. This US long-distance fighter was ordered by the RAF in early 1940 but subsequently rejected after testing.*

Source: Keystone Collection

On 25 October 1940, Air Chief Marshal Sir Charles Portal had taken over as Chief of Air Staff from Sir Cyril Newall, who had steered the RAF through the difficult early months of the war. Portal, who was soon to establish himself as a form of human dynamo in his new post, handed over his position as commander-in-chief of Bomber Command to Air Marshal Sir Richard Peirse. In July 1941, Sir Richard was directed to throw the main weight of his command against the German transportation system and to destroy the morale of the civil population, especially the industrial workers. It was reasoned that such a policy would be of maximum benefit to the Russian forces, who were falling back from the German onslaught.

Although the new C-in-C had forty-nine squadrons at his disposal in July 1941, there were formidable problems in executing the orders. Eight of the squadrons were still equipped with Blenheims, which were not capable of long-distance raids, while two-thirds of the remainder were crewed by men who were not yet fully trained. Of the 1,000 aircraft within the command, only 400 were available, and only a small proportion of these could operate each night. Another major problem was the weather over northern Germany, which was frequently unfavourable during these months. No new navigational aids had yet reached the squadrons. Long flights over Germany could be accomplished only by 'dead reckoning' navigation and any visual observation of landmarks such as rivers, or by positions obtained from sextant observations if the sky was clear enough. More often than not, the precise position of a target could not be found, even when there was a 'bomber's moon'. Similar problems faced the crews on return to England, for the eastern counties were often shrouded in fog and industrial pollution, resulting in numerous crashes when aircraft ran out of fuel or lost their way.

The effects of the bombing campaign over Germany were not impressive, in terms of damage. A post-war examination of the records of Cologne, which was attacked on thirty-three occasions between 1 June 1941 and 28 February 1942, including some 2,000 sorties, revealed that only about one sixth of the high-explosive bombs dropped fell on the city. Certainly some damage to industrial plants was caused, but the loss of production was soon made good. The limited effects of the heavy bomber campaign were appreciated at the time, for in September 1941 interpretation of photographs taken by long-range Spitfires of the Photographic Reconnaissance Unit (PRU) indicated that only one in three of the crews claiming to have scored hits had dropped their loads within five miles of the targets.

Above: *The Boulton Paul Defiant proved no match for German fighters during the Battle of Britain and many remaining machines were employed as night-fighters. Fitted with air interception radar and painted black, they gave good service until replaced with Beaufighters and Mosquitos. This photograph shows a Defiant of 151 Squadron in this night-fighter role.*
Source: RAF Museum PO19131

However, there is no doubt that the heavy bombing tied up large numbers of German personnel in defence, at the expense of the war effort against the Russians. In November 1941, Bomber Command's attacks against the German heartland were reduced in order to concentrate on the more accessible French ports in which U-boat shelters had been built. These harbours consituted a greater threat to Britain than the industry of the Ruhr, and were also very heavily defended. Moreover, it was known that new navigational instruments were in production for the RAF, as well as new four-engined bombers with enormous carrying capacity, and that these would soon transform the effectiveness of Bomber Command over Germany.

In addition to the night raids, Bomber Command began a series of daylight attacks with increasingly successful results. These were carried out in combination with Fighter Command, which had grown steadily in strength since the end of the Battle of Britain. In December 1940, formations of Spitfires and Hurricanes began cross-Channel raids known as 'Rhubarbs', designed to bring the war to enemy airfields and engage their aircraft in combat. When they escorted bombers, usually Blenheims, the fighters went out in greater strength and the operations were termed 'Circuses'. Their purposes were to cause damage to enemy ports, shipping, power supplies, airfields and transport.

Left: *The twin-engined Avro Manchester entered RAF service in November 1940 and eventually seven Bomber Command squadrons were equipped with the machine. Unhappily, the engines proved to be under-powered and there were many failures. It continued until June 1942 and was then withdrawn. The Manchester is perhaps best remembered as the forerunner of the famous Avro Lancaster.*
Source: RAF Museum P11931

Left: *Canadian airmen cleaning the Browning machine guns of a Handley Page Halifax II Series I, photographed in 1941. These machine guns fired at the rate of 1,200 rounds per minute; this Halifax was fitted with four in the tail, two in the dorsal turret and two in the nose turret.*
Source: Keystone Collection

Following the German advances into Russia, these daylight operations were stepped up. The arrival of the Douglas Boston from America in August 1941 provided Bomber Command with a light bomber which was faster than the Blenheim and also carried a heavier bomb load. From post-war records, it is possible to establish that the RAF lost slightly more aircraft than the *Luftwaffe* in these raids, but damage was caused to the targets. At the same time, Fighter Command carried out 'Intruder' raids over enemy airfields at night, using Blenheims at first but later employing the Douglas Havoc, a version of the Boston. Experienced German pilots were pulled back from the Eastern Front to meet the challenge of the RAF in France and the Low Countries.

Another task, performed by 'special' squadrons of the RAF, was the support of the Special Operations Executive (SOE), an undercover organization set up by Winston Churchill after the fall of France to 'set Europe ablaze' by sabotaging enemy communications and operations. The saboteurs and agents were landed and picked up by Lysanders, which had remarkably short take-off and landing runs, or dropped by parachute from Whitleys. Later in the war, Halifaxes, Hudsons and Wellingtons were also used. These flights were usually carried out in bright moonlight, guided by torch signals from a field, following wireless messages from a resistance group. From Britain, coded messages were sent out on the foreign news bulletins of the BBC, always preceded by the 'V for Victory' signal taken from Beethoven's Fifth Symphony. The clandestine flights were almost invariably successful and grew steadily in number throughout the war. The agents themselves carried out some great feats of sabotage, while their work helped to keep alive the spirit of hope and resistance in the occupied and oppressed countries.

The Commando organization was formed at the same time at the SOE, drawn from volunteers in all branches of the armed services. Under the new Directorate of Combined Operations, in which the RAF played its part, the initial objective was to carry out raids on the coasts of Occupied Europe. One of the achievements of this tough force took place on the night of 27/28 February 1942, after RAF interpreters at Medmenham in Buckinghamshire had identified from PRU photographs an unusual radar apparatus at Bruneval, near Le Havre. This turned out to be a German *Würzburg*, used for controlling anti-aircraft defences and night-fighters. Whitleys dropped paratroops, including some RAF men, near the site. After a stiff fight with German troops, part of the German equipment was dismantled and taken to the coast, where the survivors of the Commando force were picked up by the Royal Navy.

While Britain turned to the offensive, an event took place which expanded the conflict into a global war. On 7 December 1941, the Japanese bombed Pearl Harbor in the Hawaiian Islands, destroying a large proportion of the US Pacific Fleet. The USA was at last in a military alliance with Britain and Russia, bringing its enormous industrial strength as well as its armed forces into the war.

Left: *Polish aircrews formed squadrons with RAF numbers, after training within the RAF. However, the Polish Air Force was a separate force, with its own administration. The Poles proved to be fanatical fighters and achieved an astonishing record in combat. In this photograph three fighter pilots, wearing the Polish silver wings, had been decorated by the Polish premier in exile, General Sikorski. Polish Spitfire squadrons were employed on sweeps over northern France from the end of 1941.*

Source: Keystone Collection

Left: *The first Spitfire with a four-bladed propeller was the Mark VI, which was built with a pressurized cockpit and a Merlin engine rated at high altitude to combat German bombers and reconnaissance aircraft developed for flying at higher levels. Spitfire Mark VIs were first delivered to 616 Squadron at Tangmere in April 1942, and only three squadrons were equipped with this version. This photograph was taken on 10 December 1942.*

Source: Keystone Collection

Left: *Boeing Fortress I, serial AM528, of 90 Squadron. Twenty of these bombers, B-17c's the forerunner of the more famous B-17e's, were flown to Britain in the spring of 1941, but they did not prove successful with Bomber Command. There were many mechanical failures, the armament was inadequate and no long-range fighters were available for daylight raids. A few were sent to the Middle East and the remainder were transferred to Coastal Command for reconnaissance and meteorological work.*

Source: Keystone Collection

Right: *When the first Fortresses arrived for the RAF, servicing was undertaken by RAF ground crews. Here the .50 inch Browning gun in the ball turret of a USAA B-17e Fortress is being demonstrated by a US armourer. The turret is labelled 'Nookie'.*

Source: Keystone Collection

Left: *A view of Spitfire VB serial EN951 of 303 (Polish) Squadron, showing the 'Donald Duck' emblem.*

Source: Keystone Collection

Below: *The Supermarine Spitfire VB, fitted with two 20 mm cannons and four .303 inch machine guns, began to appear in February 1941. The Spitfire VB in this photograph, serial EN951, was one of the machines flown by Squadron Leader J. Zumbach, who commanded 303 (Polish) Squadron from May to December 1942.*

Source: Keystone Collection

Above: *On 10 May 1941 the Deputy Fuehrer of Germany, Rudolf Hess, took off from Augsburg on a flight to Dungavel House in Scotland, the home of the Duke of Hamilton, in an attempt to arrange an armistice between Germany and Britain. This is a photograph of his Messerschmitt Bf110, radio code VJ+OQ, works number 3869, at Augsburg. It was fitted with large drop-tanks containing 1,800 litres of extra fuel.*

Source: Archive Schliephake

Above right: *In the Filter Room of Fighter Command's headquarters at Bentley Priory, Corporal (later Flight Officer) Felicity Ashbee of the WAAF was on duty as a 'teller' and monitored the track of Hess's aircraft approaching the coast of Northumberland. Her information was transmitted to 13 Fighter Group at Ouston, near Newcastle upon Tyne.*

Source: Flight Officer Felicity Ashbee

Above: *Sergeant Maurice A. Pocock of 72 Squadron, based at Acklington in Northumberland, was sent up in a Spitfire IIa to shoot down the approaching aircraft, which was thought to be another German bomber. But Hess went into a steep dive when he reached the coast and managed to escape.*

Source: Flight Lieutenant Maurice A. Pocock

Above: *A Boulton Paul Defiant, similar to that in this photograph, was sent up by 141 Squadron at Ayr to attack the Messerschmitt, but Hess baled out when the RAF night-fighter was only a few minutes away from him. He landed on Floors Farm, south of Glasgow, and remained in various prisons until his death on 17 August 1987.*

Source: Aeroplane Monthly

Right: *The remains of the fuselage of Rudolf Hess's Bf110, radio code VJ+OQ, on display at the Imperial War Museum.*

Source: Roy C. Nesbit

Left: *Volunteers from the USA enlisted in the RAF before their country entered the Second World War, forming 'Eagle' Squadrons. The first was 71 Squadron, formed in September 1940 and becoming operational with Hurricanes in February 1941. The second was 121 Squadron, which was equipped with Hurricanes in May 1941. In this photograph, a pilot of 121 Squadron tries his hand at the British game of shove-ha'penny in the crew room.*

Source: Keystone Collection

Below: *As the war progressed, the RAF could look with pride on the cosmopolitan nature of its aircrews. This photograph is of a group of Hurricane pilots from Texas, Australia, Canada, The Punjab, Czechoslovakia, Poland, England, Scotland and Wales. All these men were serving in the same squadron.*

Source: Keystone Collection

Left: *US pilots of the RAF's 121 Squadron, the second Eagle squadron to be formed, photographed on 28 November 1941 while discussing aerobatics.*

Source: Keystone Collection

Right: *The Westland Whirlwind, designed as a long-range escort and night-fighter, was the first single-seat fighter to enter service in the RAF, in June 1940. It had four 20 mm cannon mounted in the nose and could also carry 1,000 lb of bombs. Whirlwinds escorted Blenheims on a daylight raid against Cologne on 18 August 1941, but they were mainly used on low-level sweeps across the Channel. The engines were underpowered and the landing speed was high, and only two RAF squadrons were equipped with the machine, which was withdrawn in November 1943. This example is a Whirlwind of 263 Squadron operating from Filton, near Bristol.*

Source: Keystone Collection

Left: *The four Hispano 20 mm guns in a Westland Whirlwind. Each carried a magazine holding 60 rounds, with a rate of fire of approximately 650 rounds per minute.*

Source: Keystone Collection

Above: *Bombing up a Lockheed Ventura with four 250 lb general-purpose and three 500 lb medium-capacity bombs.*

Source: Keystone Collection

Right: *A Canadian officer fitting his parachute harness over his Mae West lifejacket.*

Source: Keystone Collection

Left: *A photograph showing a contrast in bombs. The sergeant is holding an 11½ lb practice bomb, coloured white, while sitting on a 1,000 lb general-purpose bomb, coloured yellow. This was the largest general-purpose bomb available when this photograph was taken in early 1941. Soon afterwards, high-explosive bombs were coloured green, so that dumps were less visible from the air.*

Source: Keystone Collection

Left: *The Bell Airacobra, or P-39D. These US fighters, with their tricycle undercarriages, were delivered to the RAF's 601 Squadron in August 1941, replacing Hawker Hurricanes. The squadron operated with its new aircraft in ground attacks over the French coast, but there were major problems with unserviceability and the Airacobras were taken off operations the following December and eventually replaced with Spitfires.*

Source: Keystone Collection

Right: *The Airacobra was heavily armed, with one 20 mm cannon firing through the propeller boss, two .303 inch machine guns in the nose and four more in the wings. It was considered capable of carrying more ammunition than any other fighter at that time. This photograph, showing ammunition boxes being loaded with 20 mm shells, was taken in October 1941.*

Source: Keystone Collection

Left: *Aircrews of 408 (RCAF) Squadron walking out to their Hampden Is. One of the first Canadian bomber squadrons, 408 Squadron, began operating from Syerston in Nottinghamshire in July 1941.*

Source: Keystone Collection

Left: *After the fall of France in June 1940, those French airmen who managed to escape were at first distributed among RAF squadrons. In November 1941, however, 340 Squadron was formed at Turnhouse as the first Free French unit, equipped with Spitfires. Moving south in April 1942, 540 Squadron began sweeps over northern France, with Spitfire VBs. The Cross of Lorraine can be seen on this Spitfire, photographed in December 1942.*

Source: Keystone Collection

Right: *Many of the Free French airmen took the precaution of covering their faces with their intercom masks when being photographed, in case they were recognised by the Gestapo and reprisals were carried out against their relatives in Occupied France.*

Source: Keystone Collection

Left: *Walt Disney emblems were popular with the Free French.*

Source: Keystone Collection

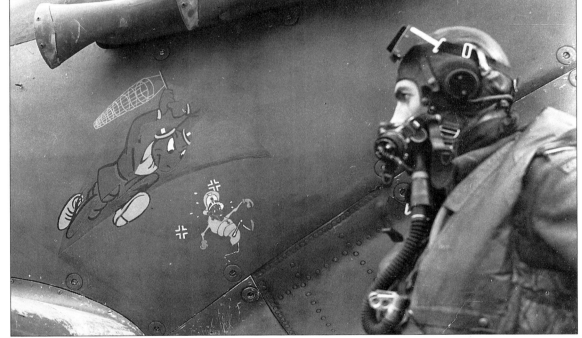

Below: *Pilots of 609 Squadron enjoying an improvised game of cricket on 30 June 1941. The squadron was based at Biggin Hill in Kent at the time, equipped with Supermarine Spitfire Vs and engaged on offensive sweeps over France.*

Source: Keystone Collection

Above: *In mid-1941 the Hawker Hurricane was modified for fighter-bomber duties. Nicknamed the 'Hurribomber', it carried two 250 lb bombs and later two 500 lb bombs. These aircraft operated over the Channel, from Malta, in the Western Desert and over Burma. This photograph shows a Hurricane IIB fighter-bomber of 402 (RCAF) Squadron, which was equipped with these machines from August 1941 to March 1942 and carried out many daylight raids over France.*
Source: Keystone Collection

Above left: *After its excellent record in the Battle of Britain, the Hawker Hurricane I became almost obsolescent. In April 1941, the Hurricane IIC, fitted with four 20 mm cannons, was supplied to 3 and 257 Squadrons.*
Source: Keystone Collection

Left: *The newly-formed RAF Regiment began to take over responsibility for the defence of aerodromes in early 1942, with officers appointed from both the army and the RAF.*
Source: Keystone Collection

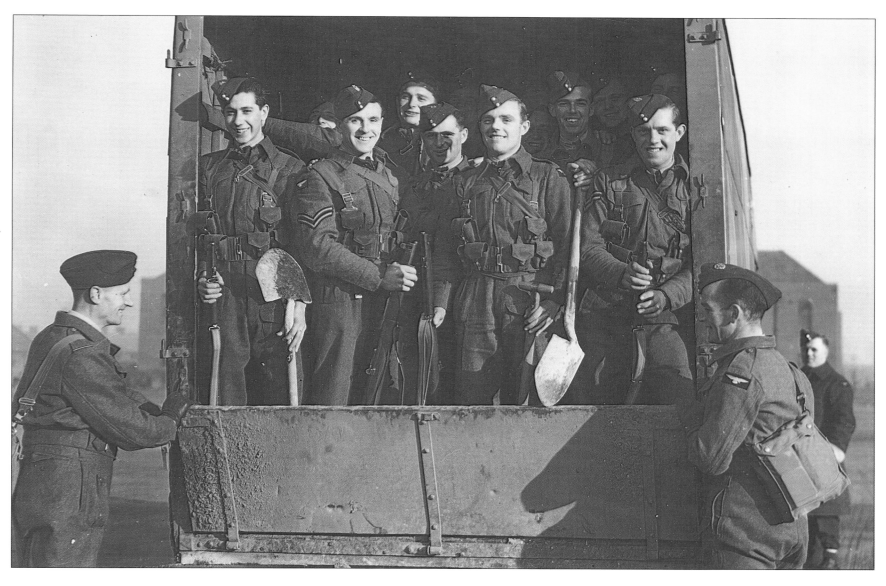

Above: *Many of the recruits for the newly-formed RAF Regiment were volunteers from the army, and wore khaki battledresses with RAF insignia as working dress. RAF uniforms were provided as "best blue".*

Source: Keystone Collection

Below: *The RAF Regiment trained dogs to help guard the lengthy perimeters of aerodromes, seen here with their handlers.*

Source: Keystone Collection

Below: *Some of the Alsatian dogs in the RAF Regiment were used to sniff out people buried in bombing attacks, seen here with their handlers setting off from an RAF depot to a bombed town in the southern counties.*

Source: Keystone Collection

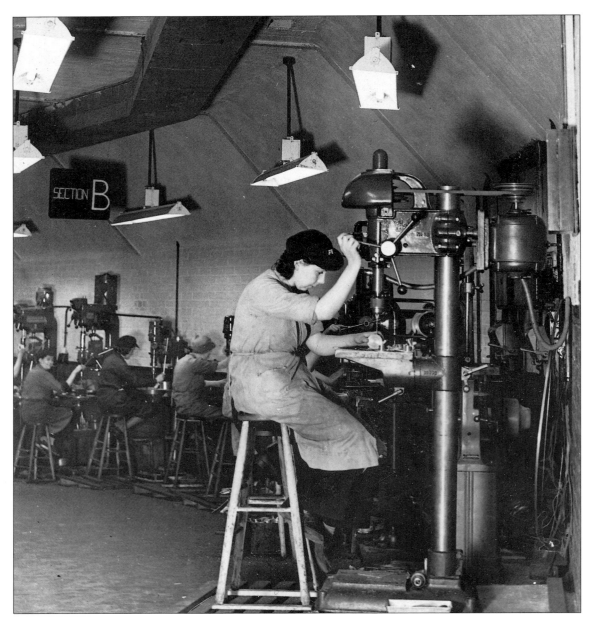

Above: *A store room containing aircraft parts, hollowed out of solid chalk.*

Source: Keystone Collection

Left: *Certain chalk mines and quarries along the banks of the lower Thames, where the product was combined with London clay for the cement industry, were used as underground works for aircraft parts. These factories, fitted with air conditioning and fluorescent lights, were almost immune from air attack. This photograph, showing a section of one of the drilling shops, was taken on 4 March 1942.*

Source: Keystone Collection

Left: *The Director of Recruiting in the RCAF during the Second World War was Air Marshal W.A. "Billy" Bishop, VC, DSO and bar, MC, DFC, Legion of Honour, Croix de Guerre with palm. One of the most famous air aces in the First World War, he had been credited with 72 victories. In September 1942, he visited 411 (RCAF) Squadron at Digby in Lincolnshire, at a time when it was equipped with Spitfire Vbs and engaged on sweeps over the Low Countries and France. Billy Bishop was immensely popular with airmen, as can be seen from this photograph of his visit.*

Source: Keystone Collection

Right: *The ground crews had to put their backs into their work, sometimes quite literally. These men were lifting up the wing of a fighter in order to change the wheel of an undercarriage, on 5 November 1942.*
Source: Keystone Collection

Below: *The North American Mustang I was designed to meet the RAF's specification and entered service in May 1942, on sweeps over the Channel. The performance was good at low altitudes but the Allison engine was under-powered for high-altitude escort of large bomber formations over Germany. This photograph shows a Mustang I of 2 Squadron, which was equipped with the machine until May 1944.*
Source: Keystone Collection

Left: *On 29 September 1942 the three Eagle squadrons, numbers 71, 121 and 133, were transferred to the USAAF and thereafter flew as US fighter squadrons over Europe. This photograph shows a number of the former Eagle pilots after returning from a raid over enemy territory in which they escorted B-17 Fortresses.*
Source: Keystone Collection

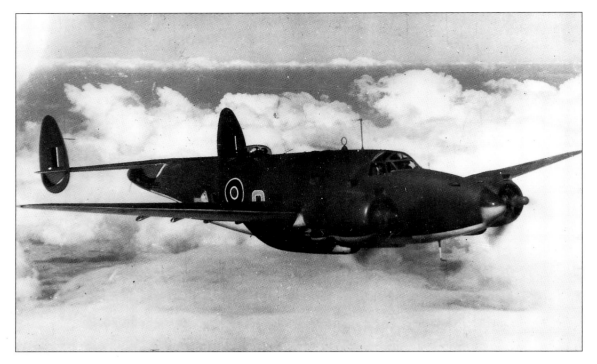

Left: *The Lockheed Ventura was similar to the Lockheed Hudson, a military development of a civilian aircraft. It was, however, more heavily armed than the Hudson, with two .50 inch machine guns in the nose as well as six .303 inch guns in three positions. It entered service with Bomber Command in May 1942, being given the unflattering nickname of 'The Pig', and was employed primarily on daylight raids. On 3 May 1943, Sqdn Ldr L.H. Trent of 487 (RNZAF) Squadron was awarded a Victoria Cross following a daylight raid which he led against a power station at Amsterdam, during which the whole formation of eleven Venturas was shot down and he was taken prisoner. The machine was withdrawn from Bomber Command in September 1943 and thereafter served with Coastal Command and the maritime squadrons overseas, on reconnaissance and meteorological flights.*

Source: RAF Museum P4537

Above: *The Douglas Boston III, or DB-7. Eight RAF squadrons were equipped with this fast US day-bomber, four in the UK and four in the Middle East. It was the first RAF machine with a tricycle undercarriage, which required a longer runway. Unusually for an RAF aircraft, all crew members sat in separate compartments, communicating only by intercom. It was the only machine in the RAF in which the pilot was not expected to be the last to bale out; a detachable control column was available in the upper gunner's compartment, in the hope that he could fly straight and level so that the pilot could avoid hitting the very high tailplane after clambering out of his top hatch and diving off the trailing edge of the wing.*

Source: Keystone Collection

Left: *Bombing up the DB-7 Douglas Boston with 500 lb bombs. The aircraft carried a maximum of 2,000 lb.*

Source: Keystone Collection

Above: *Cartoons were often used in crewroom posters. This appears to represent a high-altitude Mosquito of a photo-reconnaissance squadron and a Tiger Moth trainer. It was indeed vitally necessary to keep a continual lookout for other aircraft in the crowded skies over Britain during the Second World War.*

Source: RAF Museum (Crown copyright) POO397

Above: *A formation of DB-7 Douglas bombers in flight. The new aircraft was liked by RAF pilots, although the tricycle undercarriage required more runway for landings.*

Source: Keystone Collection

Below: *An aerial view of two Douglas Bostons of 88 Squadron.*

Source: Keystone Collection

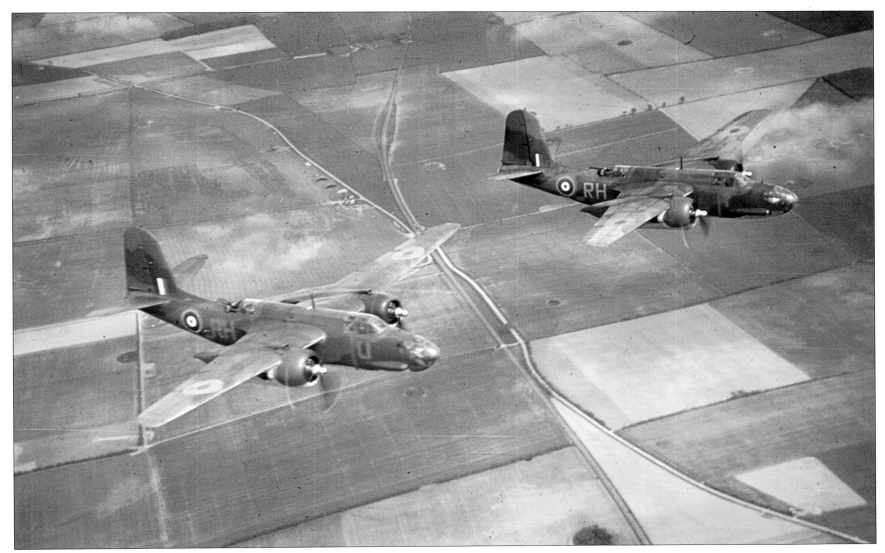

Above: *Many crashes during the Second World War occurred on high ground, sometimes on mountains where access by ambulance was impossible. The RAF formed a Mountain Rescue Service which carried out excellent work in saving the lives of injured aircrew. This photograph was taken in Wales in November 1943.*

Source: Keystone Collection

Left: *To commemorate the 25th anniversary of the formation of the RAF, the RAF Regiment took over the guard at Buckingham Palace for a period in 1943.*

Source: Keystone Collection

Left: *In retaliation for the raids by Bomber Command over Germany, Hitler ordered the Luftwaffe to carry out raids over London, which lasted from 21 January 1944 to the beginning of the following March. Many of the German raiders were shot down by RAF night-fighters. This aircraft was a Do217M of 3/Kampfgeschwader 2, shot down on the night of 24/25 February 1944 by a combination of AA fire and cannon fire from a Mosquito of 29 Squadron flown by Sqdn Ldr C. Kirkland, based at Ford in Sussex. Two of the German crew baled out and were captured, but the other two were killed in the crash, at Westcott near Dorking. In this photograph, Kirkland's navigator, Fl Off R.C. Raspin, was displaying a German radio code taken from the fin of the Dornier. All the bombs were still in the aircraft, but did not explode.*

Source: Keystone Collection

Above: *This strange aircraft, named the Libellula, was designed by George Miles, the chief designer of the company which produced the Miles Magister and Master. It was a tandem-winged and twin-engined machine which gave the pilot an excellent view, suitable for landing on aircraft carriers. This photograph was taken in August 1945, but the aircraft did not progress beyond the experimental stage. During the war, queer machines such as this could occasionally be seen by startled RAF crews flying near the experimental station of Boscombe Down in Wiltshire.*

Source: Keystone Collection

Above: *In August 1943, 464 (RAAF) Squadron received de Havilland Mosquito VIs to replace its obsolescent Lockheed Venturas, when based at Sculthorpe in Norfolk. By the end of the year, the squadron was engaged on night intruder missions with these fighter-bombers, and continued in this role until the end of the war.*

Source: Keystone Collection

Left: *The insignia on the aircraft of Sqdn Ldr E. Herbaczewski, Cross of Valour and three bars, DSO, DFC. He commanded 315 (Polish) Squadron from February to August 1944, at a time when it was equipped with North American Mustang IIIs and based at various aerodromes in southern England. Fourteen Polish squadrons flew with the RAF during the Second World War.*

Source: Keystone Collection

CHAPTER 8

REAPING THE WHIRLWIND

On 14 February 1942, Bomber Command was issued with a new directive. This stressed that the primary object of the bombing campaign was to be 'the morale of the enemy civil population and in particular of the industrial workers'. Eight days later, a new commander-in-chief replaced Sir Richard Peirse. This was Air Marshal Sir Arthur T. Harris, an able and experienced RAF officer with a strong personality and a marked gift for leadership, which was sometimes to display itself in an obstinacy which brought him into dispute with leading members of the Air Staff. Harris remained in this position for the remainder of the war and brought his command up to the massive force which demonstrated to the Germans the grim truth of the biblical message 'They have sown the wind, and they shall reap the whirlwind'.

The directive was issued in the knowledge that a new navigational aid was available to the RAF. This was 'Gee', which came into general service in the following month. Synchronized radio pulses were sent out from three radio stations in Britain, each situated about 100 miles from the next. A receiver fitted in the bomber enabled the navigator to see the time differences between the reception of the various pulses. He then plotted the results on a special Gee map and, with three stations sending out signals could ascertain the point at which the position lines intersected. For a bomber at 20,000 feet, the range was 200 miles, sufficient to reach the Ruhr.

New heavy bombers had been coming into RAF service since 1941. These were the twin-engined Avro Manchester, and the four-engined Handley Page Halifax and Short Stirling. Their increased carrying capacity was such that the old 'heavy' bombers such as the Whitley, the Wellington and the Hampden, were reclassified as 'medium', while the Blenheim became a 'light' bomber. The Manchester was not successful but gave rise to the four-engined Lancaster, the most successful and renowned RAF bomber of the war, which began to enter service at the end of 1941. At almost the same time as the Lancaster, the de Havilland Mosquito began to enter RAF service, gaining fame as the best light bomber of the war.

At the time of assuming his new command, Harris had only about fifty of the new heavy bombers and 250 medium bombers at operational readiness, but the carrying capacity had increased and, above all, they were able to find their targets with a high degree of accuracy. He made his first experiment on the night of 3/4 March 1942, against the Renault factory at Billancourt, near Paris. The heavy bombers equipped with Gee led the bomber stream, and hit the target precisely. Over 220 bombers dropped successfully and caused so much devastation that the plant was unable to return to full production for about three months. After two other successful attacks against industrial targets at Poissy in France, Harris felt the time had come to deal with Germany, principally the Ruhr and the Rhineland.

The first of these attacks took place on 8/9 March, against Essen in the Ruhr, the home of the great Krupps works. The bombers in the first wave were equipped with Gee but the incendiaries dropped were too widespread and the weight of the main force fell on the southern outskirts. Other attacks in the following days also missed the main

target. It was obvious that, although Gee was excellent as a navigation aid, it was not so precise that it could be used for aiming bombs at a specific target, especially when industrial haze limited visibility. On the other hand, the contrast between sea and land usually enabled bomb aimers to identify ports from the air, provided they were not covered by low cloud.

The most effective early raid carried out by the new bombing force took place on 28/29 March against the Hanseatic port of Lübeck on the Baltic coast. Although outside the range of Gee, the new instrument provided an aid for the majority of the flight, and the crews were able to pick out the port visually. About 190 aircraft dropped their bombs, and acres of buildings, most of which were of wood, went up in flames. Warehouses, port facilities, a power station and many factories were destroyed. Nearly 6,000 people lost their lives, and some 8,000 buildings were destroyed or badly damaged. The RAF lost five per cent of the attacking bombers, more than was considered sustainable for any length of time; with an operational tour of thirty bombing sorties, these odds were weighted too heavily against any crew's chance of survival. Nevertheless, the Nazi leaders were alarmed at the effect such raids could have on civilian morale, and braced themselves for worse to come.

For the next few weeks, raids against the Ruhr did not produce uniformly accurate results. A particularly gallant attack on 17 April against the M.A.N. Diesel Engine Works at Augsburg by twelve of the new Lancasters, in daylight at low level, resulted in some

Below: *Air Commodore John Searby, D.S.O., D.F.C. Master bomber – Lancaster over Peenemunde, 17 August 1943.*
Source: Courtesy of Frank Wootton, P.P.G. Av.A.

damage for the loss of seven aircraft. The raid created a sensation in Britain and amazement in Germany, but confirmed the view that heavy bombers should not make daylight attacks unless escorted by long-distance fighters. On the night of 23/24 April, however, the Baltic port of Rostock came under attack in clear weather and with the aid of a bright moon. Although more distant than Lübeck, the crews identified the dock area accurately. The bombers went back for the next three nights. About seventy per cent of the centre was destroyed, while severe damage was caused to a factory manufacturing Heinkel aircraft, and to some U-boat building yards. Casualties were heavy and 100,000 people had to be evacuated. Hitler was reported to have been enraged, but the next development was sufficient to bring him to a state of apoplexy.

On the night of 30/31 May, over 1,000 bombers were despatched to Cologne. Preparations for this massive attack had been made for several weeks. To make up the number, which was about four times the maximum quantity despatched on previous raids, crews and aircraft from Bomber Command's flying training group were willingly pressed into service. The first wave of aircraft was equipped with Gee, and the whole attack lasted only ninety minutes. The conflagration from the city was visible for 150 miles on the return journey, and the damage was later confirmed as immense. Over 18,000 buildings were destroyed and 9,500 heavily damaged. Nearly 500 people were killed, 5,000 injured and over 59,000 made homeless. Half the industrial plants in the city were badly damaged, and nearly 500 other businesses destroyed. Forty bombers failed to return, as well as two of the fifty engaged on diversionary work. Operation 'Millenium', as it was called, was counted a success. Even worse was in store for the Third Reich, although raids on this scale were not possible in the next few months except on rare occasions.

At the same time as the intensification of the nightly war against the German cities and towns, the cross-Channel raids in daylight were stepped up. This was the period in which the FW190, the latest German fighter, came into service. In some ways, its performance was superior to the Spitfire V, and the RAF losses mounted. However, the raids succeeded in drawing increased numbers of Luftwaffe units away from the Eastern Front.

At dawn on 19 August, a combined raid on Dieppe took place, with Canadian regiments and Commandos landed by the Royal Navy. The purposes were to experiment with a large-scale landing in preparation for the re-opening of the Second Front on the Continent, and to bring more German fighters into combat over the beachhead at a time when the RAF enjoyed a numerical superiority. The defences proved too strong for the raiding forces, which suffered over 4,000 casualties. There was a great air battle, during which the RAF lost 106 aircraft whereas the *Luftwaffe* lost only forty-eight. It was an expensive experiment, but one in which valuable lessons were learnt and later put into practice.

In July 1942, the first Boeing Fortress B-17s of the US Eighth Air Force reached Britain, and participated in the bombing of Dieppe. The machines were flown over the Atlantic from Gander in Newfoundland to Prestwick in Ayrshire, the first of a flood which would join in the air assault on Germany. It was intended that the Americans, who specialized in precision bombing in daylight with heavily armed aircraft which carried a fairly light bomb load, would join with the RAF in a 'round the clock' bombing of German targets. But this objective proved to be several months ahead.

In August 1942, Bomber Command formed the Pathfinder Force (PFF), under Gp Capt Don C.T. Bennett. At first, Harris opposed this formation, for he feared that his squadrons would be weakened when their best crews were picked for this work. The idea was to create an elite force to lead the bomber streams with the aid of Gee and then drop flares and markers to illuminate the target for the heavy bombers. However, the new PFF squadrons soon became efficient and, provided the weather was reasonably good, marked their targets accurately on about seventy-five per cent of the raids. This was in spite of German jamming of Gee, which reduced its effective range.

Two months later, Bomber Command was instructed to divert its efforts temporarily to industrial centres in northern Italy, to support the Allied landings in Morocco and the advance of British forces in North Africa. Genoa, Milan and Turin received the full weight of the heavy bombers, to the dismay of the Italian people, many of whom were waging their war with less than fervent enthusiasm.

By February 1943, a conference held by Churchill and Roosevelt, together with their Chiefs of Staff, had included in their decisions a directive to the Allied Air Forces, to the effect that the primary objective was the destruction of German economic and military system, coupled with the undermining of the morale of the German people. In descending order of priority, the targets were to be U-boat construction yards, the aircraft industry, transport, oil plants and other war industries. However, these objectives were left open to wide interpretation by the bomber force commanders, for they were dependent on weather conditions and tactical feasibility.

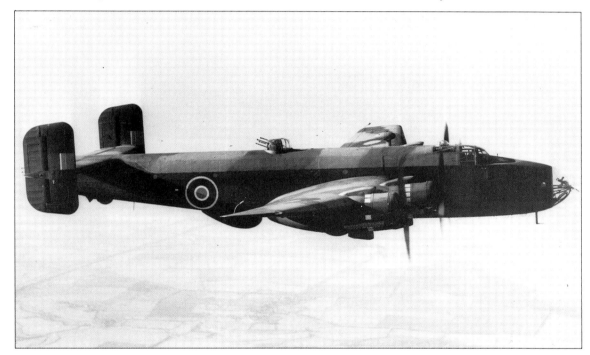

Left: *The Handley Page Halifax was the first four-engined bomber of the RAF to drop bombs in Germany during the Second World War. It first entered service in December 1940, preceding the Avro Lancaster. The Mark I acquired a poor reputation with aircrews, owing to its inability to maintain sufficient altitude during operations, but various modifications were made and the record of the Halifax in Bomber Command was exceeded only by the Avro Lancaster. Some Halifaxes were allocated to Coastal Command and made a major contribution to the war against U-boats and coastal shipping. Eventually over 6,000 of the various marks were built. This photograph shows a Halifax III of 423 (RCAF) Squadron, taken on charge on 18 November 1943. Unfortunately, it was shot down during a raid on Magdeburg on 21 January 1944 and the entire crew lost their lives.*

Source: RAF Museum PO12020

Two further navigational aids became available to Bomber Command at the end of 1942. One was 'H2S', a device in the aircraft which transmitted a signal to the surface of the earth; this was reflected back and luminised on a small screen with a revolving trace. The early version was not easy to read, but it could show up a town, or more definitely a port. It also operated through cloud and was not subject to jamming. The other aid was 'Oboe', which depended on two transmitters in the Eastern Counties. These sent out a series of pulses which the aircraft amplified and returned. One of the ground stations could tell the navigator whether he was left or right of track, while the other told him when he was at the point of intersection over the target, with a high degree of accuracy. Oboe was used by Pathfinder Mosquitos, dropping target indicators. The early transmitters could handle only one aircraft at a time but a later adaptation, called GH, involved the installation of the system in the aircraft itself, enabling many aircraft to use it simultaneously. However, like Gee, Oboe was subject to range limitation and eventually to jamming.

These new devices enabled Bomber Command to achieve some notable successes in early 1943. Among these was a series of forty-three major raids on the Ruhr, known ironically as 'Happy Valley' by the crews, between March and July, in which heavy damage was inflicted. By March 1943, Bomber Command comprised sixty-five squadrons, including light bombers and the Pathfinder Group. On the night of 16/17 May, the newly-formed 617 Squadron carried out a raid which captured the imagination of the world, the breaching of the Möhne and Eder dams with the special 'bouncing bombs' invented by the designer of the Wellington, Barnes Wallis. The raid caused havoc and temporarily brought to a halt the water supply to millions of people in the Ruhr.

A series of attacks on Hamburg were made towards the end of July, when the 'Window' technique was used. This consisted of the dropping of showers of aluminium strips which clouded the German radar screens, interrupting the control of flak and night-fighters. A great firestorm was created, resulting in devastation on a scale which had not been seen before. A small section of the U.S. Eighth Air Force also attacked the port in daylight, their first operation over German soil. About sixty-one per cent of the living accommodation of Hamburg was demolished, 41,800 people were killed and about 38,000 injured. Many of the remaining population fled from this dreadful holocaust. Manufacture almost came to a halt, including the production of U-boats, and it is estimated that between six to twelve weeks were lost in the various industries.

Right: *This early colour photograph of a Vickers Wellington III, serial Z1572 of 419 (RCAF) Squadron, was taken on 27 May 1942. The squadron was based at Mildenhall in Suffolk at the time.*
Source: RAF Musuem P100692

Above: *Vickers Wellingtons setting course at dusk, over cloud.*
Source: Keystone Collection

Left: *The crew of a Handley Page Hampden I of 83 Squadron, returning from an operational sortie over a German coastal port in October 1940. The squadron was based at Scampton in Lincolnshire at that time.*
Source: Keystone Collection

Right: *As soon as possible after landing from an operational flight, crews were always debriefed by an intelligence officer. Long flights were physically and mentally exhausting, and the strain shows on the faces of some of the men in this photograph, four of whom are wearing sheepskin Irvin jackets. A mug of tea and a cigarette were usually provided at these debriefings.*
Source: Keystone Collection

However, these operations were not an unqualified success in terms of RAF losses. These had been considered acceptable during much of 1942, but they began to rise rapidly in the spring of 1943, when the Germans began to improve their defences under *General der Flieger* Josef Kammhuber. The numbers of radar stations, searchlights and flak guns were increased, forming a 'Kammhuber Line' across the normal paths of the bomber streams from England. A network not unlike the Royal Observer Corps was expanded. The number of night-fighter units was increased, until these comprised nearly 500 aircraft in the summer of 1943. These night-fighters, mostly Bf110s and Ju88s, were equipped in the late autumn of 1942 with the *Lichtenstein Gerät* radar apparatus, which gave excellent results on the screens of the air operators. Some fighters were fitted with the deadly *Schräge Musik* (jazz music), two upward-slanting cannons firing into the blind spots of bombers, similar to the system used in the First World War.

The German night-fighters accounted for the majority of Bomber Command's losses. In the first three major attacks on Berlin at the end of August and the beginning of September 1943, 123 heavy bombers were shot down, eighty of them by night-fighters. In the subsequent attacks against Berlin, from the following November to March 1944, 1,047 RAF bombers were lost. The rate of losses, 5.2 per cent per sortie, was higher than acceptable for an extended campaign. On 30/31 March 1944, there was a catastrophic raid on Nuremberg, when ninety-four bombers were lost from the 795 despatched, a rate of attrition of nearly twenty-one per cent.

The results of raids were assessed by information brought back by the high-flying Mosquitos and Spitfires of the Photographic Reconnaissance Unit, part of Coastal Command. Highly-skilled RAF interpreters assessed the results, with considerable accuracy. In addition, cameras were installed in the bombers, taking a series of films at the same time as the bombs and a flash-bomb containing magnesium powder were released. There was a human tendency for crews to drop their bombs slightly short of the targets when under intense fire, and these night photographs showed any "creep-back", as it was termed. If a crew brought back photographs showing creep-back the sortie was not counted as one of the thirty prescribed for an operational tour.

Although Bomber Command's raids, combined with the daylight attacks of the Eighth Air Force, were steadily flattening German cities, production of war materials in the Third Reich was mounting, under the guidance of Albert Speer, the Minister of Armaments and Munitions. It is probable, however, that production would have increased at a much greater rate if the bombing campaign had not taken place. The morale of the German people did not crack in 1944, contrary to the hopes expressed at the Casablanca Conference. But the damage caused by air attacks on Germany up to this period, although immense, was dwarfed by the air assault launched in the last twelve months of the war in Europe.

Right: *Forty-seven RCAF Squadrons flew with the RAF during the Second World War. This photograph shows the mascot on a Wellington of 405 (RCAF) Squadron in July 1941.*

Source: Keystone Collection

Centre right: *The first heavy bomber squadron of the RCAF was 405 Squadron, formed on 23 April 1941 at Driffield in Yorkshire, equipped with Vickers Wellington IIs. An early example of 'nose art' can be seen here, photographed on 28 July 1941.*

Source: Keystone Collection

Far right: *Twenty-three RAAF squadrons flew with the RAF during the Second World War. The first bomber squadron to be formed in the UK was 458 Squadron, based at Holme-in-Spalding-Moor in Yorkshire in August 1941. This photograph was taken in November 1941, showing a badge on a Vickers Wellington IV.*

Source: Keystone Collection

Left: *Group Captain Hughie I. Edwards was the first Australian airman to win the VC in the Second World War, after he led Blenheims of 105 Squadron in a daylight attack on 4 July 1941 against Bremen. He was also the first man in the war to win the VC, DSO, DFC and bar.*

Source: Keystone Collection

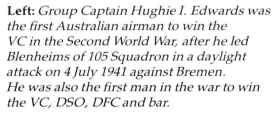

Right: *In October 1941, a Short Stirling I named 'MacRobert's Reply' began operations, following £25,000 donated by Lady MacRobert for the purchase of a bomber. Lady MacRobert had lost three sons, one in a flying accident before the war and two while serving in the RAF.*

Source: Keystone Collection

Above: *Air Marshal Sir Arthur T. Harris, who was appointed to the post of Air Officer Commanding-in-Chief, Bomber Command, on 22 February 1942.*

Source: Keystone Collection

Above: *The dispersal bays of Avro Lancasters of 50 Squadron, which was first equipped with these bombers in May 1942 and continued with them until November 1946.*

Source: Keystone Collection

Below: *Flying Officer G. Leonard Cheshire, together with his aircrew and ground crew, in front of Handley Page Halifax 'Offenbach' of 35 Squadron.*

Source: RAF Museum P000688

Heavy "Stirling" bombers raid the Nazi Baltic port of Lübeck and leave the docks ablaze

BACK THEM UP!

WINGS FOR VICTORY

MORE SAVINGS - MORE WINGS

Above left: *The 'Wings for Victory' campaign was intended to encourage saving and keep down inflation. The squadron letters on the Avro Lancasters in this poster may have been imaginery; the letters VS were not used by any RAF squadron, but the letters VN were those of 50 Squadron, which was equipped with Lancasters from May 1942 onwards.*

Source: RAF Museum (Crown copyright) P00473

Above: *The heavy attack by Bomber Command on the port of Lübeck, on the night of 28/29 March 1942, when over 200 acres were devastated by a mixture of bombs and incendiaries, inspired this poster showing Short Stirlings. At the time, the public was demanding attacks by the RAF in retaliation for the German bombing of British cities.*

Source: RAF Museum (Crown copyright) P00164

Above: *In May 1943, Air Chief Marshal Sir Arthur Harris chatted to the crew of a Halifax who were rescued from the North Sea after spending sixteen hours in a dinghy. Bomber Command aircrews were devoted to their chief, who was "Bomber" Harris to them.*

Source: Keystone Collection

Left: *The damaged rear turret of a Short Stirling after the first 1,000 bomber raid, against Cologne on 30/31 May 1942.*

Source: Keystone Collection

Right: *Bombing up Armstrong Whitleys with 250 lb general-purpose bombs, in the summer of 1942.*

Source: Keystone Collection

Right: *The first of Bomber Command's 'thousand bomber' raids took place against Cologne on the night of 30/31 May 1942. Leaflets intended to unsettle the morale of the German civilian population were dropped a few days afterwards. This leaflet read:*
"From now on we shall bomb Germany on an ever-increasing scale, month by month, year by year, until the Nazi regime has been either exterminated by us or – better still – torn to pieces by the German people themselves."
CHURCHILL
14 July 1941
ON THE NIGHT OF MAY 30/31
THERE BEGAN
THE 1000 BOMBERS A NIGHT RAIDS
TWO IN THREE NIGHTS

After the second raid, Churchill declared: 'These two great night bombing raids mark the introduction of a new phase in the British air offensive against Germany and these will increase markedly in scale when we are joined, which we soon shall be, by the air force of the United States.
'As the year advances, German cities, harbours and centres of war production will be subjected to an ordeal the like of which has never been experienced by any country in continuity, severity or magnitude.'

ENGLAND'S OFFER
JUSTICE FOR ALL, INCLUDING GERMANS
'Justice, first for the people enslaved by Germany, justice for ourselves, justice for Germany.' (Lord Cranborne)

PUNISHMENT OF THE CRIMINALS
'Justice stern and unflinching for those Germans guilty of the abominable crimes we have witnessed.' (Lord Cranborne)

ECONOMIC EQUALITY AND SECURITY
'Equal rights for victor and vanquished to free access to the raw materials of the world.

Work and social security for all.' (Churchill-Roosevelt declaration)

ENGLAND'S DEMAND
THE GERMAN PEOPLE MUST ACT THEMSELVES IN ORDER TO FREE THEMSELVES FROM HITLER'S GANGSTER RULE
'Therefore, if any section of the German people really wants to see a return to a German State which is based on respect for

law and for the rights of the individual, they must understand that no one will believe them until they have taken active steps to rid themselves of their present regime.' (Foreign Secretary, Eden)

'None can remain neutral. Everyone must show through his deeds where he stands; whether against us and freedom, or by our side in the great army of the world of the future.' (Sir Stafford Cripps)

THE GERMAN PEOPLE HAVE THE CHOICE

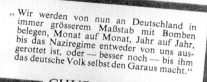

Far left: *The assembly line of a factory manufacturing de Havilland Mosquitos.*

Source: Keystone Collection

Left: *Geoffrey de Havilland (right) with the new Mosquito aircraft developed by his company.*

Source: Keystone Collection

Above right: *As Bomber Command aircraft flew over Belgium, leaflets were dropped to encourage the people in the occupied country. This leaflet was in French and Flemish, and read:*

JUST BACK FROM GERMANY!
COURAGE, BELGIAN FRIENDS!
Did you hear the drone of our engines as we flew high over your roofs the other night? We thought of you Belgians down there…. We were on our way back from Germany where our bombs left a nice mess for the Boche to clear up.
We thought you would like to know that we gave them a night of hell because they're giving you a life of hell. And now, night after night, we'll continue to pay them back in their own coin!
Courage! Together we're going to beat the Boche!
Greetings from the boys of the R.A.F. BOMBER COMMAND - Royal Air Force

On the picture of the Stirling was a box with the message
To our friends:
Please paste this up in public.

Source: RAF Museum (Crown copyright)

Right: *Avro Lancaster letter N of 50 Squadron in flight.*

Source: Keystone Collection

Left: *The de Havilland Mosquito must be classed as one of the most superb aircraft built in Britain. Constructed of wood, originally as a private venture, the bomber version of the 'Mossie' had no defensive armament but relied on altitude and speed for protection. The Mosquito IV, which carried a bomb load of 2,000 lb, first entered service in November 1941. The Mosquito XVI, with more powerful engines, entered service in December 1943 and could carry the surprisingly large load of 4,000 lb. This photograph is of serial numbers DZ353 and DZ367 of 105 Squadron, which first received Mark IVs in November 1941.*

Source: RAF Museum P9547

Right: *Detail of the assembly of a de Havilland Mosquito, which was sometimes known as 'the wooden wonder'.*

Source: Keystone Collection

Hoog de hoofden, Belgische vrienden!

BOMBER COMMAND — Royal Air Force

Left: *About 6,500 Lancasters were manufactured during the Second World War.*

Source: Keystone Collection

Below: *The Avro Lancaster justified its reputation as the finest heavy bomber employed by the RAF during the Second World War. Developed from the unsuccessful Avro Manchester, it proved easy to fly, highly reliable and capable of absorbing considerable punishment. The first Lancasters entered service in December 1941 and, before the end of the war, fifty-six squadrons of Bomber Command were equipped with these machines. In 1945, Lancasters carried the enormous 'Grand Slam', a bomb of 22,000 lbs. This photographs shows a Lancaster I, serial R5868, of 467 (RAAF) Squadron, one of the original heavy bomber squadrons, being loaded with a 4,000 lb 'cookie' and 5000 lb medium-capacity bombs. This aircraft completed 144 operations and survived the war.*

Source: Keystone Collection

Above: *The 200 foot gap in the Moehne dam after the attack by Lancasters of 617 Squadron on the night of 16/17 May 1943. Nineteen Lancasters, led by Wg Cdr Guy Gibson, attacked the Moehne, Eder, Sorpe, Lister and Schwelme dams, breaching the Moehne and Eder but losing eight aircraft. This photograph was discovered in German archives after the war.*

Source: Keystone Collection

Right: *The breached Moehne dam on 17 May 1943, the morning after the attack by 617 Squadron, photographed by Flying Officer F.D. Fray in a Spitfire PR XI of 542 Squadron. Wg Cdr Guy Gibson described the water during the attack "like stirred porridge in the moonlight, rushing through a great breach". The dam served the needs of over four million people in the Ruhr and was not fully repaired until August 1944.*

Source: Keystone Collection

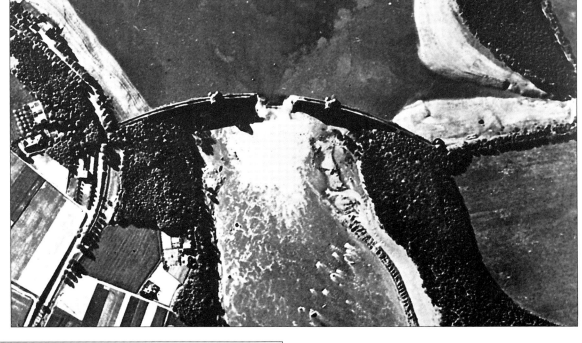

Left: *A Lancaster being fitted with a 4,000 lb blast bomb, called a 'block-buster' or a 'cookie'. The bomb exploded a few feet above the ground, causing a lateral blast, and was often dropped in combination with showers of incendiaries, to cause maximum destruction of buildings.*

Source: Keystone Collection

Left: *Wg Cdr Guy Gibson (with pipe) photographed a few days after returning from a raid on Berlin in January 1943.*

Source: Keystone Collection

Left: *Wg Cdr Guy Gibson (centre), after his investiture with the Victoria Cross at Buckingham Palace in June 1943, together with the Australian airmen who took part in the raid. Gibson lost his life during a raid on München-Gladbach on 19 September 1944, by which time he had been awarded the VC, the DSO and bar, and the DFC and bar.*

Source: Keystone Collection

Below: *A fully-laden Avro Lancaster taking off at dusk on a bombing mission.*

Source: Keystone Collection

Wer hat gesagt —
„Vor allem werde ich
dafür sorgen, dass der Feind
keine Bomben werfen kann."

WARSCHAU

ROTTERDAM

BELGRAD

LÜBECK

KÖLN

DÜSSELDORF

Above: *Bomber Command continued to drop propaganda leaflets over Germany when the major bombing attacks began against German cities. This leaflet showed Hermann Goering looking cheerful when he ordered the German bombing attacks against Warsaw, Rotterdam and Belgrade, but increasingly miserable when the RAF attacked Lübeck, Rostock and Cologne. The leaflet pointed out "Who said: Above all, I shall see to it that the enemy will not be able to drop any bombs?"*

Source: RAF Museum (Crown copyright)

Above: *The continuing destruction of German cities by Bomber Command was portrayed in this recruiting poster showing Avro Lancasters.*

Source: RAF Museum (Crown copyright) P00545

Left: *A 'cookie', or 'blockbuster', 4,000 lb blast bomb being loaded on a de Havilland Mosquito. The bomb bay of this light bomber, originally intended to carry only 2,000 lb, was modified to accommodate the extra size. A Mosquito of 692 Squadron first dropped one of these bombs over Düsseldorf on the night of 23/24 February 1944.*

Source: Keystone Collection

Right: *As the war progressed, the bombs carried by Lancasters became larger. The new 8,000 lb high-capacity bomb was first dropped on 10 February 1942. This photograph was released by the censor in September 1943.*

Source: Keystone Collection

Left: *This Lancaster force-landed in October 1943 after a raid over Germany. One engine had burnt out, the undercarriage was smashed and the propellers twisted. In this photograph it is being hoisted by self-propelled cranes on to bogies, to move it to the side of the aerodrome. Damaged aircraft such as this were dismantled and transported in parts to repair depots, where they were repaired and reassembled.*

Source: Keystone Collection

Left: *Canadian aircrews in a Mosquito squadron relaxing over cards in their crew room.*

Source: Keystone Collection

Right: *The 'Grand Slam' bomb of 22,000 lb. The first of these bombs was dropped on 14 March 1945 by an Avro Lancaster Mark I (Special) of 617 Squadron on the viaduct at Bielefeld in Germany. In all, 41 of these bombs were dropped before the end of the war. This photograph was taken in June 1946 at an exhibition in Oxford Street, showing the contrast with a cadet of the Air Training Corps. The bomb was 25 ft 5 in long and had a charge/weight ratio of 42 per cent.*

Source: Keystone Collection

Below: *A plaque in the Officers' Mess of 9 Squadron on 11 January 1944, at a time when the squadron was based at Bardney in Lincolnshire and equipped with Avro Lancaster Is and IIIs. The squadron motto was* Per noctum volamus *(Through the night we fly).*

Source: Keystone Collection

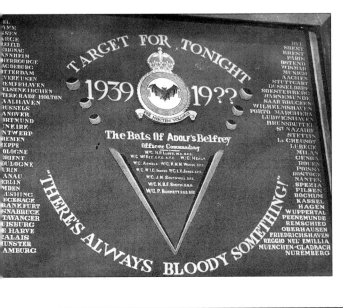

CHAPTER 9

THE ATLANTIC AND HOME WATERS

The tasks faced by Coastal Command after the German occupation of Norway, Denmark, the Low Countries and France were herculean. A coastline extending from the Arctic Circle to the Franco-Spanish border was suddenly and unexpectedly controlled by the enemy. Even ignoring long inlets and large islands, the length was 16,500 miles. In July 1940, Germany was able to ply captured enemy merchant ships along much of this coastline, almost with impunity. Moreover, U-boat shelters were built in Norwegian and French ports, giving this deadly branch of the *Kriegsmarine* improved access to arctic waters, the North Sea and the Atlantic. Together with the Royal Navy and the Fleet Air Arm, Coastal Command shared responsibility for asserting Allied control over these seas.

The U-boats found their major pickings in the Western Approaches to England, following the convoys by day and then closing in after nightfall to make their attacks, when protection from escort vessels and from the air was very limited. Other attacks were made by Focke-Wulf FW 200's, the military version of a civil airliner, which carried out very long-range work in collaboration with U-boats. Shorter-range work was carried by He111s and Do17s. In the last seven months of 1940, sinkings of British and Allied shipping rose to the appalling total of 4,500,000 tons, about 1,200 vessels, reducing essential imports by a fifth. At the outbreak of war, Britain had possessed about 21,000,000 tons of merchant shipping, including 3,000 deep-sea vessels and 1,000 coastal vessels. Since replacement during these seven months amounted to only 500,000 tons, it was evident that Britain could not last out for long, unless the U-boat menace could be overcome.

In January 1941, Coastal Command consisted of twenty-three operational squadrons within five groups, including a squadron of the Photographic Reconnaissance Unit and a squadron in Gibraltar. The principal land-based aircraft were Ansons, Hudsons, Wellingtons, and the new Bristol Beaufort torpedo bombers. The most important flying boat was the Sunderland, but there were still a few Supermarine Stranraers, while very long-range Consolidated Catalinas had been ordered from America. Some of the squadrons were based in Iceland, for the British had forestalled a German invasion by landing in that country in May 1940.

An expansion programme forecast an increase of fifteen squadrons in the command by the following June. In April 1941, it was decided that Coastal Command should come under the Admiralty's operational control, while remaining part of the RAF. In practice, the outcome was simply an improved liaison, for Coastal Command continued to conduct its day-to-day operations without interference, while conferring with the Admiralty on broad issues.

Although bad weather in the first two months of 1941 reduced the activities of German U-boats and aircraft, over 530,000 tons of shipping were sunk in March and 644,000 tons in April. There was a further threat from German surface vessels, the battleships *Scharnhorst* and *Gneisenau*, the pocket-battleship *Admiral von Scheer*, and the cruiser *Hipper*, all of which had broken out into the Atlantic and were sinking merchant ships. The resources of Coastal Command were so stretched that three

Left: *A Sunderland Mark III of Coastal Command. This type was fitted with a dorsal turret instead of beam guns, as well as a faired main step which reduced air drag by about ten per cent.*

Source: RAF Museum P020896

Below: *A Short Sunderland Mark I on a slipway.*

Source: Keystone Collection

squadrons of Blenheims were transferred to it, one from Bomber Command, one from Army Co-operation, and one from Fighter Command. In addition, a Swordfish squadron was temporarily transferred from the Fleet Air Arm. These additional squadrons took part in patrols and anti-shipping attacks over the North Sea, relieving other squadrons for duties elsewhere.

The turning point in the war against British merchant shipping came with improved tactics by naval escort vessels, the cracking of the German signal code, and the installation of new equipment in the growing number of aircraft. Also, fighters catapulted from auxiliary escort vessels gave cover to convoys and began to account for enemy bombers. During March 1941, the Royal Navy escort vessels sank five U-boats, in which three of the most experienced German commanders were lost. From the beginning of the war, the *Kriegsmarine* had lost thirty-seven U-boats, while thirty-two were still operational, and a further eighty-one were undergoing training and trials. Up to this time, the RAF had sunk no U-boats, although aircraft had shared in sinkings with the escort vessels and damaged several others.

The new equipment was an improved mark of 'Air to Surface Vessel' (ASV) radar, installed at first in Sunderlands. This consisted of a transmitter and receiving system, sending out a series of pulses which were reflected back and displayed on a screen. Ships on the surface showed up as blips along a central line, indicating the distance away and whether they were to the left or right of the aircraft's heading. Serviceability of this ASV Mark II was not perfect at first, but results were achieved. U-boats needed to come to the surface for periods during each day in order to recharge their batteries as well as to change their foul air. It was extremely unnerving to suddenly find themselves the target of an aircraft armed with depth charges and machine guns.

On 8 May 1941, a destroyer escort brought *U-110* to the surface with depth charges, and the Germans abandoned her. Their explosive charges failed and British sailors boarded the vessel, discovering code books as well as a secret 'Enigma' coding machine. From this time, the Government Code and Cipher School at Bletchley Park in Buckinghamshire knew almost as much about the movements of U-boats in home waters as the Germans themselves, as well as the times of sailing and cargoes of German coastal convoys.

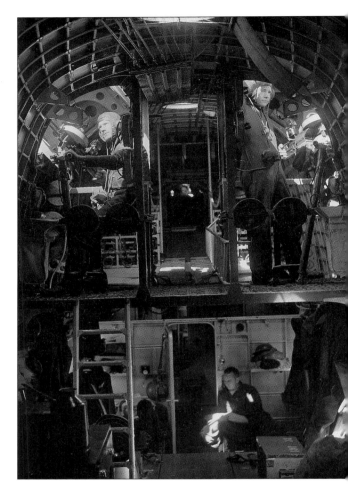

Above: *The interior of a Short Sunderland I, showing the two beam gunners and the accommodation on the deck below. In some of the Sunderland Mark IIs, the beam guns were replaced by a dorsal turret, and this became standard in the later Mark III. This photograph is dated 16 June 1941.*

Source: Keystone Collection

Later in May 1941, the U-boats were forced to cease operating in the Western Approaches, and to turn their attention to the central and southern Atlantic, outside the range of aircraft based in Britain and Iceland. Even then, they were harried off the West African coast by Sunderlands and Hudsons based near Freetown in Sierra Leone. Sinkings of Allied ships dropped dramatically to an average of 125,000 tons per month during June, July and August. The period which the U-boat commanders called 'the happy time' was over.

On 6 April 1941, *Gneisenau* was badly damaged by a torpedo dropped in a dawn attack by a solitary Beaufort, while in the roads of Brest, before the defences blew the aircraft out of the sky. On 13 June, the pocket-battleship *Lützow* off Norway was damaged by a torpedo from another Beaufort. On 27 May, the immensely powerful battleship *Bismarck* was sunk in the Atlantic by the Royal Navy and carrier-borne Fairey Swordfish of the FAA. Part of her journey from the Baltic, together with the accompanying cruiser *Prinz Eugen*, had been monitored by reconnaissance aircraft of Coastal Command and the FAA, enabling British warships to close in when the enemy formation reached the waters north of Iceland and then pursue the battleship. The threat from German surface vessels diminished, while Bomber Command continued to pound the harbours in which they and the U-boats were sheltering.

In June 1941, Air Chief Marshal Sir Frederick Bowhill left Coastal Command to form the RAF's new Ferry Command. He left behind a force of increasing effectiveness, which was taken over by Air Chief Marshal Sir Philip de la Ferté, who was familiar with the command, for he had been its chief in 1936-7. He was to remain in this post until February 1943, when Air Marshal Sir John Slessor took over.

On 27 August 1941, a Hudson based in Iceland attacked *U-570* with depth charges. The U-boat was forced to the surface and the crew waved a white shirt when treated to bursts of machine gun fire. Relays of aircraft circled the unlucky vessel until a destroyer arrived and towed her to Iceland, enabling details of her construction to be studied.

The merchant shipping losses began to mount again in September 1941, with U-boats operating outside the range of Coastal Command's aircraft. It was proposed that some of Bomber Command's heavier aircraft, such as the Halifax, should be transferred to Coastal Command, but this move was fiercely opposed by Sir Arthur Harris. Instead, an increased bombardment of the U-boat shelters in ports on the west coast of France took place, including Brest, Lorient, St Nazaire, La Pallice and Bordeaux. But so thick were the concrete roofs that almost no damage was caused to the pens, although the general port facilities were shattered.

Hitler became impatient with the role of his surface warships as targets for Bomber Command in Brest and ordered their return to German waters. He believed that the

Allies would attempt another landing in Norway and that his battleships and cruisers should be available to help repel such a move. On the foggy night of 11/12 February 1942, the battleships *Scharnhorst* and *Gneisenau*, together with the cruiser *Prinz Eugen* and a flotilla of destroyers, torpedo boats and E-boats, slipped out of the roads at Brest and began their 'Channel Dash' at high speed to the Strait of Dover, protected by relays of night-fighters and day fighters. Astonishingly, by mischances which included the failure of the ASV Mark IIs in patrolling aircraft, they reached the Strait in daylight before the FAA and Coastal Command began to make their torpedo attacks. In spite of the heroism of the crews and heavy casualties, none of these were successful. Bomber Command also flew 242 sorties over the low cloud and lost fifteen aircraft, without result. The German fleet reached its destination, although both battleships were damaged when they struck magnetic mines dropped previously by the RAF. Hitler was jubilant, but the exercise availed nothing. A few days later, *Prinz Eugen* was torpedoed by a British submarine and saw no more service. Bomber Command put *Gneisenau* permanently out of action at Kiel on the night of 27/28 February. *Scharnhorst* was sunk by the Royal Navy in a battle off the North Cape of Norway in December 1943.

In 1942, two important branches of Coastal Command were expanded. One was the Photographic Reconnaissance Unit, which had consisted of high-level and unarmed Spitfires. To these were added Mosquitos, increasing the range of PRU activities. By October 1942, five separate squadrons formed part of PRU, with over 1,000 men and women in specialized sections of the Central Interpretation Unit at Medmenham, engaged on the work of examining about 5,500 reports annually, together with almost 1,500,000 photographs. A great deal of Allied intelligence derived from this source. The other development was air-sea rescue which, in October 1941, was passed to the control of Coastal Command. During 1942, seven squadrons operated round British coasts, in co-operation with the squadrons of high-speed launches, and over 1,000 airmen were recovered from the sea.

Coastal Command also provided protection for Allied convoys on the arctic route to Murmansk, which were menaced by the presence of the battleship *Tirpitz*, sister-ship of *Bismarck*, in Trondheim fjord, as well as by other warships. Catalinas were involved in the recapture of Spitsbergen during the summer of 1942 and then, together with two squadrons of torpedo-carrying Hampdens and a flight of PRU Spitfires, flew to North Russia the following September. After providing protection for a convoy, the Catalinas flew back to the Shetlands, but the other aircraft were left behind as presents for the Russian Air Force. Detachments of PRU Spitfires also flew to North Russia in September 1943 and March 1944.

In early 1942, the U-boats found a new hunting ground off the eastern coasts of America, following the entry of that country into the war. In May, 109 ships totalling 531,000 tons were sunk in those waters, before the Americans organized convoys and patrols. Meanwhile, Coastal Command had been developing the Leigh Light, a dazzling searchlight invented by Sqdn Ldr H. de V. Leigh. These were first fitted under Wellingtons and switched before the attack, after homing with the aid of ASV on

Left: *The navigator in a Short Sunderland, sitting in the seat of the first pilot and signalling with an Aldis lamp to a convoy. All navigators were trained to proficiency with Morse code.*
Source: Keystone Collection

surfaced U-boats. Targets were found at night in the Bay of Biscay and 'kills' were made from July 1942 onwards. At the same time, new Bristol Beaufighters of Coastal Command patrolled the Bay of Biscay during daylight, scoring successes against German bombers.

By August 1942, U-boats were gathering in 'Wolf packs' in the central Atlantic, in the gaps outside the range of aircraft. This new menace was countered by the gradual introduction of small aircraft carriers in the convoys and by the employment of very long-range Halifaxes and Consolidated B-24 Liberators, mainly based in Northern Ireland and Iceland. In January 1943, Coastal Command aircraft were equipped with the new ASV Mark III, which was similar to Bomber Command's H2S navigational aid. Sinkings of U-boats mounted and, somewhat in desperation, *Grossadmiral* Karl Dönitz, who commanded the *Kriegsmarine*, ordered them to group together on the surface and fight it out with attacking aircraft. They did so during the summer of 1943, and casualties were heavy on both sides, but the effectiveness of the U-boats diminished. By the end of the war, Coastal Command had sunk, or shared in the sinking, of no less than 213 U-boats and had badly damaged 120 more. Casualties of the men in this branch of the German armed forces amounted to over seventy per cent during the war.

Another role carried out by aircraft of Coastal Command was the assault on the enemy's coastal traffic. At first, these attacks were usually made in daylight by single aircraft on 'Rover' patrols, making use of cloud cover. The aircraft involved were Blenheims, Hudsons and torpedo-carrying Beauforts. At night, magnetic mines were dropped in the approaches to enemy ports. One of the main purposes of these attacks was the interruption of the trade in iron ore between Sweden and Germany, amounted to some 10,000,000 tons per year, which was highly profitable to Sweden and helped sustain the war economy of the Third Reich. On the return journey, the vessels carried coal and coke to the Norwegian industries, as well as supplies for the German occupation forces. These convoys were heavily defended by flak-ships and fighter escorts.

These anti-shipping attacks were by far the most dangerous of all the RAF's activities. In November 1942, it was calculated that the chance of survival of an operational tour in a torpedo bomber squadron was below eighteen per cent, compared with sixty-six per cent in Sunderlands and over seventy-seven per cent in Catalinas. The equivalent figures in the other commands were forty-three per cent in fighters and forty-four per cent in medium and heavy bombers.

In the spring of 1942, the Beaufort squadrons were sent out to the Mediterranean, to attack the Axis ships carrying supplies to North Africa. Their place was taken by Hampdens coverted into torpedo bombers, while Hudsons continued low-level bombing attacks on shipping. By the following June, Coastal Command was losing one aircraft in four on low-level attacks and was forced to order crews to attack only at

Above: *The Sunderland V was fitted with Pratt & Whitney Twin Wasp engines instead of the Bristol Pegasus XVIII and entered RAF service in February 1945. Painted 'Coastal white', it remained in service until May 1949. This photograph shows the crew of a Sunderland V of 10 (RAAF) Squadron, which was equipped with this mark of the flying boat from May 1944 to June 1945, while based at Mount Batten in Devonshire. The RAAF uniforms, which were dark blue, can be distinguished on some of the crew members, with the letters RB on the Sunderland.*

Source: Keystone Collection

Right: *The Bristol Beaufort was employed as a low-level bomber and torpedo bomber by Coastal Command and the maritime air forces overseas, first entering service in November 1939. The targets were enemy warships and merchant ships, but Beauforts also bombed ports and laid mines outside entrances. Fl Off Kenneth Campbell of 22 Squadron was awarded a posthumous VC for a dawn torpedo attack on the German battleship* Gneisenau *at Brest on 6 April 1941. In statistical terms of losses, the operations carried out by Beauforts were the most dangerous of all RAF activities during the Second World War. This photograph was taken in 1941 and shows a Beaufort I, serial L9878, flying over St Eval in Cornwall. The author flew in this aircraft on a number of operational sorties.*

Source: RAF Museum colour slide P100079

Left: *The Consolidated Catalina, otherwise the PBY-5 of the US Navy, began to arrive in Coastal Command early in 1941. Slow but highly reliable, it could stay in the air for about 27 hours when fitted with extra fuel tanks. RAF Catalinas served in the North Atlantic, the Arctic, the Mediterranean, the Indian Ocean and the Far East. Detachments were also sent to North Russia to protect the arctic convoys. This photograph of a Catalina armed with four 250 lb depth charges was taken at moorings in Iceland.*

Source: Aeroplane Monthly

medium level, resulting in a decrease in effectiveness. A post-war analysis of the period from January 1940 to March 1943 revealed that the RAF sank only 107 enemy vessels, totalling 155,076 tons, by direct attack in European waters. It lost 648 aircraft in the process, giving an average of 239 tons sunk per aircraft lost. On the other hand, aerial mines sank 369 vessels totalling 361,821 tons for the loss of 329 aircraft, giving an average of 980 tons per aircraft lost.

This unhappy state of affairs was transformed in early 1943 by the use of the Beaufighter as an anti-shipping aircraft, with some aircraft in the role of torpedo bombers while others carried cannons and machine guns to suppress the flak ships. Special 'Strike Wings' were formed, each consisting of two or three squadrons, and their combined attacks in daylight were protected by Spitfires. The Germans suddenly began to lose heavily, while the Swedes became less enthusiastic about using their ships on the 'gold run', as they called this trade. In April 1943 the rocket projectile arrived, eight of these being fitted under the wings of a Beaufighter. Rockets were aimed at the sea in front of the target and the warheads were capable of sinking any merchant ship or escort vessel if they struck below the waterline.

By June 1944, other Strike Wings were formed from Mosquito squadrons, initially operating over the west coast of France. Some of the Mosquitos carried cannons and rockets while others were fitted with anti-tank guns of 57 mm calibre, firing six-pounder shells. These squadrons accounted for U-boats as well as warships and merchant vessels. Before the end of the war the Strike Wings, consisting of nine squadrons of Beaufighters and Mosquitos, almost obliterated the German coastal traffic, sinking over 300,000 tons and badly damaging another 118,000 tons.

Above: *The pilot of a Bristol Beaufort, with the navigator at his chart table in the nose of the torpedo bomber.*

Source: Keystone Collection

Left: *The author's crew in front of Beaufort I of 217 Squadron, photographed in July 1941 at St Eval in Cornwall. Left to right: Sgt 'Davy' Davies, wireless operator: Fl Off John 'Percy' Percival, pilot: Sgt Ken Reeves, gunner: Plt Off Roy Nesbit, navigator. The crew survived their tour, but Percival was killed later in the war, while Reeves survived a very bad crash. The fate of Davies is unknown, and the author was not harmed.*

Source: Flt Lt K. Reeves

Left: *A Mark XII torpedo of 1,610 lb, with a contact warhead, being loaded into the bomb bay of a Bristol Beaufort. The bomb doors could be only partially closed when the torpedo was in place.*

Source: Keystone Collection

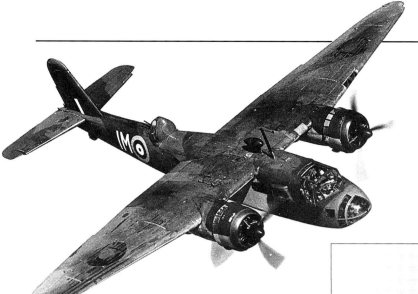

Below: *A crewroom poster showing views, dimensions, speeds and ceilings of German flying boats and floatplanes.*
Source: RAF Museum AD1359

Above: *The Blackburn Botha was designed as a torpedo bomber for Coastal Command and was delivered to 608 Squadron in June 1940. However, it proved to be underpowered and was withdrawn five months later. Thereafter it was employed as an operational trainer, in numerous schools and units, but it was not at all popular with aircrews. It was declared obsolete in August 1943.*

Source: Aviation Bookshop

Above: *A soldier of the Royal Corps of Signals with a pigeon named "Beachcomer" which brought news of the Dieppe landings of 19 August 1942. Pigeons were used in the RAF, particularly by Coastal Command, being carried in wicker baskets. Flying at a speed of about 50 m.p.h., they could carry news of aircrews in dinghies after 'ditching' in the sea.*

Source: Keystone Collection

GERMAN AIRCRAFT

SHEET 4

BLOHM & VOSS Ha 138 (3-JUMO 205)
FUNCTION: RECONNAISSANCE SPAN: 88' 7" MAXIMUM SPEED: 190 m.p.h. LENGTH: 65' 4" CRUISING ,, : 170 m.p.h.

BLOHM & VOSS Ha 139 (4-JUMO 205)
FUNCTION: COASTAL-RECONNAISSANCE SPAN: 80' 7" MAXIMUM SPEED: 215 m.p.h. LENGTH: 64' CRUISING ,, : 190 m.p.h.

BLOHM & VOSS Ha 140 (2-B.M.W. 132)
FUNCTION: TORPEDO-RECONNAISSANCE SPAN: 69' MAXIMUM SPEED: 200 m.p.h. LENGTH: 57' 9" CRUISING ,, : 180 m.p.h.

DORNIER Do 18 (2-JUMO 205 OR B.M.W. 132)
FUNCTION: RECONNAISSANCE SPAN: 77' 8" MAXIMUM SPEED: 155 m.p.h. LENGTH: 63' 2" CRUISING ,, : 135 m.p.h.

DORNIER Do 24 (3-B.M.W. 132)
FUNCTION: RECONNAISSANCE SPAN: 88' 6" MAXIMUM SPEED: 210 m.p.h. LENGTH: 72' CRUISING ,, : 170 m.p.h.

DORNIER Do 26 (4-JUMO 205)
FUNCTION: RECONNAISSANCE SPAN: 98' 6" MAXIMUM SPEED: 210 m.p.h. LENGTH: 80' 6" CRUISING ,, : 185 m.p.h.

HEINKEL He 59 (2-B.M.W.)
FUNCTION: GENERAL PURPOSE FLOAT PLANE SPAN: 77' 6" MAXIMUM SPEED: 135 m.p.h. LENGTH: 56' 6" CRUISING ,, : 120 m.p.h.

HEINKEL He 114 (BRAMO 323)
FUNCTION: COASTAL-RECONNAISSANCE SPAN: 44' 7" MAXIMUM SPEED: 210 m.p.h. LENGTH: 39' CRUISING ,, : 185 m.p.h.

HEINKEL He 115 (2 B.M.W. 132)
FUNCTION: TORPEDO-RECONNAISSANCE SPAN: 73' MAXIMUM SPEED: 220 m.p.h. LENGTH: 56' 8" CRUISING ,, : 185 m.p.h.

OFFICIAL USE ONLY
AIR DIAGRAM 1359 4.41

Above: The pilot of a Lockheed Hudson turning round to speak to the navigator.
Source: Keystone Collection

Above: The Lockheed Hudson, a military version of the Lockheed 14-WF62 Super Electra airliner, was the first American-built aircraft to serve on operational duties with the RAF during the Second World War. In May 1939, Hudsons began to replace the Avro Ansons of Coastal Command as reconnaissance and anti-submarine aircraft. Three Hudsons of 224 Squadron scored the RAF's first aerial victory of the war when they shot down a Do18 flying boat on 8 October 1939. After the fall of France, Hudsons were also employed on anti-shipping strikes, a role for which they were not entirely suitable. This photograph shows a Hudson of 320 (Royal Netherlands Air Force) Squadron. Three Dutch squadrons served with the RAF during the war, many of the personnel being former members of the Royal Netherlands Air Service.
Source: RAF Museum P8143

Right: Three of the crew of a Lockheed Hudson of 206 Squadron, based at St Eval in Cornwall, playing a game of draughts in front of their aircraft. This Coastal Command squadron was at St Eval during July and August 1941, engaged on bombing the German battleships Scharnhorst and Gneisenau in the French port of Brest.
Source: Keystone Collection

Right: *The wireless operator of a Lockheed Hudson operating an F24 camera from the port side.*

Source: Keystone Collection

Below: *WAAF instrument repairers with the aerial cameras on which they worked. The P14 camera on the left was the forerunner of the standard F24 which took a series of 5 inch by 5 inch exposures from a magazine and could be either cranked manually or operated automatically when installed in a fixed position. The G28 gun cameras, centre and left, were based on the Vickers machine gun and produced negatives of about 2½ inch by 2½ inch from a roll film.*

Source: Keystone Collection

Above: 'Tea Wagons' were much appreciated by aircrews and ground crews alike. This was one of four allocated to Coastal Command from a batch of fifty donated to Britain by the British War Relief Society of America. The photograph was taken on 10 December 1941, four days after America entered the war, and shows a lieutenant of the USNAF finishing a design on the wagon.

Source: Keystone Collection

Left: An air gunner of 206 Squadron, carrying two Vickers .303 machine guns.

Source: Keystone Collection

Left: The mascot of 407 (RCAF) Squadron was named "Squadron Leader Bill", photographed at Bircham Newton on 24 July 1941. The squadron was formed as an anti-shipping squadron in May 1941 and equipped with Lockheed Hudsons. It carried out a series of successful attacks against German shipping off the Dutch coast until October 1942, and then concentrated on anti-submarine patrols from Cornwall. Eventually, forty-five RCAF squadrons flew alongside the RAF in Europe and the Mediterranean, apart from those Canadians who served in the RAF itself.

Source: Keystone Collection

Right: *The only RAF squadron to be equipped with Northrop N3P-Bs was 330 (Norwegian) Squadron, which flew these US seaplanes from Iceland on reconnaissance work from June 1941 to May 1943. Five Norwegian squadrons served with distinction as part of the RAF during the Second World War.*

Source: RAF Museum PO17844

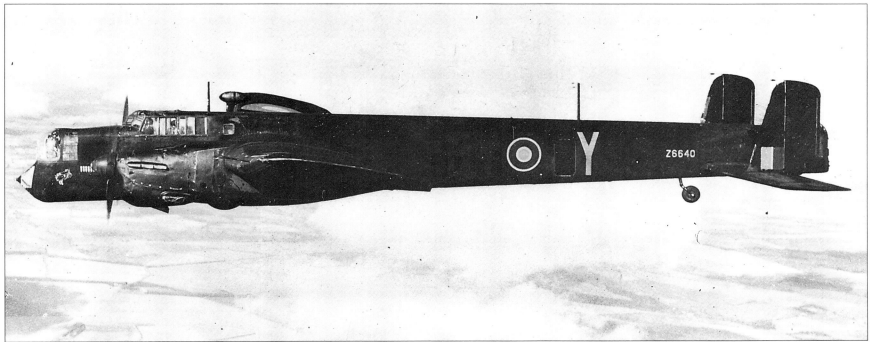

Above: *An Armstrong Whitworth Whitley V, serial Z6640, of 1484 Flight at Driffield in Yorkshire, where it was used for target-towing, bombing and gunnery. This machine had served with 78 Squadron at Croft in Yorkshire, which was re-equipped with Handley Page Halifaxes during March 1942.*

Source: RAF Museum P788

Left: *A magnetic mine being transported to the bomb bay of a Handley Page Hampden in November 1942.*

Source: Keystone Collection

Left: *A magnetic mine being loaded on the Handley Page Hampden. These mines, each of 2,000 lb, descended with the aid of their parachutes and rested on the sea bed, where they were activated by metal in the hulls of vessels passing overhead. They were code-named 'cucumbers', while the operation was 'gardening'. Although the operations were less dramatic than direct attacks on enemy vessels during daylight, the results were often more effective since RAF losses were lower. The mines were dropped by both Coastal and Bomber Command.*

Source: Keystone Collection

Left: *On 26 April 1942, 455 (RAAF) Squadron was transferred from Bomber Command to Coastal Command, together with its Handley Page Hampden Is. The squadron then trained in torpedo bombing and operated mainly along the Norwegian coast. This colour photograph of a Hampden T.B.1, serial AT137, of 455 Squadron was taken in 1942.*

Source: RAF Museum colour slide P100325

Right: *A Canadian navigator in the nose of a Handley Page Hampden, showing bomb release switches (top right) and ammunition pans (bottom right) for the forward-firing Vickers K gun.*

Source: Keystone Collection

L'alliance des peuples français et britannique continue. Vive la Victoire!

F.88

HOMMAGE DE LA R.A.F. AU SOLDAT INCONNU DE FRANCE

Le Flight Lieutenant Gatward, survolant l'Arc de Triomphe le 12 juin 1942, a laissé tomber le drapeau tricolore sur la dalle sacrée.

Left and above: *On 12 June 1942, Flight Lieutenant Ken Gatward and his navigator Sergeant George Fern flew in a Beaufighter IC of 236 Squadron, Coastal Command, on a daring daylight raid over Paris. The intention was to attack a German parade in the Champs Elysées, but on arrival there were no troops in sight. Instead, they dropped a tricolour over the Arc de Triomphe, then roared down the Champs Elysées at roof-top height and attacked with cannon fire the headquarters of the Kriegsmarine in the Place de la Concorde, where they dropped another tricolour. The episode caused astonishment in France, and the RAF dropped showers of these leaflets soon after the event.*

Source: RAF Museum (Crown copyright)

Above: *A Westland Lysander dropping dinghies into the sea.*
Source: Keystone Collection

Right: *An airman practising in an 'H-type' dinghy while wearing his 'Mae West' lifejacket, and obviously enjoying the experience. This round dinghy was stowed in the wing of most RAF bomber aircraft, and inflated automatically when a handle was pulled. It had a drogue and paddles, but only minor progress could be made against wind and currents. Most survivors simply drifted until help appeared.*
Source: Keystone Collection

Left: *A Supermarine Walrus amphibian flying boat has cruised to the rescue, and a crew member is pulling in the dinghy with a boathook. Although these photographs merely show practice, they are representative of many genuine rescues of downed airmen.*
Source: Keystone Collection

Left: *The airborne lifeboat was carried under the fuselage of an aircraft and dropped by a cluster of five parachutes near survivors in the sea. It was designed so that it could not capsize. The equipment consisted of an engine which gave a range of about eighty miles, together with wireless, sails, food and water. The Vickers Warwick was often used on this type of air-sea rescue work. This photograph was taken in October 1944 and shows a Warwick with the black and white 'invasion stripes'.*

Source: Keystone Collection

Above: *The Leigh Light was first devised in 1940 by Sqdn Ldr H. de V. Leigh, who had been a pilot in the First World War. It consisted of a searchlight which gave out a brilliant beam, used to illuminate a U-boat at night in the final stage of attack after initial detection by air-to-surface vessel radar. It did not come into operation until June 1942 but proved immediately successful. This photograph, taken in October 1944, shows a test being made by an RAF B-24 Liberator.*

Source: Keystone Collection

Left: *The amphibian Supermarine Sea Otter was designed as a replacement for the Walrus and served as air/sea rescue aircraft with Coastal command from April 1944 as well as in Burma and the Far East. This photograph is of the prototype, serial K8854, which first flew in September 1938.*

Source: RAF Museum P806

Left: *Air-Sea Rescue proved its worth during the Battle of Britain, when Westland Lysanders and Walruses worked effectively with high-speed launches in rescuing 'ditched' airmen. In August 1941, the U.K. rescue services came under the direction of Coastal Command. If weather permitted, high-speed launches remained in positions near flight paths, waiting for 'crash calls' over the W/T or R/T before speeding to the rescue. Hundreds of airmen were rescued by these RAF marine craft from the seas around Britain and from the Mediterranean.*

Source: RAF Museum colour slide P100747

Below: *The Vickers Warwick 1, a larger version of the Vickers Wellington, served in Coastal Command squadrons at home and maritime squadrons abroad as an air-sea rescue aircraft, from November 1944. Another version, the Warwick III, served as a transport aircraft. The Warwick V was modified with a longer nose and radome, as well as a Leigh Light under the roundel, for anti-submarine duties. This photograph of a Warwick V, serial PN811, of 179 Squadron, was taken on 15 December 1945. Warwicks did not continue in service beyond 1946.*

Source: RAF Museum colour slide P100687

Right: *The ability of the de Havilland Mosquito to fly at high altitudes and at high speeds for long distances proved a godsend to the RAF's photographic reconnaissance squadrons. The machines were stripped of armament and all possible equipment, being fitted with extra fuel tanks which gave ranges of about 3,500 miles. They carried out magnificent work in all theatres of war. This photograph of Mosquito XVI, serial NS502, of 544 Squadron was taken in 1944.*

Source: RAF Museum PO16733

Below: *The Supermarine Spitfire XI was one of the machines used by photographic reconnaissance squadrons, for shorter range work than the Mosquitos. It was stripped of armament and fitted with extra fuel tanks. This photograph of serial PL775 of 541 Squadron was taken in 1944.*

Source: RAF Museum PO16732

Above: *The German U-boat pens built on the west coast of France, at Brest, Lorient, St Nazaire, La Pallice and Bordeaux, proved resistant to much of the Allied bombing. However, one well-aimed bomb penetrated the concrete roof of one of the pens in Brest. This photograph was taken on 23 September 1944, shortly after the German garrison capitulated.*

Source: Keystone Collection

Left: *The rocket-firing Bristol Beaufighter TFX, specially designed for Coastal Command, was one of the most effective aircraft used by the Strike Wings. It carried eight rockets as well as four 20 mm cannons and was flown with devastating effect against German coastal shipping. This Beaufighter was on the strength of 455 (RAAF) Squadron, based at Langham in Norfolk from April to October 1944, operating in partnership with 489 (RNZAF) Squadron along the Dutch and German coasts.*

Source: RAF Museum PO19119

Left: *The pilot's cockpit of a Strike Wing Beaufighter with the reflector gunsight locked into a central position.*

Source: British Aerospace

Below: *The Strike Wings of Coastal Command employed the de Havilland Mosquito VI as a fighter-bomber from early June 1944 to the end of the war. This photograph shows serial RF610 of 248 Squadron, one of the first squadrons to be equipped with the machine.*

Source: RAF Museum PO21827

Above: *An attack on 2 May 1945 by Mosquitos of the Banff Strike Wing on U-boats in the Kattegat.*

Source: The late Wg Cdr F.E. Burton, OBE, DFC.

Above: *An attack by the Banff Strike Wing, consisting of Beaufighter TFXs of 144 and 404 Squadrons and Mosquito VIs of 235 Squadron, off Stong Fjord in Norway on 19 September 1944. Two merchant ships were sunk, Lynx of 1,367 tons and Tyrifjord of 3,080 tons.*

Source: RAF Museum PO21837

Below: *The Danish freighter* Java *in Nakskov harbour in Denmark, under attack by rocket-firing TFXs of the Dallachy Strike Wing on 3 May 1945. These rockets had 25 lb solid-shot warheads designed to penetrate below the waterline. The* Java *sank and the two freighters behind her were damaged.*

Source: The late Wg Cdr F.E. Burton, OBE, DFC.

CHAPTER 10

NORTH AFRICA, MALTA AND ITALY

At the outbreak of the war with Germany, nineteen RAF squadrons were stationed in what may be loosely termed the Middle East and the Mediterranean. Fourteen of these were based in Egypt and the Sudan, one in Palestine, one in Iraq, three in Aden and one in Malta. They were commanded by Air Chief Marshal Sir William Mitchell, who handed over to Air Chief Marshal Sir Arthur Longmore in May 1940, shortly before Italy entered the war. By this date, the aircraft, numbering some 300, were an extraordinarily assorted collection. There were Blenheims, Lysanders, Gladiators, Battles, Wellesleys and Sunderlands, but also a miscellany of obsolete bombers, transports and biplane fighters. Against these were ranged about 500 Italian machines in Libya, East Africa and the Dodecanese. These were roughly equal to the RAF aircraft in performance, but to their numerical superiority was added ease of reinforcement from Italy, where their home strength was about 1,200.

The RAF went on to the offensive immediately, operating over Libya, but resources were too limited for large-scale attacks and there was a major difficulty with reinforcement. Long-range aircraft could fly from Cornwall to Gibraltar and then via Malta to Egypt, but fighters were usually crated and sent by sea, and the route through the Mediterranean was subject to attack. To overcome this problem, an air route was devised from the Gold Coast port of Takoradi, where the crated aircraft were assembled and fitted with long-range tanks, to Nigeria and then across French Chad to the Sudan. RAF ferry pilots flew the aircraft on this route, which served well until the Axis was finally cleared out of Africa.

The geographical position of Malta was to prove one of the most decisive factors of the war in the Mediterranean, but when Italy entered the war the only operational aircraft on the island were four FAA Gladiators, apart from five Swordfish target-towers. One of the Gladiators was damaged, and the remaining three, nicknamed Faith, Hope and Charity, constituted the only defence of Malta against the *Regia Aeronautica* until a few Swordfish and Hurricanes arrived at the end of June. These were followed by more Hurricanes in August and November. Three Marylands arrived in September, and a squadron of Wellingtons in November. With these scanty forces, the RAF in Malta went on to the offensive, primarily against the Italian forces in Libya.

In the Western Desert, as the vast area of Libya was called, the British scored considerable successes at first. In November, two Wellington squadrons arrived in Egypt from the U.K., as well as a squadron of Hurricanes via Takoradi. Another Hurricane and three Blenheim squadrons were switched to the front from the defence of Egypt and the Canal Zone. The British began to attack on 9 November and by early February had chased the Italians all the way past Benghazi to El Agheila on the Gulf of Sirte, taking 130,000 prisoners. Both the ground and air forces were then weakened by the withdrawal of some of their strength to the defence of Greece. In February 1941 the *Deutsches Afrika Korps* arrived in the Western Desert and, headed by the dynamic *General* Erwin Rommel, began to fight in a way which outwitted its opponents. The co-ordination of *Panzers*, artillery, infantry and aircraft sent the British reeling back across the desert. By April 1941, the British were back behind the Egyptian border, leaving only some well-defended positions around the port of Tobruk.

Strong Italian forces were concentrated in Abyssinia, Eritrea and Italian Somaliland, heavily outnumbering British forces on the ground but roughly equal in the air. The Italians overran part of British Somaliland, but their success was short-lived. British ground forces were supported by RAF squadrons based in the Sudan, Aden and Kenya, and the Italians were subjected to some very effective bombing attacks. British reinforcements arrived by sea in January 1941 and a three-pronged invasion began from the Sudan, British Somaliland and Kenya. Four Italian destroyers off Eritrea were sunk by the RAF and the FAA, while two others were scuttled. In the south, the invading forces were supported by squadrons of the South African Air Force (SAAF). On 6 April, the British entered Addis Ababa, and a mopping-up began, which lasted until the last Italian troops capitulated in the following November.

In other areas, the British met with disaster. Mussolini's invasion of Greece on 28 October 1940 resulted in a request from the Greek government to support the Royal Hellenic Air Force, which numbered only seventy-five aircraft. Three Blenheim and three Gladiator squadrons were sent to ill-prepared bases near Athens, from where they were engaged in bombing enemy airfields and repelling air attacks, with considerable success. But the humiliating reverses which the Italian forces suffered at the hands of the Greek army drove Hitler to despair. In any event, he had planned to move southwards into the Aegean, having entered Romania in October 1940 and Bulgaria in March 1941. On 6 April 1941, the *Wehrmacht* invaded Yugoslavia and Greece. By then,

Below: *The more seriously wounded prisoners were repatriated to their own countries. Here, a sergeant observer of the RAF who had lost a leg is arriving at Lisbon on 22 April 1943, after repatriation from Italy. He is being attended by Portuguese medical orderlies.*

Source: Keystone Collection

four Commonwealth divisions had arrived in Greece, while two more Blenheim squadrons were on their way, together with three squadrons equipped with a mixture of Gladiators, Hurricanes and Lysanders. Two temporary detachments of Wellingtons followed. But nothing could stop the massive assault of the *Wehrmacht*, which included twenty-seven divisions and 1,200 aircraft. The German forces swept into Yugoslavia and Greece, crushing the determined opposition. After nine days of fighting against impossible odds, only forty-six RAF aircraft remained serviceable, while the Royal Yugoslav and Royal Hellenic Air Forces were all but wiped out. On 20 April, the surviving aircraft were withdrawn to Crete, while the surviving Commonwealth troops sailed for that island, covered by the remnants of the RAF to the best of their ability.

Worse was to follow when *General* Kurt Student's airborne troops began to descend on Crete on 20 May. The *Luftwaffe* mustered about 650 aircraft for the attack, as well as over 700 air transports and gliders to carry an invading force of 15,000 men. Although the defending troops were numerically superior, they had left most of their equipment behind in Greece. The only air cover that could be provided was twenty-four aircraft of the RAF and the FAA, consisting of Hurricanes, Gladiators and Fulmars. The island was outside the range of fighters in Egypt. Nevertheless, the outcome of the battle hung in the balance for several days. At the expense of enormous casualties, the Germans finally overcame the defenders. The Royal Navy evacuated half the survivors, at the cost of three cruisers and six destroyers sunk.

These setbacks threatened to undermine the position of Iraq, where Britain was responsible for internal security, and in Syria, where there was a possibility that the controlling French Vichy government might be forced to make available airfields for the *Luftwaffe*. A German presence in these countries would constitute a serious threat to Britain's oil supplies in the Middle East. In Iraq, the pro-British government was ousted at the end of 1941 by Rashid Ali, who supported the Axis. At the end of the following month, about 9,000 Iraqi troops laid siege to the RAF base at Habbaniya, near Baghdad, subjecting the camp to artillery fire. The RAF and local levies put up a defence which was classed as a minor epic of the Second World War. Wellington bombers from Shaibah on the Persian Gulf bombed the Iraqi positions, while Gladiators and Audaxes from the RAF Flying School at Habbiniya delivered strafing attacks. After several days the Iraqis decided they had had enough and retired to Baghdad, where they were defeated by a British column at the end of May. The previous government in Iraq was restored. The British then turned their attention to Syria, advancing into that country with the support of about sixty RAF and FAA aircraft. The Vichy French forces resisted fiercely, supported by about a hundred aircraft, but capitulated on 14 July.

The battle lines in the Mediterranean were thus more clearly drawn. The British 8th Army faced the Axis forces in the Western Desert, where Rommel threatened Egypt, the Suez Canal and eventually India, while Malta provided a strategic base from which the RAF and FAA could attack enemy positions and supply lines. On 1 June 1941, Air Marshal Sir Arthur Tedder took over the RAF's Middle East Command, and a few weeks later the *Luftwaffe* began withdrawing some of its strength for the invasion of Russia. By the following November, the RAF and FAA numbered about 660 aircraft in the Western Desert with another 120 in Malta. These included Blenheims, Wellingtons, Marylands, Hurricanes, Tomahawks, Swordfish, Albacores, Beauforts and Beaufighters. The *Luftwaffe* mustered 180 aircraft in Greece, while *Fliegerführer Afrika* supported Rommel with 240 aircraft in Libya. The *Regia Aeronautica* in Libya possessed about 300 aircraft. Although outnumbered, the rate of serviceability of the RAF was higher than that of its opponents, and it was more capable of moving bases rapidly.

The 8th Army opened the 'Crusader' offensive on 18 November, following a fierce bombardment of the enemy's airfields and land transport by the RAF, including low-level attacks by cannon-firing Beaufighters and continued assaults on sea supplies from the air and by British submarines. The British had an advantage which Rommel would have considered incredible had he known. Using a captured 'Enigma' coding machine, they were decrypting regularly the messages which the Germans were passing to their forces in North Africa. They knew the state of the *Afrika Korps* and the dates of sailing of almost all Axis convoys, as well as the contents of their cargoes. PRU aircraft based at Malta knew where to hunt for the convoys and the RAF was able to concentrate its few anti-shipping aircraft at critical times. In November, fourteen of the twenty-two supply vessels sent from Italy were sunk. The Axis forces fell back to Agedabia and Tobruk was relieved by the 8th Army. But in December two large convoys, heavily escorted by most of the Italian Fleet, succeeded in reaching North Africa. In the following month, 400 German aircraft arrived in Sicily, under the command of *Generalfeldmarschall* Albert Kesselring. Rommel went over to the offensive and by 6 February the 8th Army had retreated as far as Gazala.

Meanwhile, Malta underwent the protracted agony of an intense bombardment, and, in spite of the arrival of a handful of Spitfires, only six serviceable fighters and a handful of bombers remained by the end of March 1942. Forty-seven Spitfires were

Above: *One of the most unusual fighter aces of the war was George Frederick Beurling, known as "Screwball" from his frequent use of the name and his craving for combat. He was a Canadian of Anglo-Swedish parentage, and qualified as a pilot when too young to hold a licence. He tried unsuccessfully to join various air forces, but then worked his passage to England in 1941 , where he enlisted in the RAF and became a sergeant pilot. After flying Spitfires with 41 Squadron he was posted to Malta, where he came the top-scoring Spitfire pilot during the siege of the island. He later flew Spitfires with 412 (RCAF) Squadron in the 2nd Tactical Air Force. By the end of the war, his score was 31 1/3 aircraft destroyed and he had been awarded a DSO, DFC, DFM and bar. He lost his life in 1948 in an air crash, while ferrying a North American B-25 Mitchell to Israel.*

Source: Keystone Collection

Right: *A German airman posing on a Bristol Blenheim IV of 11 Squadron, letter V serial T2177, captured after the Germans conquered Greece in April 1941.*

Source: Keystone Collection

Above: *Three Hawker Hurricane IIB fighter-bombers of 1 (SAAF) Squadron, photographed in May 1941 while flying over the Sudan from Amriya in Egypt. This South African squadron had been equipped with Hurricanes during the previous month. It eventually moved up to the Western Desert and began ground attacks against the Axis forces. Twenty-eight SAAF squadrons flew with the RAF, mainly in the Mediterranean theatre of war.*

Source: Keystone Collection

flown to the island on 20 April from the US carrier *Wasp* but most of these were destroyed by air attack on the following day. The Axis had plans to invade Malta in its weakened state, but these were abandoned owing to pressure of events in Russia and the need to defend Germany from attacks by Bomber Command. However, supplies streamed across the Mediterranean for the Axis forces, while the Allied forces were supplied from the route round the Cape of Good Hope and via Takoradi.

In the Western Desert, Rommel struck again, on 26 May. This time, he met with enormous success, capturing Tobruk, taking 45,000 prisoners and capturing 1,500,000 gallons of precious fuel. With its remarkably efficient organization, the RAF fell back in good order to prepared airfields, while the 8th Army took up new positions at El Alamein.

There was then a period of stalemate on the ground, while the RAF shot up Axis road convoys and bombed airfields and ports. Fighters intercepted Ju52 air transports flying between Libya and Crete. U.S. bomber and fighter squadrons began to arrive in Egypt, to serve alongside the RAF. By October, the RAF and FAA in the Middle East controlled ninety-six operational squadrons, including thirteen American, thirteen South African, five Australian, one Rhodesian, one Canadian, two Greek, one French and one Yugoslav. At the same time, Malta began to receive air reinforcements, including Spitfires, as well as some sea-borne supplies. In June, the Beaufort squadrons in the U.K. flew out to the island and immediately began to attack, escorted by Beaufighters and guided by the PRU squadron. Torpedo-carrying Wellingtons from Malta and Egypt also joined in these attacks, using ASV at night. By August the Axis convoys began to suffer heavy losses, both from aircraft and submarines. Although the anti-shipping squadrons lost many aircraft, the attacks continued, while RAF medium bombers pounded the enemy ports. Once again, Rommel began to run short of fuel and military supplies in his advanced positions.

When the British opened their bombardment at El Alamein on the evening of 23 October 1942, they were supported by about 1,200 first-line aircraft based in Egypt and Palestine and another 300 in Malta, whereas only about 690 Axis aircraft supported Rommel in Africa. The bombing and strafing attacks from the air and the weight of armour contributed to the Allied victory, but perhaps the decisive factor was the almost complete destruction of the Axis vessels attempting to reach North Africa, which were attacked from both Malta and Egypt. With only a couple of days fuel in hand, Rommel was forced into a fighting retreat, still in good order in spite of severe losses, all the way along the North African coast to Tunisia.

On 7 November, the landings of Anglo-American forces at Oran and Algiers, under the code-name of operation 'Torch', transformed the military situation in North Africa. The RAF provided cover for these landings, primarily from Gibraltar, where the runway of the airfield had been lengthened, and then flew to forward bases in Algeria in support of the ground forces. The Axis responded by occupying Vichy France and setting up bases in Tunisia. Supplies for the Axis began to pour across the 100 miles of sea which

LIBYA
Help them finish the job

separate Tunisia and Sicily, while *Fliegerkorps II* increased its transport aircraft from 250 to about 750. Spitfires, Beauforts, Beaufighters and FAA Albacores from Malta kept up constant attacks against these sea and air supply routes, shooting down many Ju52s and sinking many ships, while bombers from Libya and Malta began to lay waste to the ports in Sicily and Tunisia. Nevertheless, the *Panzerarmee Afrika* put up a fierce and skilful defence until the last remnants surrendered on 14 May, bringing the total of prisoners taken in Tunisia to 250,000.

Air Chief Marshal Sir Arthur Tedder had been appointed on 17 February 1943 as C-in-C of the new Mediterranean Air Command, controlling the whole of the Allied air activities in that vast area. The next task of the Allies was the invasion of Sicily, under the code-name of operation 'Husky', preparatory to an invasion of the Italian mainland. This operation began with sustained air attacks on the enemy airfields in Sicily, Sardinia and southern Italy, as well as ports and industrial targets. On 10 July, airborne troops were landed in the south of Sicily by Waco and Hadrian gliders towed by Dakotas, Halifaxes and Albemarles, while others parachuted in. At dawn on the same day, troops

Right: *The Martin Baltimore, a development of the Martin Maryland, was produced in the USA to meet a British specification for a light bomber. It first entered service with the RAF in January 1942. Baltimores were used exclusively in the Mediterranean theatre of war, by nine RAF squadrons as well as two RAAF and three SAAF squadrons. The original Wright engines gave some trouble in the desert, but later Pratt & Whitney engines stood up well to these conditions. Although the machine was heavy and crew conditions were cramped, the Baltimore was strongly constructed and could take a fair amount of punishment. This photograph shows a formation of 55 Squadron, which was equipped with these aircraft from May 1942 to October 1944.*

Source: RAF Museum PO14682

Left: *Curtiss Kittyhawks, designated P-40D onwards by the USAAF, served only in the Mediterranean when delivered to the RAF from late 1941 onwards. With a more powerful engine and heavier armament than the Tomahawk, they were employed as interceptors and fighter-bombers until the end of the war in Europe. This photograph shows a Kittyhawk Mark III, or P-40M, serial FR452, of 112 Squadron, which adopted the famous shark's head motif.*

Source: RAF Museum P10159

from convoys amounting to about 2,000 vessels landed on the southern tip of the island, under constant air cover. The Germans resisted fiercely, although their air support was noticeably weaker. Within hours, RAF fighters landed on Sicilian airfields. On 25 July, the dictator Mussolini was arrested and imprisoned by the Fascist Grand Council, although he was later rescued by German paratroops and taken to Germany, where he formed a puppet 'government'. The Allies steadily advanced through Sicily and drove out the last of the defenders on 17 August, capturing many Italian prisoners. The wreckage of some 1,100 enemy aircraft was left on Sicilian airfields.

Elements of the British 8th Army crossed the Strait of Messina on 3 September and landed on the "toe" of Italy. On 8 September, the terms of an armistice arranged between the Allies and the Italian government were announced, the day before divisions of the U.S. Fifth Army landed at Salerno in Campania. By then, the *Luftwaffe* in Italy had been almost neutralised by air attacks and air combats, but the invaders on the beach-head met with determined opposition from German *Panzers*. The weight of the Allied air force fell upon the German counter-attacks, while airborne troops were dropped behind enemy lines. By 15 September, the Allies were more firmly established and began to advance. On 1 October, the vital port of Naples was captured, enabling all-important military supplies to be landed.

In the Aegean, however, the Allies met with a reverse. Their objective was the capture of the Italian Dodecanese Islands, as a prelude to an invasion of Greece. The enterprise bypassed the island of Rhodes, which was strongly held by the Germans. On 13 September, British troops landed on the island of Kos, followed by paratroops dropped from Dakotas. The island of Leros and Samos were also occupied, without opposition from the Italian garrisons. Spitfires of the SAAF landed at Kos, and the airfield was protected by units of the RAF Regiment. However, the *Luftwaffe* withdrew units from other areas and, with its short lines of communication, began to bomb and strafe the British positions. The RAF responded by bombing the enemy airfields near Athens and on Crete and Rhodes, but on 3 October German troops landed by sea and air on Kos, over-running the island. Leros received the same treatment on 12 November and Samos fell ten days later. It was generally agreed that the Allied venture had been unwise, since insufficient resources had been allocated and distances were too great for the RAF to provide adequate air cover.

The Allied troops continued the hard slog up the peninsula of Italy, against skilful and determined opposition from the *Wehrmacht* and hampered by the unexpectedly bad weather which restricted the activities of the air force. Another important capture, on 28 September, was the group of airfields around Foggia in Apulia. This made possible the strategic bombing of the oil fields of Romania as well the industrial areas of Czechoslovakia, Austria and southern Germany, a task which was carried out by the U.S. Fifteenth Air Force and the RAF's 205 Group. The bases were also ideal for the sorties of the Balkan Air Force, an organization which was formed in June 1944 to support the guerilla war being waged by the Yugoslav Partisan Army.

Another development which became possible after the *Luftwaffe* had been almost eliminated from the skies was the 'Cab Rank' system of army co-operation, whereby fighter-bombers patrolled over army positions, waiting to be called upon to attack specific targets with bombs or cannon. The Allies advanced steadily, if slowly, and entered Rome on 4 June 1944.

Right: *The Curtiss Tomahawk was the RAF's name for the P-40A and the P-40B of the USAAF. These pursuit aircraft were first delivered to the UK at the end of 1940, where they were employed mainly on reconnaissance. When they arrived in the Western Desert during the following July, however, they soon proved successful as ground attack aircraft and as interceptors of Axis supply aircraft. This photograph shows Tomahawks of 414 (RCAF) Squadron in April 1942, when the squadron was based at Croydon, with a IIB in the lead and on its port, and a IIA on its starboard.*

Source: RAF Museum P9548

Above: *Curtiss Tomahawk IIs of 3 (RAAF) Squadron, taking off in January 1942. At the time, the squadron was based at LG110 in the Western Desert and engaged on escorting bombers on daylight raids, on low-level ground attack, and on escorting Allied shipping to and from Tobruk.*

Source: Keystone Collection

Left: *El Aouina aerodrome near Tunis suffered intensive attacks by Allied aircraft during the final stages of the campaign in North Africa. By the time the Axis was cleared out of Africa, in May 1943, the aerodrome was a graveyard for destroyed Axis aircraft.*

Source: Keystone Collection

Right: *The crew of an RAF aircraft, probably a Wellington, being debriefed after return from an attack against the port of Tunis in December 1942.*

Source: Keystone Collection

Left: *The Martin Marauder, or B-26 in the USAAF, was employed by only two RAF squadrons, both operating in the Mediterranean. It first arrived in April 1942 and was employed on maritime reconnaissance as well as bombing and mine-laying.*

Source: Aeroplane Monthly

Below: *The Armstrong Whitworth Albemarle was originally built as a reconnaissance bomber but by the time production lines were flowing it was already superseded by more advanced machines. Albemarles entered service in November 1942 as transport aircraft. Others were used as glider-tugs in the invasion of Sicily in July 1943. They also took part in the Normandy invasion and at Arnhem. This photograph of serial P1372 was taken in March 1942.*

Source: RAF Museum P6155

Left: *Posters encouraging young ladies of 18 to 40 years to join the WAAF were displayed in Egypt. This invited volunteers to seek information from centres in Cairo and Alexandria.*

Source: RAF Museum (Crown copyright) P00543

Left: *The Douglas Dakota, a military version of the DC-3 airliner, first entered service with the RAF in the Mediterranean during March 1943. Normally unarmed, Dakotas were used as transports in every theatre of war and earned their place in the affections of RAF aircrews as highly reliable and faithful workhorses. These Dakota IIIs of 267 Squadron at Bari in Italy during 1944 were lined up with little fear of air attck.*

Source: RAF Museum P1691

Left: *Wrecked Ju52 transports in Libya, photographed in January 1943 during the advance of the 8th Army after the Battle of El Alamein. The aircraft in the background is a Lockheed Hudson VI of the RAF, used for transport purposes over the Western Desert.*
Source: Keystone Collection

Below: *This photograph was taken early in 1943 at Malta and shows a march past of soldiers at Luqa aerodrome prior to the invasion of Sicily the following July. Inside the blast pen, to the top left of centre, is a Beaufort torpedo bomber of 39 Squadron. These blast pens were usually made of limestone blocks salvaged from the building destroyed by enemy bombing of the island.*
Source: Keystone Collection

Left: *A Spitfire being refuelled at Taranto in October 1943, shortly after the Allied invasion of the Italian mainland.*
Source: Keystone Collection

Right: *Taylorcraft Austers, designed in the USA but built under licence in England, were supplied to the RAF for 'air observation post' duties. These duties included artillery spotting, reconnaissance and communication. This photograph was taken in February 1944, near the front in northern Italy, and shows an Auster used in co-operation with New Zealander gunners of the 8th Army.*
Source: Keystone Collection

Right: *The German* Kreigsmarine *employed heavily defended barges of over 200 tons for supply purposes in the Mediterranean. Known as F-boats, they were regularly attacked by Beaufighters with cannons and bombs. In this photograph, which was taken in January 1944 south of Kalino in the Dodecanese, the bombs can be seen falling away from the racks of a Beaufighter while cannon and flak shells are splashing in the sea.*
Source: Keystone Collection

Left: *Two Martin Baltimore bombers of the RAF silhouetted against the snow-covered Apennine Mountains in central Italy, photographed in March 1944 while on their way to bomb targets in the north.*
Source: Keystone Collection

Right: *DC-3 Dakotas were employed in transporting supplies to the front line in Italy. Mount Vesuvius, near Naples, is in the background of the Dakota taking off in this photograph.*
Source: Keystone Collection

CHAPTER 11

D-DAY TO VE-DAY

The planning for the Anglo-American assault on Hitler's 'western wall' began in April 1943 and continued for over a year. After considerable discussion it was agreed that the supreme commander should be an American, General Dwight Eisenhower, who had led the successful expedition to North Africa, while his deputy should be an Englishman, Air Chief Marshal Sir Arthur Tedder, the former chief of the Mediterranean Air Command. The choice of an RAF officer for this post was a recognition of the important part which the air forces would play in the enterprise, which was code-named operation 'Overlord'. Eisenhower and Tedder presided over Supreme Headquarters, Allied Expeditionary Force (SHAEF). The naval forces were commanded by Admiral Sir Bertram Ramsay, the land forces by the victor of the Western Desert, General Sir Bernard Montgomery, and the air forces by Air Chief Marshal Sir Trafford Leigh-Mallory.

On 15 November 1943, Leigh-Mallory controlled the 2nd Tactical Air Force, the U.S. Ninth Air Force (which was also tactical), and the Air Defence of Great Britain (as Fighter Command was renamed). Bomber Command, under Air-Chief Marshal Sir Arthur Harris, and the U.S. Strategic Forces in Europe, under General Carl Spaatz, were not under his control; instead, both reported directly to the Combined Chiefs of Staff.

The preliminary objective of the air forces was the destruction of the French transportation system. With the agreement of the Chiefs of Staff, Tedder issued on 15 April 1944 a list of targets for the heavy bombers to attack. Lancasters and Halifaxes of Bomber Command began destroying marshalling yards and railways centres at night, and U.S. B-24 Liberators and B-17 Flying Fortresses joined in with daylight attacks, escorted by fighters. The Spitfires, Typhoons and Mustangs of the 2nd Tactical Air Force, under Air Marshal Sir Arthur Coningham, has been reinforced with the Bostons and Mosquitos of Bomber Command's 2 Group, and also shared in these attacks. To these massive operations was added the sabotage carried out by the French Resistance. By June, thousands of photographs taken by the reconnaissance squadrons showed that the French railway system had been seriously damaged. Allied aircraft losses had been relatively slight.

As the day for the landings drew near, rocket-firing fighter-bombers were directed against the chain of radar stations constructed by the enemy along the coasts of north-west France and the Low Countries, while larger W/T stations were put out of action by Bomber Command. Road and rail bridges leading to the invasion area were also destroyed, and major airfields and maintenance depots also came under low-level strafing as well as heavy bombing. Lastly, the coastal batteries were subjected to bombing attacks, both within and outside the areas where the invasion forces intended to land. Meanwhile, Coastal Command and the FAA carried out patrols over both ends of the Channel, hunting and sinking U-boats as well as any surface vessels which dared put out to sea.

In the late evening of 5 June the first Albermarles of Leigh-Mallory's Allied Expeditionary Air Force took off with airborne soldiers of the Parachute Regiment, heading for dropping zones behind the German lines. Dakotas, Stirlings and Halifaxes

followed, dropping paratroops or towing gliders carrying troops, guns, jeeps and motor cycles. At the same time as the great invasion armada sailed to the beaches of Normandy, spoof flights were made by Lancasters and Stirlings of Bomber Command, dropping 'Window' aluminium strips to confuse the German radar, and circling ships which emitted signals designed to indicate that large convoys were approaching other areas. The radar stations had been conveniently left functioning in these coastal areas. Other Halifaxes and Stirlings dropped dummy paratroops and firecrackers which simulated the noise of gunfire. The main force of Bomber Command was directed at the coastal batteries where the landings were to take place. These batteries were also shelled from the sea.

By dawn the first landing parties were ashore and fighting their way over the beaches. In the skies above, no fewer than 171 squadrons provided cover for the invading forces and naval vessels, co-ordinated from three specially fitted 'fighter direction' ships. The *Luftwaffe*, already reduced on this front to barely 500 aircraft, was overwhelmed. On the flanks of the invasion fleet, Coastal Command successfully kept the seas clear of the *Kriegsmarine*. More towed gliders arrived, heavily escorted by fighters, bearing reinforcements and supplies. By the end of D-Day, 6 June, the beachheads were secure.

Air cover continued from English bases, with Typhoons, Spitfires and Mustangs shooting up enemy columns approaching the combat area and knocking out hundreds

Below: *Ground crew servicing the engines of a Short Stirling.*

Source: Keystone Collection

of trucks and armoured fighting vehicles. On 7 June, the RAF's Servicing Commando and Construction Wings began setting up airstrips in France. These were used as refuelling depots at first but were soon expanded into air bases. Bomber Command continued to pound the remnants of the railway system, while fighter-bombers ensured that the Germans could move only in the hours of darkness. Within three weeks, thirty-one Allied squadrons were operating in France, using the 'Cab Rank' system which had been developed in Italy. Further behind the lines, fighters as well as Mosquitos pounced on columns trying to reach the battle area. The German commander, *Feldmarschall* Erwin Rommel, was wounded in one of these attacks, and was later forced to commit suicide when accused of complicity in the plot to kill Hitler of 20 July. Coastal Command continued to defend the approaches to the Allied convoys and within four days after D-Day attacked twenty-five U-boats, while its Strike Wings scored numerous successes against German coastal convoys off the Low Countries, Norway and western France.

The German air fleet in the area, *Luftflotte 3*, was so reduced that its activities became limited to defensive patrols, while its units continued to suffer heavy casualties. However, the defending German ground forces did not break under the colossal attack, and Bomber Command was directed to attack their positions on the battlefield itself. On the evening of 7 July, 457 bombers dropped their loads on targets north of Caen, before an infantry attack. Ten days later, 1,919 RAF and U.S. bombers delivered an even heavier attack, but the tenacious Germans somehow held out amid the heaps of rubble. Four similar attacks were made before they were dislodged. Nevertheless, the remaining *Panzers* contrived to make a determined counter-attack, designed to cut off American forces from their beach-heads, until they were decimated by waves of RAF Typhoons and the assault came to a halt. On 9 August, American armoured divisions broke through and began to sweep round the rear of the German positions, towards Paris and Belgium. The encircled Germans tried to extricate themselves but were harried remorselessly by marauding aircraft. Their commander, *Feldmarschall* Günther von Kluge, committed suicide after being dismissed by Hitler. Paris was liberated on 25 August, and British forces entered Brussels on 3 September.

Before the opening of this Second Front, it was known from reconnaissance photographs and intelligence sources that Germany possessed special weapons designed to bombard England. The centre of development was Peenemünde, on the Baltic coast, where activities were kept under constant surveillance by PRU Mosquitos. Bomber Command set back the progress of the German scientists with an accurate attack by 597 aircraft on the night of 17/18 August 1943, but a ramp with an object similar to a jet aircraft was identified the following October by the Central Photographic Interpretation Unit. In the following months, seventy-two similar ramps were identified in northern France. These sites came under continuous attacks by fighter-bombers as well as medium and heavy bombers, and about two-thirds of them were destroyed before May 1944. But others began to spring up, faster than they could be destroyed. In May, a prototype flying bomb crashed in Sweden and the details were passed to British Intelligence, and the threat of this indiscriminate weapon to British civilians became fully understood.

The first flying bomb, the V.I 'doodlebug', arrived over England on 12 June 1944. By the end of the month, over 2,000 had been despatched against London. At first, the air forces were fully occupied in supporting the invasion force and only a few aircraft could be diverted from this all-important task to attack the launching sites. But masses of balloons were deployed to the south-east of London together with lines of anti-aircraft guns. Areas in which fighters of the Air Defence of Great Britain patrolled were designated. The bombs usually flew at altitudes up to 4,000 feet, but with speeds of up to 400 m.p.h. they were difficult to catch. However, accurate interceptions were made with the help of radar and the Royal Observers Corps. Anti-aircraft guns also shot down a large number, but about half the V.Is reached the London area. As soon as they could be spared, heavy and light bombers began to knock out the sites in France, and by 5 September the advancing Allied armies had overrun most of these. Thereafter, flying bombs were launched at night from Heinkel 111s flying over the North Sea, but these aircraft suffered severely from the attentions of RAF Mosquito night-fighters and achieved very limited results. New launching sites were built in Holland, and some V.Is continued to be despatched until March 1945. Over 4,000 of these bombs were destroyed by British defences, but the remainder killed more than 6,000 people in England.

On 8 September 1944, the first V.2 rocket arrived, at Chiswick. The Germans had experimented with these at Blizna, west of Warsaw, and the site was not identified until PRU brought back photographs in March 1944. Polish agents discovered some important details and one man was picked up by an RAF Dakota and flown to Italy. It was revealed that the V.2 had a range of about 200 miles. Rockets which lifted off vertically and then flew through the sound barrier, controlled by radio, could not be pursued by aircraft. However, rocket sites were identified in northern France and heavily bombed. Then it was realized that others were being launched from Holland,

Below: *It was considered that the North American Mustang III, the RAF equivalent of the P-51 B or C, was the fighter which finally established Allied air supremacy in the skies over Germany. The combination of the Packard Merlin engine and the superbly aerodynamic airframe gave the aircraft a performance at long range which was more than a match for any German piston-engined fighter in 1944. Mustang IIIs were first delivered to the RAF in December 1943. This photograph is of serial FB353 of 315 (Polish) Squadron, which was first equipped with Mustang IIIs in March 1944 when based at Heston.*
Source: RAF Museum PO17036

Right: *The Central School of Aircraft Recognition was set up to teach instructors in the Allied air forces, including the RAF, RCAF, RAAF, RNZAF, RAF Regiment, Royal Observer Corps, the US Eighth Air Force and the US Ninth Air Force. This photograph, in which an RAF sergeant is demonstrating an He111, is dated 4 April 1944.*

Source: Keystone Collection

and these sites were attacked by Spitfire fighter-bombers. The rockets continued intermittently and with no great accuracy, but they resulted in 2,855 deaths before the last fell on 27 March 1945.

As the Allied armies swept through France and into Belgium and Holland, the Germans continued to hold out in a few ports which Hitler called 'Fortresses'. These were eliminated in turn by Bomber Command. Le Havre, Boulogne and Calais surrendered in September, but other ports such as Dunkirk and Brest still held out, while the invasion armies had more important business elsewhere. On 17 September, Albemarles, Stirlings, Halifaxes and Dakotas of the RAF's Transport Command carried airborne soldiers to the town of Arnhem in Holland, behind the Rhine and the German lines. Other lifts took place over the next two days, against intense light and heavy flak. Thereafter, supply drops were attempted but, in spite of heavy losses, only a small proportion fell in the area occupied by British troops, who were overwhelmed.

Another enterprise in which the RAF was involved, with far more success, was the reduction of Hitler's 'fortress' of the island of Walcheren, in the estuary of the Scheldt. In this instance, Bomber Command breached the dyke holding back the North Sea, on the afternoon of 3 October, and the waters rushed in. Other inundations were caused in the south and north-east, while German batteries were attacked by fighter-bombers and heavy bombers. The island was finally overrun by the infantry on 8 November, after tough and difficult fighting. In the course of these battles, Leigh-Mallory was posted to command the Allied Air Forces in the Far East, but unhappily was killed en route when his aircraft crashed. His command in Europe was absorbed into SHAEF.

On 16 December, the Germans delivered their last major offensive of the war, against the American forces in the Ardennes. With the advantage of fog and low cloud which restricted flying for over a week, the *Panzers* advanced rapidly. Then the weather lifted and both Bomber Command and the U.S. heavy bombers were able to bring their weight on to the attackers. The 2nd Tactical Air Force also went out in strength. One of the German aircraft shot down was a new jet fighter, the twin-engined Messerschmitt 262, with a speed of over 500 m.p.h. On 1 January 1945, the *Luftwaffe* made a last desperate effort against Allied air strength, sending over 800 aircraft on low-level attacks against airfields. They succeeded in destroying 144 aircraft on the ground, damaging many more, but also lost heavily from their remaining units.

By now, the enemy was in retreat on all fronts. On the night of 14/15 August 1944, the USAAF had dropped paratroops in the south of France, having taken off from Corsica, an island which the Allies had occupied at the end of the previous September. These were followed by over 400 gliders and a sea-borne invasion force. The U.S. troops encountered only slight opposition on the beaches before racing northwards, to join up with their victorious counterparts from England on 12 September. Meanwhile, the U.S. Fifteenth Air Force and the Wellingtons and Liberators of the RAF's 205 Group continued their long-distance strategic attacks from the airfields around Foggia. The RAF also scored notable successes during 1944 by mining the Danube and thus interrupting Germany's oil supplies from Romania. These sorties continued until the Red Army captured the oilfields at the end of August.

The Allied advance up the Italian peninsula was slowed by the withdrawal of American troops for the invasion of southern France. It was also hampered by mud from continuous rain and by the stubborn and skilful defence of the German troops, who had little support from the air. The Allied air forces gave these troops little respite, and attacks were delivered with mounting intensity and concentration. By April 1945, the Germans had fallen back to the river Po and were beginning to crack under the intense bombardment. On 28 April, the former dictator Mussolini was captured and shot by Italian partisans.

Meanwhile, Bomber Command's assault on Germany mounted in intensity. With the liberation of most of France and Belgium, the ground control stations for 'Gee' and 'GH' navigational aids were moved much closer to enemy territory. In addition to night bombing, attacks could also be made in daylight, escorted by long-range Mustangs of the 2nd Tactical Air Force or home-based fighters of Fighter Command, as the Air Defence of Great Britain was named once again. The Ruhr was one of the main objectives, but most major German towns were gradually obliterated by the RAF and the USAAF. Of the total tonnage of bombs used in raids on Germany throughout the war, the greater part was dropped after 1 July 1944, causing enormous destruction. Apart from towns, oil installations and transport facilities came under attack. The battleship *Tirpitz* was sunk in Tromsö in Norway on 12 November 1944 by Lancasters operating from Lossiemouth. It was obvious even to the most determined Nazis that the end was near, but the *Wehrmacht* still fought on.

On 22 February 1945, the whole of the Allied air forces, numbering nearly 9,000 aircraft, began a concentrated effort to wipe out Germany's remaining transport. A month later, the Allied forces crossed the Rhine at Wesel, while airborne troops parachuted in or landed by glider. Allied armies then broke through all along the German frontier and raced through the country. The First U.S. Army linked up with the Red Army at the Elbe on 23 April, while the Second British Army reached Lübeck on 2 May. Hitler killed himself in his Berlin bunker on 30 April. His successor, *Grossadmiral* Karl Dönitz, surrendered unconditionally on 7 May and VE-Day was celebrated on the following day. Meanwhile, the war with Japan continued.

Right: *Mosquito night-fighters, designated Mark IIs, began to replace Bristol Beaufighters and Douglas Havocs in 1942, and served in all the RAF's theatres of war. Other improvements in air interception radar followed. This photograph shows a Mosquito XIII of 604 Squadron, with a radome in the nose and aerials on the wings. This squadron was equipped with Mosquito XIIIs from April 1944 to the end of the war.*

Source: Keystone Collection

Below: *Although the RAF Regiment was formed originally to protect airfields, its scope was widened later into attack roles, such as capturing enemy airfields. The Regiment was then equipped with armoured fighting vehicles. This photograph of Morris 'Type E' armoured cars, which were fitted with Boys anti-tank rifles and Bren guns, was taken in England in April 1944.*

Source: Keystone Collection

Source: Keystone Collection

Above: *A photograph taken on D-Day, 6 June 1944, showing Short Stirlings towing Airspeed Horsa gliders across the English Channel for the airborne landings.*

Source: Keystone Collection

Left: *The devastating effect of the Allied bombing attacks against the French transport system is shown by this photograph of rolling stock at the town of Vire in Lower Normandy, at the base of the Cherbourg Peninsula. The Allies occupied the town on 7 August 1944.*

Source: Keystone Collection

Above: *As the Allies advanced in France and the Low Countries, they left behind centres of resistance which Germans described as 'fortresses'. One of these was Calais, seen here under attack by Halifaxes on 25 September 1944. The Germans surrendered a few days later.*

Source: Keystone Collection

Above: *A bomb dump containing American semi-armour piercing bombs of 1,000 lb, used by fighter-bombers of the 2nd Tactical Air Force to pulverise installations in the German enclave of Boulogne. Each bomb had two protective rings which were removed before being fitted to the aircraft. The photograph was taken two days before the German garrison surrendered on 26 September 1944.*

Source: Keystone Collection

Left: *Special RAF squadrons were formed to supply resistance forces in France. A Stirling of 138 Squadron is shown here dropping containers to the Armée Blanche, the Belgian Resistance Movement.*

Source: Keystone Collection

Left: *DC-3 Dakotas were used to carry casualties from Normandy to England. Three WAAF flew operationally in this aircraft on 14 June 1944, to tend the wounded, and were the first servicewomen to land in France after D-Day.*

Source: Keystone Collection

Left: *Airmen attaching the tubes and stabilising fins of rocket projectiles to 60 lb warheads containing high explosive, for use against armoured fighting vehicles and ground troops. Typhoon fighter-bombers of the 2nd Tactical Air Force used these weapons. The other type of warhead, not shown here, was the 25 lb solid-shot used for sinking ships. This was photographed in France, about a week after the D-Day landings.*

Source: Keystone Collection

Below: *The Hawker Typhoon was fitted with four 20 mm cannons and could also carry eight rockets with 60 lb warheads.*

Source: Keystone Collection

Above: *This attack by rocket-firing Typhoons of the 2nd Tactical Air Force, against Carpiquet aerodrome, near Caen in Normandy, was photographed by the RAF Film Unit on 4 July 1944.*

Source: Keystone Collection

Left: *As an alternative to carrying eight 60 lb rockets, the Typhoon had provision for two 500 lb bombs under the wings. It was the only Allied fighter-bomber which could carry such a load. In this form, it was sometimes known as a 'Bombphoon'. This photograph of airmen rolling a 500 lb medium-capacity bomb near a Typhoon of 193 Squadron, was taken in Holland in December 1944.*

Source: Keystone Collection

Left: *Loading 1,000 lb medium-capacity bombs under a Hawker Typhoon of 175 Squadron, which was based in Belgium in September 1944.*

Source: Keystone Collection

Right: *The Hawker Tempest V was developed from the Hawker Typhoon, being faster and with a longer range. It was known as a 'Tiffy with the bugs removed', being responsive and with an excellent combat vision. The first machines were delivered to the RAF in January 1944, and the Tempest squadrons became celebrated for success against V1 flying bombs, destroying 632 in all. Later, Tempest Squadrons formed part of the 2nd Tactical Air Force in Europe, achieving much success in air combat and in the ground-attack role.*

Source: Aviation Bookshop

Left: *One of the most celebrated of the fighter pilots in the 2nd Tactical Air Force was Gp Capt J.E. "Johnny" Johnson, DSO and two bars, DFC and bar. He was the RAF's top British scorer, with thirty-eight confirmed victories. Here he is the central figure, in a reunion of 83 Group held on 29 March 1946.*

Source: Keystone Collection

Below: *The RAF set up Construction Wings and Servicing Commandos in order to provide airfields for the 2nd Tactical Air Force as the Allies advanced. Runways were sometimes made of steel wire netting, similar to those constructed in England, as shown in this photograph.*

Source: Keystone Collection

Right: *Pegging down the portable runway, which was known as the Sommerfield Track.*

Source: Keystone Collection

Left: *The North American Mitchell, designated B-25 by the USAAF, entered service with the RAF in September 1942 and eventually equipped six squadrons of Bomber Command and the 2nd Tactical Air Force. The RAF pilots liked flying this light day-bomber, which proved fast, highly manoeuvrable and easy to handle, in spite of its unfamiliar tricycle undercarriage. The Mitchell remained in RAF service until the end of the war. This photograph shows a bombing attack by a Mitchell of 98 Squadron.*

Source: RAF Museum P7449

Right: *The General Aircraft Hotspur was the standard training glider used in the Second World War. RAF instructors trained NCOs of the army's Glider Regiment at five schools, after which the pilots earned their wings.*

Source: Keystone Collection

Above: The Hotspur was towed by Hawker biplanes or Miles Master monoplanes, and was able to glide for up to 80 miles if released from 20,000 feet. About 1,000 were built, but the machine was not used operationally.

Source: Keystone Collection

Above: The Airspeed Horsa was the standard operational glider used for carrying troops of the Airborne Divisions of the British Army during World War Two. Horsas landed in Sicily during June 1943, in Normandy during June 1944, and at Arnhem in September 1944. They were usually towed by Stirlings, Halifaxes, Dakotas and Albemarles of the RAF's Transport Command. This photograph was taken half an hour after the paratroops had jumped from Dakotas over Arnhem on 17 September 1944. They are clearing the bushes of any enemy opposition while a Horsa comes in to land.

Source: Keystone Collection

Right: The mass of gliders at Arnhem after the landings. Over 500 Horsas landed on 17 and 18 September 1944, as well as twenty-eight General Aircraft Hamilcars carrying vehicles.

Source: Keystone Collection

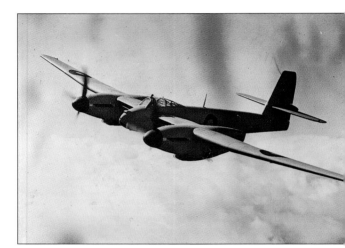

Left: *An army pilot in a Hotspur glider.*

Source: Keystone Collection

Above: *The Westland Welkin was intended as a high-altitude fighter for the RAF. It had a service ceiling of 44,000 feet but, although sixty-seven were built, it was never used operationally.*

Source: Keystone Collection

Below: *A B-25 Mitchell of the RAF in a camouflaged hangar captured from the Germans during the final stages of the war.*

Source: Keystone Collection

Right: *Fl Officer David S.A. "Lumme" Lord (right) photographed in the Middle East. On 19 September 1944 he was a pilot of a Dakota of 271 Squadron over Arnhem when his starboard engine was hit twice by flak and set on fire. Nevertheless he continued to fly over the dropping zone until most of the containers had been pushed out. He then ordered his crew to bale out while he remained at the controls. There was only one survivor from his crew. Fl Lt David Lord, who had already been gazetted with the DFC, was awarded a posthumous Victoria Cross.*

Source: Keystone Collection

Below: *A B-25 Mitchell of 180 Squadron, based at Melsbroek in Belgium, being repaired on 14 December 1944. In the background is a camouflaged building used by the Germans as a workshop, and an RAF 'Queen Mary' low-loader.*

Source: Keystone Collection

Above: *Several German aircraft which crash-landed in Britain were restored to flying condition. These were air tested by 1426 (Enemy Aircraft) Flight and the results were sent to the Air Ministry and the Royal Aircraft Establishment for analysis. Flying the machines over England could be dangerous and they were given RAF markings. At first, the Flight was based at Duxford in Cambridgeshire but it was transferred to Collyweston in Northamptonshire on 24 March 1943. This photograph, taken on 7 March 1944, shows (left to right) a Ju88, a Bf110, a Bf109G, an FW190 and an Hs129.*
Source: Keystone Collection

Left: *The Ju88 at Collyweston, with RAF markings.*
Source: Keystone Collection

Above right: *Four of the pilots at Collyweston, with a Bf110 in the background.*
Source: Keystone Collection

Left: *The Hs129 at Collyweston, still with German markings, undergoing examination.*
Source: Keystone Collection

Right: *On 14 April 1944, the RAF's Gunnery Research Unit arrived at Collyweston from Exeter. A collection of German aerial guns can be seen in this photograph, with a poster of a Do217E-2 in the background.*
Source: Keystone Collection

Left: *Pilots of 439 (RCAF) Squadron building their own dispersal huts in January 1945. The squadron was equipped with Typhoon IBs as part of the 2nd Tactical Air Force, based at the forward aerodrome B.78 Eindhoven in Holland.*
Source: Keystone Collection

Above: *All airmen who were 'demobbed' were able to choose a specified number of civilian clothes from a selection at each centre. This photograph was taken on 18 June 1945. Some men were demobilised after VE Day and before the end of the war with Japan.*
Source: Keystone Collection

Left: *The first helicopter to enter service in the RAF was the Sikorsky Hoverfly I, in May 1945. This photograph was taken at the Helicopter Training Flight at Andover in Hampshire. Only 529 Squadron, based at Henley-on-Thames, was equipped with this machine, but the squadron was disbanded in October 1945.*
Source: RAF Museum PO21609

Right: *Part of the celebration in Whitehall, London, during VE Day on 8 May 1945.*

Source: Keystone Collection

Below: *The 'nose art' on the Handley Page Halifax III 'Friday the 13th', which made 118 operational flights. In addition to the ominous message "As ye sow, so shall ye reap", the art included paintings of the VC, DSO and DFC won by members of the aircrews who flew in the machine. This bomber formed part of an exhibition "Britain's Aircraft" on a bombed site in Oxford Street, London, during June 1945.*

Source: Keystone Collection

Above: *The devastation at Magdeburg, on the river Elbe, photographed in April 1945, shortly before the end of the war. The cathedral had largely escaped the worst of the blast bombs and incendiaries.*
Source: Keystone Collection

Above left: *The view from Cologne Cathedral towards the wrecked Hohenzollern Bridge over the Rhine.*
Source: Keystone Collection

Left: *The ruined heart of Essen in the Ruhr, showing a path cleared through the rubble. This was photographed shortly after the end of the war.*
Source: Keystone Collection

Top right: *The remains of the railway station at Potsdam, to the south-west of Berlin. This photograph was taken on 24 July 1945, during the Potsdam Conference in which one of the matters discussed by the USA, Britain and Russia was the future of defeated Germany.*
Source: Keystone Collection

Right: *The march past of the RAF in Brussels on 8 July 1945 on the occasion of leaving Belgium. The RAF had been presented with a flag, carried by the flight lieutenant in front of the parade. The salute was taken by Air Marshal Sir Arthur Coningham, who commanded the 2nd Tactical Air Force, and the Burgomaster of Brussels.*
Source: Keystone Collection

CHAPTER 12

THE FORGOTTEN AIR WAR

One of the greatest disasters ever to befall British arms stemmed from the failure of the government to recognise the capacity of the Japanese to wage war against a western power. On 8 December 1941, when the Japanese landed at Kota Bahru on the north-east coast of Malaya, the defending Commonwealth forces were woefully ill-equipped. The troops had no tanks, very few anti-tank weapons, and little training in jungle warfare. They had minimal support from the Malayan or Chinese population. The RAF was hopelessly outnumbered and outclassed. Air Chief Marshal Sir Robert Brooke-Popham, the C-in-C Far East, had been presented with an impossible task. His meagre air forces consisted of only 362 aircraft, mostly outdated, of which about two-thirds were serviceable. Of these, two squadrons were equipped with obsolete Vildebeest torpedo bombers, four with Blenheims, two with Hudsons, four with Brewster Buffalo fighters, and one with Catalinas. These included squadrons of the RAAF and RNZAF, but there were insufficient pilots and some had not been trained on operational machines. There were four airfields in Singapore, but most of those in the Malayan archipelago were poorly constructed and ill-defended, while servicing facilities were inadequate. The radar system was extremely patchy, most of the stations being still under construction.

The invading Japanese included battle-hardened troops who had been imbued with a fanatical desire to die in the service of their country. They were lightly equipped for jungle warfare, but well-trained and supported by numerous land-based aircraft. Of their aircraft, the Mitsubishi A6M2 Zero outclassed every Allied fighter in the Far East or Pacific and was far superior to the Buffalo. There were two Japanese Air Forces, one subordinate to the army and the other to the navy. Both performed a formidably aggressive role. The pilots were skilled and their commanders had studied the tactics used in Europe, particularly those of their allies in the *Luftwaffe*, on which their command structure and air formations were largely based. Later in the war, there was no shortage of volunteer suicide pilots, who were known as *Tokkatai* in the Army Air Force and *Kamikaze* in the Navy Air Force. There was, however, no long-range strategic bombing force.

On the day of the landings, a badly crippled Beaufort of PRU (the only machine of this type to serve in South-East Asia) flew into the small airfield of Kota Bahru, carrying photographs of a Japanese landing further north at Singora and Patani in Siam, as well as revealing the presence of about sixty Japanese aircraft on the airfield. Kota Bahru was invested by the invaders and overrun the following day, shortly after the remaining RAF aircraft were evacuated. On the night before, Singapore had undergone its first bombing attack. The city was not fully blacked out and thus presented an excellent target. Next, the airfields in Malaya were attacked continuously by bombers escorted by fighters, resulting in the destruction of aircraft and numerous casualties. Although the number of RAF aircraft in northern Malaya was reduced to about fifty, the enemy airfield at Singora was attacked and some Japanese aircraft destroyed. But the majority of the surviving RAF bombers soon succumbed to further attacks on their airfields.

Japanese bombers and torpedo aircraft then scored a resounding success by sinking

Above: *A Brewster Buffalo I of 71 Squadron, the first Eagle Squadron manned by US personnel. Buffaloes were received in October 1940, at a time when the squadron was based at Church Fenton in Yorkshire, but these were used only for training before being shipped out to the Far East.*

Source: RAF Museum P5253

the two British battleships *Prince of Wales* and *Repulse*, which had steamed up the east coast of Malaya to intercept the invasion fleet, without the benefit of long-range fighter escort, which was not available. After this disaster, the Japanese controlled the seas as well as the air. The British troops and the RAF had no option but to pull back, destroying installations as best they could, while the few surviving Buffalos tried to support rearguard actions. The Malayan Volunteer Air Force, flying light aircraft, helped with liaison work, reconnaissance and jungle rescue.

Meanwhile, Hong Kong and Borneo were captured by the Japanese, neither having any air support. Brooke-Popham was replaced by Lieutenant General Sir Henry Roydes Pownall, but the new C-in-C was similarly unable to perform a miracle. Reinforcements arrived in Singapore in the form of fifty-one Hurricanes in crates, while twenty-four pilots were either flown in or arrived by sea. Apart from these, only seventy-five twin-engined aircraft and twenty-eight fighters remained in service. The Hurricanes achieved successes by shooting down a number of bombers over Singapore but the escorting Zeros were faster and more agile at the low levels in which most combats took place. Twenty-two bombers of the Netherlands Indies Army Air Corps also arrived in Singapore.

The Vildebeests lost five out of nine aircraft during a torpedo attack on a further Japanese landing on the east coast of Malaya. By the beginning of February 1942, the last of the exhausted troops were back over the causeway connecting Singapore with the mainland.

It soon became apparent that the island could not hold out against the continual shelling and air bombardment. Only twenty-one of the Hurricanes remained serviceable, while there were six Buffalos left. Apart from a token force, evacuation of the remaining RAF to the Dutch island of Sumatra was ordered. The operation lasted for a fortnight, employing a motley selection of shipping for the ground personnel. On 15 February the remaining troops on Singapore under Lieutenant General A.E. Percival, surrendered. They numbered 70,000, and over half these later died as a result of the brutish and cruel treatment to which they were subjected as prisoners-of-war.

Only forty-eight RAF aircraft were present in Sumatra and many of these were in poor condition. They supported the Dutch and British forces by carrying out reconnaissance flights and bombing raids, but there was little they could do to prevent another Japanese invasion. On 14 February, enemy paratroops descended on the fighter airfield of Palembang, where they soon overpowered the defences. A secret airfield had been built in the jungle, and the remaining RAF aircraft operated from there, attacking with considerable success a Japanese invasion fleet. But the military situation on the island became hopeless and another withdrawal was ordered, to Java, which was completed on 18 February. By then, eighteen Hurricanes remained serviceable, with twelve Hudsons and six Blenheims. The situation there became untenable after an entire fleet, commanded by the Dutch, was sunk in an engagement in the Java Sea on 27 February. The Japanese landed on Java on 1 March and the handful of surviving aircraft were flown to Australia. The RAF aircrews and ground personnel were evacuated by ship, so far as possible. Some reached Australia, while a few even arrived in Ceylon, after many privations.

The Japanese plans for further conquest were carried out with remorseless purpose, seeking and exploiting the weaknesses of their opponents. The occupation of Burma was of great importance to Japan, for it would cut the supply route of the western powers to China, where their armies were still engaged in bitter fighting. This 'Burma Road' was protected by an American Volunteer Group, consisting of three squadrons of Curtiss P-40s (known to the RAF as Tomahawks) based at Kunming. The RAF was represented by 221 Group, with headquarters in Rangoon, where they were joined by the Americans. Unlike Malaya, there were a number of well-constructed airfields in Burma, with good runways and accommodation for personnel, as well as positions for ground defences. Unfortunately, by Christmas 1941, when the Japanese Air Force began to attack Rangoon, only a handful of RAF aircraft occupied these bases, supported by liaison aircraft of the Burmese Volunteer Air Force. The only fighters were a few Buffalos, while there were almost no anti-aircraft guns together with a patchy system of observer posts. The officer commanding the RAF in Burma was the energetic and resourceful Air Vice-Marshal D.F. Stevenson.

Against this little force, the Japanese were able to pit about 400 bombers and long-range fighters, based in Siam. However, the aggressive tactics of the Anglo-American fighters proved surprisingly effective, for they gained altitude and then went into steep dives in order to tear into the enemy formations. After suffering many losses over Rangoon, the Japanese drew off for a few weeks, and in this period about thirty Hurricanes and a squadron of Blenheims arrived in Burma. Stevenson immediately sent these into the attack, the bombers against Bangkok and the fighters against advanced airfields, achieving considerable success until the operations were hampered by shortage of spares. The Japanese came back with increased force, but failed to achieve air superiority.

However, the limited air operations were unable to do more than postpone the advance of the Japanese army. Rangoon was finally evacuated on 7 March, but not before British sappers had wrecked and set on fire the oil installations in the area. The army withdrew northwards, following the trail of panic-striken refugees who had fled the city, while the remnants of the air force flew to the island of Akyab, from where they attacked Mingaladon, the airfield at Rangoon, and destroyed many Japanese aircraft. But the Japanese delivered mass air attacks on Akyab and wiped out the remainder of the RAF and American fighters. The only possible course of action for the RAF was retreat to India, behind the range of mountains which separate the two countries, and attempt to build up strength. From here, the remaining Blenheims gave what support they could to the retreating army and the refugees, but the Japanese Air Force was able to attack with impunity town after town in Burma. A few Dakotas dropped supplies to the army and took out the sick and wounded, while Lysanders were converted into light bombers. By May 1942, the remnants of the army reached Imphal in Manipur, and Burma had fallen to the enemy. The Japanese were within air striking range of Calcutta.

Ceylon was threatened with the Japanese Fleet, but this strategically important island was protected by the British Far Eastern Fleet and reinforced with four squadrons of Hurricanes. On 5 April, Japanese aircraft flew from carriers to bomb Colombo and the airfield at Ratmalana; several were shot down for the loss of fifteen Hurricanes and four FAA Fulmars. But on the same day, Japanese dive bombers sank the cruisers HMS

Above: *The Chindits led by Brigadier Charles Orde Wingate were supplied by C-47 Dakotas during their excursions behind Japanese lines in Burma during February to June 1943.*

Source: Keystone Collection

Above: *The Curtiss Mohawk IV, the American P-36A, served with the RAF solely in the Burma theatre of war, being first delivered to 5 Squadron at Dum Dum in India in December 1941. The fighter continued with some success on this front with three RAF squadrons, continuing until January 1944. The Mohawk in this photograph was serial AR645.*

Source: RAF Museum PO19168

Right: *One of the effective aircraft in the Burma campaign was the Vultee Vengeance dive bomber, flown by four RAF squadrons and supplied under Lend-Lease by the USA. Later Vengeances were employed in the U.K. as target-towers. This photograph of a Vengeance II, serial AN609, was taken in November 1942.*

Source: RAF Museum P9245

Right: *Indian paratroops lining up to enter a Douglas Dakota, for their first flight in an aircraft, with a Lockheed Hudson in the background. The photograph was taken in early November 1943.*

Source: Keystone Collection

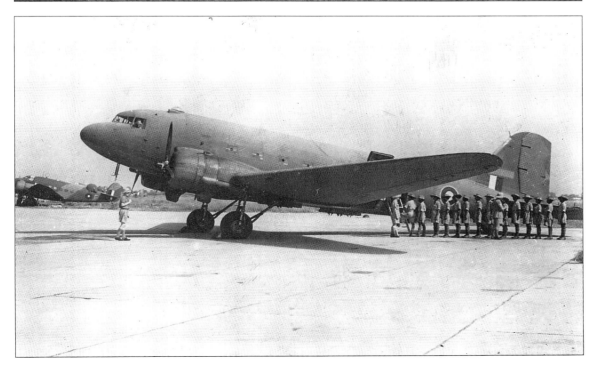

Left: *Two of Wingate's Chindits brought out from a landing strip in Burma in July 1943. According to publicity at the time, they were examining a grenade which had fallen out of a pack and which they had found rolling about on the floor of the fuselage.*

Source: Keystone Collection

Cornwall and HMS Dorsetshire in the Indian Ocean. On 9 April, Trincomalee was bombed, while the aircraft carrier HMS Hermes was also sunk by dive bombers. However, after these successes, the Japanese fleet withdrew to the Pacific, where its presence was urgently required.

The Japanese Air Force, with many commitments in the Pacific, did not begin attacks against Calcutta until December 1942. Although only a few bombs were dropped, all at night, about a million and a half Indians fled the city in panic. During the next month, a flight of Beaufighter night-fighters arrived and soon shot down five of the raiders. The Japanese did not persist, and the mollified citizens returned to their normal dwellings.

With the Burma Road cut, an alternative method of carrying troops and military equipment to China was found by the USAAF, by flying from airfields near Calcutta across the Patkai mountains to Kunming. RAF Dakotas also flew on this hazardous route which, beset by towering clouds and great mountain peaks, became known as the 'Hump Run'. General Sir Archibald Wavell took over command of the British army in India while the RAF was commanded by Air Chief Marshal Sir Richard Peirse. One of Wavell's main tasks was to convince his troops that the Japanese were not invincible, while Peirse built up his squadrons, which by December 1942 amounted to 1,443 aircraft. These included three operational groups, two in India and one in Ceylon, equipped with Hurricanes, Blenheims, Hudsons, Vultee Vengeances, Catalinas, Lysanders, Dakotas, Wellingtons and Beauforts. It was intended to increase the number of squadrons to eighty-three, after the Axis forces had been cleared out of North Africa.

In December, Wavell opened an offensive, with the limited objective of seizing the island of Akyab. The troops moved down the coast unopposed as far as the port of Indin, which they reached on 27 December, while the RAF and USAAF carried out bombing attacks against Japanese positions and transports further south. Eventually, the troops met stiff resistance and did not reach their objective. At same time, a force trained to operate behind the Japanese lines, known as the Chindits and led by Brigadier Orde Wingate, set off for a long-range penetration into the interior of Burma. These columns, which depended wholly on supplies dropped from the air, cut railway lines, destroyed bridges, and caused confusion among the Japanese forces. The operations came to an end with the monsoon which began in June 1943, having attained limited results, but the ground forces now knew that they could beat the enemy, provided they could be supported by air supplies. The immediate need was to build up the air transport squadrons. This expansion took place at such a pace that by January 1944 it was possible to transport whole divisions by air. By this time, no fewer than 275 airfields had been built, and South East Asia Command had been created, under Lord Louis Mountbatten, controlling the whole of the RAF in north-east India as well as the U.S. Tenth Army Air Force and including a Tactical Air Force, a Strategic Air Force and a Photographic Reconnaissance Force.

By early 1944, there were forty-eight RAF and seventeen USAAF squadrons in the new command. The Japanese possessed about 370 aircraft in Burma, and the first task of the Allies was to obliterate these. Spitfire VIIIs proved more than a match for the Japanese Oscars, and air supremacy over northern Burma was established. Beaufighters and Hurricanes shot up Japanese transport while Vengeances dive-bombed installations and Liberators carried out long-distance bombing attacks. The 14th Army, under General Sir William Slim, penetrated once more down the Arakan coast towards Akyab. When in February 1944 their headquarters and advanced troops were surrounded in a village named Sinzweya – known as the 'Admin Box' – they were successfully supplied from the air and fought their way out. A Japanese counter-attack was destroyed with the help of air support.

Above left: *B-24 Liberator bombers were ferried from the USA via Canada, Britain and Africa to India or Ceylon, from where they were employed on long-distance raids against Japanese positions in south-east Asia. This Liberator was snowbound at Montreal in April 1944, but a blower removed the foreground snow and trenches were cut for the wheels. An hour after the photograph was taken, the aircraft was on its way.*
Source: Keystone Collection

Above: *A Douglas Dakota III, serial FL512, at Myitikyina airstrip in northern Burma. The largest air base in northern Burma, Myitikyina was recaptured from the Japanese on 17 May 1944 and Dakotas immediately flew in troops and supplies.*
Source: RAF Museum P3506

Right: *The desperate attempts by Blenheims of 221 Group to halt the Japanese invasion of Burma in early 1942 were somewhat imaginatively portrayed in this poster.*
Source: RAF Museum (Crown copyright) P00167

Left: *A Hurricane fighter-bomber attacking a bridge on the road from Tiddim to Kalemyo in Burma during the retreat of the Japanese Fifteenth Army in the monsoon period of 1944.*
Source: Keystone Collection

Below left: *In April 1945, the RAF continued to make daylight attacks against the infamous railway which the Japanese had built with forced labour between Bangkok in Thailand and Moulmein in Burma. The main problem was the distance, involving over seventeen hours of flight. On the bombing attack shown in this photograph, the crews saw prisoners waving to them from the railway sidings.*
Source: Keystone Collection

Blenheim bombers of the Royal Air Force destroyed a large convoy of Japanese supply barges on the Chindwin river in Burma.

SMASH JAPANESE AGGRESSION!

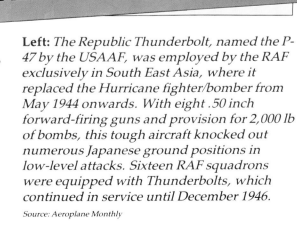

Left: *The Republic Thunderbolt, named the P-47 by the USAAF, was employed by the RAF exclusively in South East Asia, where it replaced the Hurricane fighter/bomber from May 1944 onwards. With eight .50 inch forward-firing guns and provision for 2,000 lb of bombs, this tough aircraft knocked out numerous Japanese ground positions in low-level attacks. Sixteen RAF squadrons were equipped with Thunderbolts, which continued in service until December 1946.*
Source: Aeroplane Monthly

On 8 March, the Japanese opened a major offensive with three divisions against Kohima and Imphal. By diverting transport aircraft from the 'Hump Run', a whole division was transferred from the Arakan to reinforce the threatened areas, while other units and supplies were flown from India. There was extremely fierce fighting at close quarters, during which large numbers of British and Indian troops were surrounded by the Japanese, but Dakotas and C-46 Commandos supplied them from the air while Hurricanes and Vengeances attacked the enemy positions. RAF Spitfires, with U.S. Lightnings and Mustangs, strafed enemy airfields and ensured that air supremacy was maintained.

Meanwhile, over 9,000 Chindits were flown in troop carriers or towed in gliders to positions well behind the Japanese front, while other Chindits set off on foot. The columns were accompanied by RAF officers equipped with R/T and W/T sets, entrusted with the tasks of guiding the supply aircraft and directing the tactical fighter-bombers. At the same time, a Chinese division under the U.S. General J.W. Stilwell pushed southwards, supplied from the air, to capture the vital airfield of Myitkyina, even further east. By the end of May 1944, the Japanese around Imphal and Kohima began to weaken, and a retreat turned into a rout, harried from the air. In the three months before mid May, the Japanese had lost 30,000 men in northern Burma. They were being outclassed and outfought.

More Liberators arrived, while Hurricanes were replaced with Thunderbolts and Vengeances with Mosquitos. The Japanese had been reduced to no more than 125 aircraft. In November 1944, Air Chief Marshal Sir Richard Pierse's successor, Air Chief Marshal Sir Trafford Leigh-Mallory, was killed en route to take up his new command. The post was filled temporarily by Air Marshal Sir Guy Garrod until Air Marshal Sir Keith Park arrived in February 1945. The Japanese supply lines came under continual attack, including the railway line from Bangkok to Moulmein, built at the cost of thousands of lives of Allied prisoners of war. The photographic squadrons carried out extensive operations, including a survey of fifty-seven per cent of the entire area of Burma, which had never been adequately mapped. Japanese U-boats were hunted, while coastal and river shipping came under low-level attack.

In January 1945, the Japanese withdrew from Akyab, and the island was used by the Allies for an amphibious assault on the mainland. At the same time the armies broke through from the north, closely supported by the air forces, and began to sweep down the central plain of Burma. The liquid fire bomb of napalm was first used in these attacks. By April, the Japanese were in full retreat and within a few weeks had evacuated Rangoon, which was occupied by the 14th Army without a fight. From this time, the war became a form of massacre, with the tattered and starving remnants of the Japanese army ruthlessly cut down as they attempted to retreat to Siam.

After the end of the campaign in Burma, the next stage was the preparation for an invasion of Malaya, under the code-name of operation 'Zipper'. But this was not necessary. On 6 August 1945 the first atomic bomb fell on Hiroshima and three days later the second was dropped on Nagasaki. On 14 August the Japanese surrendered unconditionally and the Second World War was at an end.

Above: *Wing Commander R.R.S. Tuck, DSO, DFC and two bars, who achieved fame flying Hawker Hurricanes in 257 Squadron during the Battle of Britain, carrying the RAF Ensign into Westminster Abbey on 13 September 1946, during a rehearsal for the Battle of Britain ceremony the following day.*

Source: Keystone Collection

Far left: *On 15 September 1945, a great flypast took place over London to commemorate the end of the Second World War. This photograph shows 'The Few', those who flew in the Battle of Britain, led by Group Captain Douglas Bader, over St. Paul's.*
Source: Keystone Collection

Left: *Group Captain Douglas Bader, the celebrated air ace who lost his legs before the Second World War, climbing into a Spitfire to lead the flypast of 15 September 1945.*
Source: Keystone Collection

Right: *A contingent of RAF men arriving from the West Indies on 21 September 1945 for demobilisation.*
Source: Keystone Collection

Right: *A contingent from the RAF Regiment marching along Parliament Street as part of the Victory Parade of 8 June 1946.*
Source: Keystone Collection

Above: *In November 1947, Gp Capt Douglas Bader unveiled a new engine named 'Fighter Pilot' for Southern Railway. Also present were Wg Cdr W.G. Clouston and the former commander of Fighter Command's 11 Group during the Battle of Britain, Air Chief Marshal Sir Keith Park.*
Source: Keystone Collection

CHAPTER 13

THE COLD WAR

Above: *The Gloster Meteor F.4 first entered service in November 1947 and eventually twenty-one RAF squadrons were equipped with the machine. This photograph is of Meteor F.4, serial EE521.*

Source: RAF Museum colour slide P100283

The enormous size of the air force with which Britain had ended the Second World War was obviously impractical for the years of peace which everyone hoped would stretch ahead. Many squadrons were disbanded while large numbers of aircraft in service or on the production lines were scrapped. In any event, the economy of the country was in a parlous state and the political climate was averse to spending on defence. By 1948/9, the budget for the RAF had been reduced to only £173 million.

Air Chief Marshal Sir Arthur Tedder, who had taken over as Chief of Air Staff from Marshal of the Royal Air Force Lord Portal in January 1946, was well aware that the United States was continuing with atomic research and that the Soviet Union would soon develop similar weapons. Conventional defence of the U.K. had lost much of its meaning in the knowledge that the use of atomic bombs in another war could result in the annihilation of the entire population. The government had to make up its mind whether Britain should develop its own nuclear capability or stand on the sidelines of world events.

In October 1947, the government announced that it intended to fund atomic research and that the RAF would be the carrier of the resulting weapons. In the same year, the Air Staff put forward 'Plan E', which proposed fifty-one fighter squadrons, forty-one bomber squadrons, thirteen maritime squadrons, forty-two transport squadrons and a reserve of twelve squadrons. These totalled about 1,500 aircraft, but a cutback of about 240 aircraft resulted from a limit on the air estimates, falling mainly on Transport Command.

But whatever the plan, the reality depended partly on the availability of trained men, and almost all the experienced wartime entrants had disappeared into civilian life. Moreover, many of the aircraft were outmoded and remained suitable only for some of the commitments outside Europe. Although Britain possessed excellent aeronautical designers, the U.S. had forged well into the lead with aircraft production. The RAF was still mainly equipped with piston-engined aircraft, although some jet aircraft such as the Gloster Meteor and the de Havilland Vampire had entered service. The piston-engined Avro Lincoln was being produced to replace the Lancaster, but a strategic jet bomber was required for nuclear weapons. In 1948 the RAF at home consisted of eighty squadrons, with twenty more in the Royal Auxiliary Air Force. Overseas, there were thirty-three squadrons. Meanwhile, although events in the Middle and Far East were looking ominous, it was in Europe that the RAF was suddenly needed.

On 24 June 1948, six months after the breakdown of a Four-Power Conference on the future of Germany, the Soviet Union closed all road and rail communications with West Berlin, thus denying access to the British, American and French sectors of the former capital. This move had been anticipated by the West, and both the RAF and the USAF were prepared to mount an airlift designed to keep their garrisons supplied. Dakotas immediately began ferrying supplies into Gatow in the British sector and Tempelhof in the American sector of the city. However, the British and American governments then decided that their air forces should supply the needs of the entire civilian population of

West Berlin, numbering over two million people, as a bargaining counter with the Russians. Such a colossal task seemed impossible of achievement, for the required load was 4,000 to 5,000 short tons per day, but both air forces rose magnificently to the occasion.

By 29 July, the entire Dakota fleet of the RAF's Transport Command, numbering sixty-four aircraft, had arrived at the base of Wunstorf, near Hanover, in the British zone of occupied Germany. Two days later, the RAF's fleet of fifty-six Avro Yorks also arrived. Ten Sunderlands of Coastal Command flew to Hamburg, from where they could carry loads to Havel Lake in Berlin, a small but impressive contribution. The Americans were able to muster an even larger transport force of C-47 Dakotas and Douglas C-54 Skymasters at their bases of Wiesbaden and Rhein/Main in their zone of Germany. Operation 'Plain Fare', as it was called, was under way.

Congestion in the airports in West Berlin and in the occupied zones of Germany presented a major problem. There was also the limitation of only three permitted air corridors, each twenty miles wide. The northern corridor was used by the British, the southern by the Americans, and the central by returning aircraft. The four-engined C-54 Skymasters could carry about ten tons, the Yorks about eight and a half tons, and the Dakotas about three and a half tons. In order to increase carrying capacity, the Americans soon withdrew their Dakotas and brought in more Skymasters. The RAF Dakotas moved to Lübeck, to relieve congestion at Wunstorf.

Below: *The Avro Lincoln was intended to succeed the Avro Lancaster but did not arrive in the RAF until August 1945, too late to serve in the war. It was armed with 20 mm cannons and .50 inch machine guns, and could carry 14,000 lb of bombs. It flew on operations against terrorists in Malaya and Kenya, and continued in RAF service until 1963. This photograph shows a Lincoln of 7 Squadron, which was equipped with the machine from August 1949 to December 1955.*

Source: RAF Museum P11922

During July, the combined air forces carried an average of 2,226 short tons a day to West Berlin, of which the RAF contribution was forty-two per cent. The average daily tonnage rose to 3,839 tons in August and 4,641 tons in September. This increased tonnage was mainly carried by the USAF, with the advantage of the larger payload of the C-54 Skymasters. However, in September, British charter aircraft carried an additional 177 tons a day, and continued until the end of the operation.

The main cargo in terms of weight was coal, which was urgently required with the onset of winter. Of course, foodstuffs were also required, and these were dehydrated where possible, in order to save space. An airfield in the British zone, Fassberg, was opened in August for the American C-54 Skymasters. The average tonnage carried in October rose to 4,760 per day, but there was dip to 3,786 tons in November, owing to fog. The new Handley Page Hastings began to join in during that month, but the RAF's contribution did not increase; instead, improved facilities were provided for USAF aircraft in the British zone. In December, the new airport of Tegel was opened in the French sector of Berlin, having been built since the beginning of the operation. Another air base for the American C-54 Skymasters was opened at Celle in the British sector. The tonnage then rose steadily from 4,563 tons in December to 5,546 tons in January, 6,327 tons in March and 8,091 tons in May. In January, Air Chief Marshal Sir John Slessor took over from Lord Tedder as Chief of Air Staff, to preside over the RAF's contribution to this success.

The capacity of the USAF and RAF amazed the Russians, who were losing face in the eyes of the world and particularly the delighted West Berliners. They lifted their blockade on 12 May 1949, after 'Plain Fare' had been in operation for over ten months. However, the airlift continued for another four months, to build up a stockpile in case the Russians decided to renew their interference. The operation demonstrated that the run down of the RAF had been allowed to go too far, but that the personnel were capable of rising to an emergency, given reasonable backing. The close collaboration of the RAF and the USAF was also a contributory factor in the formation of the North Atlantic Treaty Organization, which came into being on 24 August 1949. Four weeks later, the Federal Republic of Germany was also established, marking a new solidarity among western nations against the Communist bloc.

These events gave impetus to the establishment of a strategic deterrent. By 1949, Bomber Command had been reduced to only about 150 aircraft, Lincolns and Mosquitos, but during the following year was reinforced by Boeing B-29 Superfortresses, which were called Washingtons by the RAF. Canberras began to enter service in 1951, but this otherwise excellent tactical bomber could not carry an atomic bomb. The RAF was awaiting its V-bombers, as these were called. The first of these, the four-jet Vickers Valiant, began to arrive in 1955, and eventually equipped ten squadrons. Meanwhile, the Blue Danube plutonium bomb had been developed by British scientists and tested in the Monte Bello Islands, off Western Australia, in October 1952. The first of these bombs became available to the RAF in November 1953, ten months after Air Chief Marshal Sir William Dickson took over as Chief of Air Staff. Ten airfields were enlarged in England for the new V-bombers, and a dispersal system in other airfields was also arranged, to give the bombers protection against a 'first strike'. The crews underwent intensive training in high-level operations, in collaboration with the USAF.

In 1956, the year in which Air Chief Marshal Sir Dermot Boyle took over as Chief of Air Staff, the delta-winged Avro Vulcan V-bomber arrived, and the first squadron became operational with these the following year. The third of the V-bomber trio, the Handley Page Victor entered squadron service in 1958. In the same year, sixty Thor intermediate-range missiles from the U.S.A. were installed on dispersed sites, operated by the RAF in conjunction with the Americans. Defence of airfields was provided by Bloodhound ground-to-air missiles, together with an efficient guidance system. By 1959, those V-bombers at readiness were capable of flying clear within three minutes and then setting off in retaliation. An early warning station was completed in 1963 at Fylingdales in Yorkshire, by which time the nuclear deterrent force consisted of fifteen squadrons, equipped with the more powerful hydrogen bombs. During this period there were two further appointments as Chief of Air Staff, Air Chief Marshal Sir Thomas Pike on 1 January 1960 and Air Chief Marshal Sir Charles Elworthy on 1 September 1963.

As a counter to the surface-to-air missiles which the Soviet Union was known to have developed, the V-bombers were equipped in 1963 with the Blue Steel 'stand-off' missile, capable of being launched a hundred miles from the target. As an additional counter to enemy radar and defensive missiles, the Vulcan and Victor crews trained in low-level approaches, climbing up at the last moment to launch their missiles. In the same year, the RAF's V-bomber force came under the authority of NATO for nuclear strikes, while retaining its conventional bombing capacity for any national needs. However, a change of policy followed the introduction of Polaris missiles launched from submarines, and in this year the RAF began to wind down its nuclear strike force. In 1964, the British Aircraft Corporation TSR 2, a tactical strike and reconnaissance bomber

Above: *The Gloster Meteor was the first jet aircraft to enter service in the RAF, in July 1944, and the only Allied jet aircraft to fly operationally in the Second World War. Its main role was to intercept V.1. flying bombs, thirteen of which were destroyed. In 1945, a Meteor achieved the record speed of 606 m.p.h. This photograph of a Meteor F.3 of 74 Squadron was taken at Colerne in Wiltshire on 30 August 1945.*

Source: Keystone Collection

Below: *The Boeing B-29 Superfortress was named the Washington by the RAF when supplied from the USAF in 1950. It was gradually replaced by the English Electric Canberra, but continued with the RAF until 1958. This photograph shows a Washington with engines prepared for storage.*

Source: Aviation Bookshop

Above: *The first production batch of de Havilland Vampires, one of which is shown in this photograph, entered 247 Squadron in April 1946, too late for war service. The new jet fighter-bomber gained a high reputation for its aerobatic qualities as well as reliability and ease of access for servicing. The first RAF jet crossing of the Atlantic was made by six Vampires of 54 Squadron in July 1948. Although several overseas squadrons were equipped with the Vampire, only those in Malaya and Singapore flew operationally, on anti-terrorist strikes. Other Vampires served as night-fighters. As trainers, a few continued in RAF service until 1969.*

Source: RAF Museum PO12562

which had been under development for five years, was cancelled. Some of the V-bombers were retained for reconnaissance purposes and as conventional bombers, while others entered a new life as in-flight tankers and receivers.

In common with Bomber Command, Fighter Command was wound down rapidly after the end of the Second World War. By early 1947, it consisted of under 200 aircraft, mainly Meteors, Vampires, Hornets and Mosquitos, together with a small but efficient Control and Reporting system. In parallel with Bomber Command, an expansion programme began when operation 'Plain Fare' emphasised the seriousness of the Cold War, and by 1952 the number of aircraft had doubled, while there were about 160 additional Meteors and Vampires in the Royal Auxiliary Air Force. These aircraft could not match the Russian MiGs, however, and in 1952 the swept-wing North American Sabre entered service as a stop-gap jet until modern British jet fighters came off the production lines. These arrived two years later in the form of the Supermarine Swift and the Hawker Hunter, both swept-wing and subsonic in level flight. The Hunter proved the more successful and became the RAF's standard single-seat fighter until 1960. The two-seat Gloster Javelin, also subsonic, entered service in 1956; this was the first RAF fighter to carry an air-to-air missile, the heat-seeking Firestreak, as standard armament. By the end of that year, Fighter Command numbered 600 aircraft in thirty-five squadrons.

After this expansion, military thinking favoured the use of surface-to-air missiles for defence of the U.K., together with the introduction of a supersonic fighter, the English Electric Lightning, armed with air-to-air missiles. Moreover, it was believed that there was no defence against the new Russian surface-to-surface intercontinental missiles and that fighters were consequently losing much of their relevance for the defence of the U.K.

The Lightning, capable of achieving twice the speed of sound, came into service in 1960. Five years later Fighter Command was reduced to only sixty aircraft, all Lightnings and Javelins, fitted with the more powerful Red Top air-to-air missile. At this time, however, incursions by Russian reconnaissance aircraft in air space around the British Isles caused some alarm. The early warning system was improved by the employment of Avro Shackletons, while the number of fighter aircraft was gradually increased to seventy-six by 1975. One new aircraft was the McDonnell Douglas Phantom, which arrived in squadron service in 1968, replacing some of the ageing Lightnings. In April of the same year Fighter Command was combined with Bomber Command to form the RAF's new Strike Command. Air Chief Marshal Sir John Grandy took over as Chief of Air Staff in April 1967, followed by Air Chief Marshal Sir Denis Spotswood in April 1971, Air Chief Marshal Sir Andrew Humphrey in April 1974 and Air Chief Marshal Sir Neil Cameron in January 1976.

In addition to commitments at home, the RAF continued as a potent force in West Germany. In July 1945 the 2nd Tactical Air Force was renamed the British Air Forces of Occupation (BAFO), consisting of thirty-four front-line squadrons. In common with the RAF practise everywhere, these squadrons were rapidly wound down, until only ten remained at the end of 1947. With the beginning of the Cold War in 1948 and the formation of NATO the following year, these squadrons were moved to bases along the eastern frontier and an expansion began. By 1951, there were sixteen squadrons in BAFO, equipped with Vampires and Meteors, under the control of NATO. By the following year there were two divisions, the 2nd Allied Tactical Air Force (2ATAF) and the 4th Allied Tactical Air Force (4ATAF), the former consisting mainly of RAF squadrons.

The 2ATAF grew rapidly to twenty-five squadrons, in which Venoms replaced the Vampires, and Sabre squadrons were formed. In 1954 four squadrons of Canberras arrived, 'on loan' from Bomber Command. Over the next few years Javelins replaced the Vampires, and Hunters began to replace the Sabres. In 1958 the number of front-line squadrons was reduced to eighteen, with economic problems at home and the advent of the V-bomber nuclear deterrent. By the end of 1962, there were only twelve RAF squadrons in Germany. In 1965, Wessex helicopters replaced the Whirlwinds which had arrived two years earlier, while Lightnings equipped two squadrons as replacements for the Javelins. Phantoms began to take over reconnaissance duties from Canberras in 1970, and the Harriers and Buccaneers first arrived in that year, replacing Hunters. By 1972, there were four squadrons of Phantoms, three of Harriers, two of Buccaneers, two of Lightnings and one of Wessex helicopters. Jaguars began to replace the Phantom squadrons in 1975, and in turn the Phantoms were sent to the Lightning squadrons.

Above: *A poster inviting donations for the RAF Benevolent Fund, the best known of all the RAF charities, sponsored by Rolls Royce.*
Source: Vintage Magazine Co. colour slide

Right: *The Vickers Valiant was the RAF's first four-jet bomber and entered squadron service in April 1955. Its introduction gave rise to the V-bomber force, Britain's strategic nuclear deterrent. Valiants dropped bombs on Egypt during the Suez Crisis and also dropped Britain's atom and hydrogen bombs during nuclear trials in the Pacific. They continued as front-line aircraft for ten years and then some were adapted to the role of in-flight refuelling tankers. Valiants were withdrawn from service in May 1965. This photograph of serial WB215, the second prototype, was taken on 23 September 1953.*
Source: RAF Museum colour slide P100635

Left: *When the English Electric Canberra B.2 first entered service in May 1951, with 101 Squadron, it marked the beginning of jet bombers in the RAF. With its sleek lines and speeds in excess of 500 m.p.h., the aircraft proved one of the most durable and versatile bombers in aeronautical history. It flew on bombing attacks against terrorists in Malaya and against Egyptian aerodromes during the Suez crisis. Later variations of the Canberra were phased out as front-line bombers at the end of 1961, but until recently others were employed for photographic reconnaissance and jamming enemy radar. Some are still in service as trainers. Ironically, Canberras were employed by the Argentine Air Force in the Falklands War. This photograph, of two Canberras of 61 Squadron and one of 109 Squadron, was taken in July 1955.*
Source: RAF Museum colour slide P100257

Right: *The Handley Page Hastings became the standard long-range transport in the RAF after 47 Squadron was first equipped with the machine at Dishforth in Yorkshire in September 1948. It operated throughout the Berlin airlift, and continued in first-line service until 1967. This photograph, of the prototype Hastings C.1, was taken on 23 May 1946.*

Source: RAF Museum colour slide P100326

Right: *The de Havilland Venom, designed as a successor to the Vampire, first entered RAF service in August 1952 as a fighter bomber. The engine gave a far greater thrust, while long-range tanks were fitted to the wingtips. The aircraft proved to have a good rate of climb and be very manoeuvrable at high altitudes. This photograph shows the two-seat night-fighter version, serial WL830 of 23 Squadron, which was equipped with NF.2s from November 1953 to March 1956 while stationed at Coltishall in Norfolk.*

Source: RAF Museum P019078

Below: *The Avro York flew in Transport Command, most of the handful built during the Second World War serving as VIP aircraft. It was a development of the Avro Lancaster, but the fuselage was deeper and wider to give double the cubic capacity. After the war, large-scale production resulted in Yorks being delivered to six RAF squadrons. They came into prominence during the Berlin airlift, from 1 July 1948 to 12 May 1949, when they made 29,000 flights to the beleaguered city. It was a slow aircraft, but regarded as docile and reliable. The last York was withdrawn from service in 1957. This photograph, of a York of 511 Squadron, serial MW102, was taken at Northolt.*

Source: Keystone Collection

Opposite: *The Avro Vulcan B.1, serial VX777, was the second prototype and made its maiden flight on 3 September 1953. The Vulcan was the first large bomber in the world with the delta-wing. It entered service in Bomber Command in July 1956 as part of the 'V' Class of long-range bombers. Range was extended in 1959 by in-flight refuelling from Valiant tanker aircraft.*

Source: Aviation Bookshop

Below: *The Avro Vulcan, the first large strike aircraft in the world designed with the delta wing, or V-bomber, entered service with the RAF's Bomber Command squadrons in July 1957. The B.1 version could carry a bomb load of 21,000 lb and proved easy to handle and maintain. The B.2 version followed in 1960, as shown in this photograph. This was larger, more powerful and capable of flying for about 4,600 miles without refuelling. Vulcans remained in service until the end of 1982.*

Source: RAF Museum PO21342

Above: *The prototype Vulcan B.1, serial VX770, photographed in September 1952.*

Source: RAF Museum P100457

Left: *The Handley Page Victor B.1 followed the Vickers Valiant and the Avro Vulcan as the last of the trio of V-bombers. This graceful four-jet aircraft first entered squadron service in April 1958 and continued until 1964 when the B.2 began to replace the earlier version. The Victor B.2 carried the Blue Steel air-to-surface nuclear missile, which had a range of 200 miles. Victors were phased out of the bomber role in 1968 but continued as in-flight refuelling tankers. This photograph of a Victor B.1, serial ZA918, was taken in January 1957.*

Source: RAF Museum P100354

Left: The Times *marked the air display of 7-13 September 1953 at Farnborough with a special 'Survey of British Aviation'. Their poster showed the prototype Avro Vulcan bomber, serial VX770.*

Source: RAF Museum P100163

Below: *The larger missile in this photograph, taken at Farnborough, was the air-to-surface Blue Steel, manufactured by Hawker Siddeley Dynamics. Carrying a thermo-nuclear warhead for a range of about 200 miles, it became the main strategic weapon of Britain's V-bombers from February 1963. It continued until 1970. The smaller missile was the air-to-air Firestreak of British Aerospace Dynamics, which first came into service with Fighter Command in 1958. It had a high-explosive warhead and a range of about five miles.*

Source: RAF Museum P36046

Right: *The first Handley Page Victor B.1 with under-wing fuel tanks and facilities for in-flight refuelling was serial XA930.*

Source: RAF Museum P100359

Right: *The Beagle Basset C.C.1 was a communications aircraft, adapted from the executive jet Beagle B.206 and first supplied to the RAF in 1965 for the transport of V-bomber crews. The twenty which were supplied suffered from some technical problems and the last was withdrawn in May 1974.*
Source: RAF Museum PO21677

Below: *The Douglas Thor was a surface-to-surface missile with a nuclear warhead and a range of 1,725 miles. The length was 65 feet and the speed at burn-out was up to Mach 15. It entered RAF service in August 1958 and eventually twenty squadrons of Bomber Command were each equipped with three of these missiles. They were withdrawn in 1963.*
Source: RAF Museum PO15249

Right: *The Supermarine Spitfire F.21 was one of the later versions powered by the Rolls Royce Griffon instead of the Merlin, entering service in January 1945. This photograph shows a Spitfire F.21 of 602 (City of Glasgow) Squadron, squadron letters RAI, which was equipped with these fighters from April 1947 to May 1951.*

Source: RAF Museum P7202

Below: *The North American Sabre was supplied to the RAF from the beginning of 1953 as a stop-gap before the arrival of swept-wing fighters manufactured in Britain. Squadrons in Germany and in the UK were equipped with Sabres, which gave good service until superseded by Hawker Hunters by the summer of 1956. This photograph is of Sabre serial XD727 of 92 Squadron, based at Linton-on-Ouse in Yorkshire.*

Source: Aeroplane Monthly

Above: *The* Evening News *marked the air display of 7-13 September 1953 at Farnborough with a series which included combat stories from Battle of Britain pilots. Their poster showed a Hurricane I of 87 Squadron.*

Source: *RAF Museum PIC75/15/14*

Left: *The Bloodhound surface-to-air missile was first deployed in 1958 to protect V-bomber and Thor surface-to-surface missile bases. It was fitted with a proximity-fuse nuclear warhead and was directed to the target by radar. Fifteen Air Defence Missile Squadrons of Fighter Command were equipped with the Bloodhound Mark 1, in groups of sixteen. The Bloodhound Mark 2 was introduced in 1964, using continuous-wave radar instead of pulse radar, and is still part of Strike Command's defence system. This photograph shows Bloodhound Mark 2s of B Flight, 25 Squadron.*

Source: T. Malcolm English

Above: *The Hawker Hunter F.6 entered service in October 1956 and became the RAF's standard single-seat interceptor, capable of Mach 0.95 at 36,000 feet. It was beloved by pilots for its superb handling capabilities as well as its elegant appearance. The formation flying and aerobatics of 111 Squadron's Black Arrows and 92 Squadron's Blue Diamonds were regarded as breathtaking by spectators. The Hunter F.6 was phased out at the end of 1962.*

Source: RAF Museum colour slide P36033

Right: *An unfortunate pilot in a state of indecision as to which handle to pull to operate his ejector seat, shown on a crewroom poster in 1967.*

Source: RAF Museum (Crown copyright) P00409

Left: *The Supermarine Swift F.1 was the RAF's first swept-wing fighter to enter frontline squadron service, in February 1953. It was built in case the Hawker Hunter proved unsatisfactory but in fact it was the Swift which was outclassed. On 25 September 1953, however, the prototype Swift F.4 established a World Air Speed Record by flying to North Africa at 737 m.p.h., photographed here at Idris in Libya.*

Source: RAF Museum P3510

Above: *Some Supermarine Swift F.1s were employed in the fighter-reconnaissance role, and proved satisfactory at low-level tactical work. This photograph of Swift F.R.5, serial XD922, of 2 Squadron, was taken at Geilenkirchen in West Germany. Swift F.R.5s remained in service until March 1961.*

Source: RAF Museum P10086

Right: *The Hawker Hunter F.G.A.9 was a development of the F.6, fitted with extra drop-tanks and weapon points beneath the wings for the ground attack role. It entered squadron service in September 1961 and continued until December 1971, although some continued as trainers until June 1976. This photograph is of an F.G.A.9 of 79 Squadron.*

Source: RAF Museum P3475

Left and below: *The Gloster Javelin was the first delta-winged twin-jet fighter as well as the largest fighter employed in the RAF. It was introduced to the RAF in February 1956, as a high performance aircraft capable of flying at great altitude. Extra radar made it highly suitable for night fighter interception. However, the machine had its faults, one of which was poor recovery from stalls, which was probably responsible for several accidents. There were nine marks, and the aircraft continued in service until April 1968. In these photographs, WT827 was the third prototype which first flew on 7 March 1953, while XH966 was Javelin FAW 8 which first flew on 9 May 1958.*

Source: Aviation Bookshop

Right: *When the British Aircraft Corporation Lightning was delivered to the RAF in December 1959, it marked the beginning of single-seat fighters which exceeded the speed of sound in level flight. The Lightning could reach Mach 2, whereas the machine it began to replace, the Hawker Hunter, reached Mach 0.95. It also contained sophisticated guidance systems, and at the time was regarded by the RAF pilots as the finest interceptor in the world. This photograph, of a Lightning F.6 of 5 Squadron, shows the machine about to land and carrying the Red Top air-to-air missiles, which have a speed of Mach 3, and a range of seven miles.*

Source: RAF Museum colour slide PO18668

Left: A Red Top air-to-air missile being fitted to a Lightning F.6 of 5 Squadron.

Source: T. Malcolm English

Right: *The McDonnell Douglas Phantom F.G.1 entered service with 43 Squadron in February 1969 as an interceptor. The F.G.R.2 followed in May 1969 in the reconnaissance and ground attack role, and eventually fourteen RAF squadrons were equipped with this version. Although it is heavier and less manoeuvrable than most aircraft in the same role, it is considered easy to fly and can carry up to eight tons of weaponry. It is also equipped with excellent radar systems. This photograph, of an F.G.R.2 serial XV407 of 41 Squadron, shows the aircraft fitted with four Raytheon Sparrow air-to-air missiles; these have a range of twenty miles and reach the speed of Mach Four. It is also carrying four BL755 cluster bombs, each of 600 lb and carrying 147 small bomblets. The squadron badge on the tail is a 'double armed cross'.*

Source: RAF Museum colour slide PO12638

Left: *The Hawker Siddeley Buccaneer I first entered service with the Fleet Air Arm as a strike aircraft designed to fly at less than 200 feet, beneath radar screens. When aircraft carriers were phased out in 1968, however, existing contracts for Fleet Air Arm Buccaneers were added to those intended for the RAF. The first aircraft began to arrive in the RAF in October 1969 and replaced Canberras as low-level strike aircraft with advanced instrumentation and guidance systems, capable of flying close to Mach 0.85 while retaining excellent manoeuvrability. This photograph of Buccaneer XK490, Fleet Air Arm, was taken in September 1959.*
Source: RAF Museum colour slide P100414

Right: *The first aircraft capable of vertical take-off and landing in the RAF, or any of the world's air forces, was the British Aerospace Harrier G.R.1, originally manufactured by Hawker Siddeley. It was delivered to 1 Squadron in July 1969. Although sub-sonic, the Harrier has proved one of the most remarkable and successful ground-attack aircraft. The Harrier G.R.3, with a more powerful engine, a lengthened nose and more advanced systems for naviation and ground attack, updated the G.R.1. This photograph shows Harrier G.R.1s, serials WV746 and WV753, of 1 Squadron.*
Source: RAF Museum colour slide PO18654

Left: *A Hawker Siddeley Harrier G.R.3 of 4 Squadron.*
Source: T. Malcolm English

CHAPTER 14

MARITIME AND TRANSPORT

y the end of 1946, Coastal Command had been whittled down to a front-line strength of no more than fifty aircraft within eight squadrons, together with a meteorological squadron and two long-distance photographic reconnaissance squadrons. The command was divided into 18 Group with headquarters in Scotland and 19 Group with headquarters in Devon, together with RAF Northern Ireland and the Central Photographic Establishment at Benson in Oxfordshire. Of its commitments, meteorological reconnaissance over the Atlantic was considered of major importance for weather forecasting; this task was carried out by Halifaxes until Hastings arrived in 1950. The photographic squadrons, equipped with Spitfires, Mosquitos and Lancasters, were frequently engaged on air survey work. The anti-submarine squadrons, numbering six, were equipped with Sunderlands and Lancasters, armed for the most part with the equipment of the Second World War. This was in a period when it was known that the Soviet Union was already engaged on a massive expansion of her submarine fleet and surface warships.

Coastal Command was allowed to expand after the Cold War began in 1948. The first Avro Shackletons arrived in 1951, giving the anti-submarine squadrons a much longer range. Production of these was inadequate, however, and Lockheed Neptunes were imported as stopgaps. Three years later, Coastal Command consisted of thirteen squadrons, equipped with Shackletons, Neptunes and Sunderlands. An important development was the introduction of the Mark 30 homing torpedo. These were used in conjunction with sonobuoys, which detected underwater noises and transmitted their direction by radio. When two or more sonobuoys were dropped in the vicinity of a submarine, the aircrew could work out an accurate position and the homing torpedoes gave them an excellent chance of a 'kill'. Armed with this strike capability, Coastal Command operated in conjunction with NATO. In 1955, Whirlwind helicopters arrived for search and rescue operations, beginning a new phase of this highly-regarded RAF activity around the coasts and in the mountain areas of the U.K.

The contraction of the RAF in the second half of the 1950s affected Coastal Command somewhat less than the other commands, since the expansion of the Russian Navy was continuing at such a pace. However, the Neptune and Sunderland squadrons were disbanded in 1956 and 1957. More problems arose with the advent of Soviet nuclear submarines in the early 1960s, since these were capable of much higher speeds and were also able to travel underwater at greater depths for many days. Improved radar and navigational equipment was installed in the Shackletons, while some squadrons were transferred to more northerly airfields, in order to detect Soviet submarines and surface vessels moving into the North Atlantic.

A replacement for the Shackleton was found with the introduction in late 1970 of the Hawker Siddeley Nimrod, an adaption of the de Havilland Comet airliner. With the arrival of this aircraft, the front-line squadrons were reduced to only four, together with two helicopter squadrons equipped with Whirlwinds. However, in October 1969, a Buccaneer squadron of the RAF's new Strike Command was converted to the maritime strike role. A month later, Coastal Command itself was absorbed into Strike Command, becoming 18 Group with headquarters at Northwood in Greater London.

Transport Command had experienced an enormous increase during the last years of the Second World War, growing to a force of 1,200 aircraft in 1945, little more than two years after its formation in March 1943. It was poised for further work in carrying troops to the Far East when the atom bombs dropped on Japan put an end to the war. The main task then was the repatriation of prisoners of war and the return to the U.K. of servicemen for demobilisation. Thereafter, Transport Command maintained a regular but small air service with British bases overseas; in this period, sea transport was the more normal method employed by the armed forces. As with all other RAF commands, Transport Command also faced the problem of insufficient trained aircrews and ground personnel as well as the lack of new aircraft.

The Dakotas, which had formed the mainstay of Transport Command during the war, had been supplied under Lend-Lease and were due for return to the U.S.A. As a temporary measure, Britain purchased some of these and renewed the leases of others. In addition, Avro Yorks were produced in greater numbers, a few having been used primarily for V.I.P. work in the final years of the war. Other than these, Transport Command relied on a mixture of converted heavy bombers which were not ideal for its tasks.

In Germany, much of the work of Transport Command was taken over by British European Airways, although Dakotas continued to supply freight and to carry

Below: *The Bristol Brigand was intended as a successor to the Bristol Beaufighter T.F.X. torpedo-bomber of Coastal Command. The prototype, serial MX988, first flew on 4 December 1944, but production aircraft were too late to serve in the Second World War.*
Source: RAF Museum P5273

passengers to the occupying British forces. Other Dakotas served on routes to Austria, the Balkans and Malta. The Yorks were employed on long-distance routes to the Far East, via the Middle East and India or Ceylon. In the absence of full radar coverage as aids for navigation, some stretches of these routes could be difficult in poor weather.

Some training with airborne forces were also carried out, but these were severely limited as a result of defence cuts. When the Cold War began, with the airlift to Berlin from June 1948, the whole of Transport Command's resources were transferred to Europe for over a year and the overseas routes were temporarily abandoned. Even when they were resumed, the command was whittled down drastically while available finance went into expansion of the other commands. By 1951, only fifty aircraft remained, mainly Yorks, Hastings and the new Vickers Valettas.

When the Korean War broke out in June 1950, Transport Command's tasks were increased with the need to extend the Far East route to Japan from Singapore, in order to carry the British troops who served in this theatre. At the same time, political troubles in the Middle East placed extra burdens on the command in transporting troops and supplies. Training with paratroops also increased, as did 'mercy missions' such as carrying relief supplies to Greece after a volcano erupted.

Somewhat paradoxically, it was the withdrawal of British forces around the world which determined an expansion of Transport Command, for it became necessary to carry a small but highly mobile force at speed to trouble spots in the Commonwealth when the need arose. Moreover, it was realized somewhat belatedly that it was more economical to transport troops by air than on lengthy sea journeys. The need to expand the command also coincided with the completion of re-equipment in other commands, releasing finance for the creation of a modern fleet of strategic and tactical air transports. This began in early 1956 with the arrival of de Havilland Comets for long-range work and Blackburn Beverleys for shorter ranges. Three years later, Bristol Britannias entered service, giving Transport Command the impressive total of ten Comets and twenty-three Britannias as a strategic force, within four squadrons. These were kept fully employed, not only on the regular routes but also on carrying troops to such trouble spots as Cyprus, the Middle East and Borneo. In 1966, ten Shorts Belfasts arrived to give the command the benefit of a long-range strategic freighter, and in the following year fourteen Vickers VC10s provided another addition to the long-range passenger and freight service.

Below: *The Avro Shackleton was designed to replace Avro Lancasters, Consolidated Liberators and Boeing Fortresses in the anti-submarine role, but entered RAF service in April 1951 as a long-range maritime reconnaissance aircraft. Eleven Coastal Command squadrons were equipped with this reliable machine, as well as three maritime squadrons serving overseas. The marine reconnaissance version continued until 1972 but an 'airborne early warning' Shackleton was developed in 1971 and 8 Squadron will remain equipped with these machines until the arrival of the Boeing E-3 Sentry. This photograph of Avro Shackleton M.R.1 serial VW135, one of the prototypes, was taken on 18 April 1950.*

Source: RAF Museum colour slide P100447

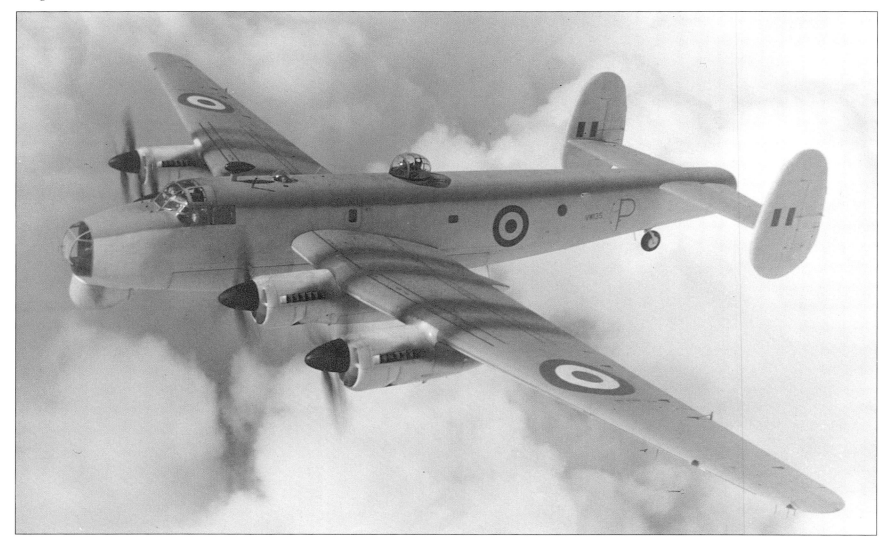

By the middle of the 1960s there were five squadrons in the shorter-range tactical force, equipped with Beverleys, Hastings and the new Armstrong Whitworth Argosy. For short-range work in the 1960s, there were five helicopter squadrons, equipped with Scottish Aviation Pioneers and Sycamore and Whirlwind helicopters. Westland Wessex helicopters arrived in 1964. These performed army co-operation duties in the U.K. but were sometimes detached for duties in Germany and Borneo. The tactical squadrons trained in paratroop work and in the air lifting of heavy equipment for the army, as part of a NATO force. Two squadrons of Hunters were transferred from Fighter Command, to give striking power to the tactical group.

In August 1967, Transport Command was renamed Air Support Command. In this new role, which included a more aggressive element, it was augmented in 1969 by a squadron of Harriers and two squadrons of Phantoms. Another Phantom squadron was added in 1972. Meanwhile, the shorter-range tactical squadrons were re-equipped with the arrival of Hawker Siddeley Andovers in 1966 and the very important introduction of Lockheed C-130 Hercules transports a year later. These gradually replaced the remaining Argosies, Hastings and Beverleys. Two Westland Puma helicopter squadrons were added in 1971, while the Whirlwinds were withdrawn.

In September 1972, Air Support Command was absorbed by Strike Command. Three years later, the two support groups within this overall structure reached a peak of twenty-one squadrons with 227 aircraft, including sixty aircraft in the offensive role and fifty-two helicopters. By this time, the RAF's need for scheduled services to small garrisons in the world had diminished, while its participation in NATO was increasing. Troops were flown on a regular basis to and from Germany, as well as Gibraltar and Cyprus. Training exercises involved the air transport of large contingents of paratroops to Denmark, Germany and Turkey.

In 1976, the transport support groups were assigned to NATO, serving its Allied Command Europe Mobile Force as well as the home-based United Kingdom Mobile Force. At the same time, there was an increased need to transport troops and military supplies to Northern Ireland. Many of the long-distance strategic squadrons were wound down and disbanded, beginning with the Comet and Britannia squadrons in 1975 and the Belfast squadron in the following year. The Hunters and some of the Hercules also disappeared, while a Puma squadron was transferred and the two air support groups in Strike Command were combined into one. Following other reductions, the number of aircraft in the transport element fell to 145 in that year.

Above: *The Hawker Siddeley Nimrod, a maritime reconnaissance aircraft derived from the famous Comet airliner, entered service with maritime squadrons of Strike Command from October 1970, replacing Avro Shackletons. Equipped with Sidewinder missiles, they took part in the Falklands War, but their primary role remains anti-submarine with Harpoon air-to-surface missiles and sophisticated radar equipment. The early-warning development of the Nimrod was cancelled in December 1986, but the reliable maritime version remains in service. This photograph of a Nimrod M.R.2, serial XV250, of 42 Squadron, was taken in September 1986.*
Source: RAF Museum colour slide PO51748

Above: *The flight deck of a Hawker Siddeley Nimrod.*
Source: T. Malcolm English

Above: *The first production Bristol Brigand T.F.1 was serial RH742, as shown in this photograph. The machine was armed with a Mark XVII torpedo and eight rockets with 25 lb solid-shot warheads. However, the Brigand did not serve in the role of a torpedo-bomber, partly because it was realized that this form of attack against surface vessels armed with radar-controlled anti-aircraft guns had become suicidal. Instead, the Brigand entered RAF service in early 1949 as the last piston-engined light bomber in the RAF. From early 1950 to late 1952, Brigands of 45 and 84 Squadrons flew operationally with bombs and rockets against terrorists in the Malayan jungle.*

Source: BAC via Roger Hayward

Right: *From January 1952 onwards, Lockheed Neptune M.R.1s were delivered to four Coastal Command squadrons, as a stop-gap until Avro Shackletons arrived. The aircraft was armed with two .50 inch machine guns in a mid-upper turret, with twin 20 mm cannons in a nose and a tail turret, and it could also carry rockets and bombs. Four Neptunes were converted to operate as early warning aircraft. All these maritime reconnaissance aircraft were phased out by March 1957.*

Source: Aeroplane Monthly

Above: *The RAF's premier operational aerodrome off the north Cornish coast is St. Mawgan, photographed here in 1960. Established in 1943 and used principally by ferrying aircraft, it fell into disuse in 1946 but was reopened in 1951. Nowadays, it is the home of 42 Squadron and 236 Operational Conversion Unit, both equipped with Hawker Siddeley Nimrods.*

Source: *RAF Museum PO17587*

Right: *The Vickers Valetta C.1, a military version of the Viking airliner, entered RAF squadron service in May 1949, being employed as a troop or freight carrier and for casevac operations. Valettas were active in Malaya during the anti-terriorist war, mainly dropping supplies to troops. A later Valetta version, the T.3, was used for navigation training. Valettas continued in service until April 1966. This photograph of serial VL263, the second Valetta C.1 to enter RAF service, was taken over Southampton docks on 2 February 1949.*

Source: *RAF Museum P100628*

Above: *The de Havilland Comet Series 2 was the RAF's military version of BOAC's turbojet airliner. First delivered to Transport Command in July 1956, Comets brought Australia within thirty hours flying time of the U.K. All were given the names of star constellations, the Comet 2 in this photograph being serial XK695 'Pegasus' of 216 Squadron. The stretched version, Comet Series 4, was delivered to the Transport Command from February 1962. Comet 2s were withdrawn in April 1967 and Comet 4s in June 1975.*

Source: RAF Museum colour slide P100421

Below: *The Blackburn Beverley was the first RAF transport aircraft designed to off-load equipment through "clam shell" rear-loading doors. It was also the largest aircraft to enter service with the RAF when first delivered to 47 Squadron at Abingdon in March 1956. As a medium-range aircraft capable of carrying very large loads, it continued in service with Transport Command until 1968. This photograph, of Beverley C.1 serial XB283 of 47 Squadron, was taken in November 1956.*

Source: RAF Museum colour slide P100238

Above: *The first turboprop transport aircraft introduced into the RAF was the military version of the Bristol Britannia airliner, which arrived at 99 Squadron in June 1959. Twenty-three Britannias in all were delivered, and all were given the names of stars. This Britannia, XL639 Atria, saw service with both 99 and 511 Squadrons, the two Transport Command (later Air Support Command) squadrons equipped with the machine until January 1976.*
Source: RAF Museum colour slide PO18660

Left: *The Short Belfast, first delivered to 53 Squadron of the RAF's Transport Command in January 1966, was designed specifically as a strategic freighter, the payload being 22,000 lb over a range of 3,600 miles. They were withdrawn from service at the end of 1976. The ten which served in the RAF were given names from the Bible or from Greek and Roman mythology. The Belfast Mark I in this photograph was serial XR368 'Theseus'.*
Source: RAF Musuem colour slide PO18672

Above: *The British Aerospace VC10, a military version of a civil airliner, began to enter service with the RAF's Transport Command in 1966. It proved capable of carrying 150 troops and their kit for nearly 3,700 miles. All the VC10s in the RAF were named after holders of the Victoria Cross; the aircraft in this photograph, serial XR806, was named after Flight Sergeant George Thompson, a wireless operator in a Lancaster of 9 Squadron, who was awarded a posthumous Victoria Cross after a raid over Germany on 1 January 1945. The VC10 remains in service with 10 Squadron, based at Brize Norton in Oxfordshire.*

Source: RAF Museum PO22051

Below: *The Andover C.1, a military version of the turboprop Avro 748 civil transport, first entered service in December 1965 with 46 Squadron at Abingdon in Berkshire. Andovers served as multi-purpose transports with four RAF squadrons. They are still in service with 115 Squadron at Benson in Oxfordshire, engaged on radar calibration. This photograph, of Andover C.1, serial XS596, of 115 Squadron, was taken at Alconbury in Huntingdonshire in August 1982.*

Source: RAF Museum PO18081

Above: *The Scottish Aviation Twin Pioneer C.C.1 was the military version of the civil transport and entered RAF service in 1958. Like its predecessor, the single-engined Pioneer, it was capable of short take-off and landing. Six squadrons were equipped with the machine, which was nicknamed 'The Twin Pin'. The last Twin Pioneers continued in squadron service until December 1968. This photograph, of serial XM286, was taken on 22 July 1958.*

Source: RAF Museum P100534

Left: *The Lockheed Hercules C.1 is the RAF's equivalent of the USAF's C-130E turbo-prop transport. With the shrinking of Britain's overseas territories, it became necessary to acquire a long-range aircraft to transport troops and supplies over great distances, and the Hercules supplied this need, first entering RAF squadron service in August 1967. It is able to carry almost 100 passengers and their kit over a range of nearly 5,000 miles, and at the same time is easy to handle and service. Sixteen modified aircraft, known as Hercules C.1Ks, entered service as flight refuellers from May 1982, during the Falklands War. In addition, twenty-six Hercules were 'stretched' from 1980 onwards, designated Hercules C.3s.*

Source: RAF Museum PO15217

CHAPTER 15

ON WORLD SERVICE

T he commitments of the RAF in the Far East did not end after Japan surrendered on 14 August 1945. The existence of the atom bombs had been such a well-kept secret that South East Asia Command was prepared for the war continuing for at least another year. One immediate task of the RAF was to help in the repatriation of thousands of debilitated Allied prisoners of war and internees, and this was completed by the following December. At the end of the war, the RAF component of SEAC numbered seventy-three squadrons, but of course many of the wartime entrants among the servicemen were either due for demobilisation or their release dates were coming up. The area allocated to it included Siam, Malaya, French Indo-China south of the 16th parallel, Borneo, Java, Sumatra, Hong Kong, the Dutch East Indies and the Celebes, in addition to the old area of India, Burma and Ceylon. Some of these areas were expected to resist the reimposition of colonial rule, and the RAF was faced with some difficult and delicate tasks at the same time as it was being run down.

Small RAF contingents were sent to Siam but soon withdrawn when the government resumed control. Similarly, two squadrons sent to Indo-China were withdrawn when the French Air Force took over in January 1946. In Java, however, a British division was involved in fighting with extremists, supported by RAF Spitfires, Mosquitos, Thunderbolts and Dakotas. These operations continued until November 1946, when the Dutch resumed responsibility for their colonial possessions until these achieved independence. The RAF's Air Command Far East was created in the same month.

In India, the remaining RAF squadrons were withdrawn soon after the country was partioned and gained its independence in August 1947, both India and Pakistan remaining in the Commonwealth. In Burma, the Dakota squadrons were progressively reduced and the remainder finally withdrawn when the country gained independence and left the Commonwealth in January 1948. In Ceylon, the RAF was able to retain a staging post after the country became independent within the Commonwealth in February 1948.

In Malaya, there was an emergency which began in 1948 and lasted for several years. In China, an RAF Sunderland was involved in the 'Yangste incident'. The frigate HMS *Amethyst* was damaged by Chinese gunfire on the river in April 1949 and, before the warship made its escape, the flying boat made several attempts to transfer medical supplies and a doctor. Following this, three RAF Sunderland squadrons as well as two Auster flights operated in the Korean War, which lasted from June 1950 to July 1953. The Sunderlands helped in the blockade of the Korean coastline, while the Austers were used in army co-operation.

The RAF contribution to the anti-guerrilla war in the Malayan jungle began with detailed reconnaissance of much of the country by Mosquitos and Spitfires, enabling maps to be constructed. Transport was provided by Dakotas, while Beaufighters, Tempests and Harvards strafed terrorist camps and Lincolns made bombing attacks. Meteors, Hornets and Valettas also arrived, and Sunderlands maintained coastal patrols. Dragonfly, Sycamore and Whirlwind helicopters proved their worth, as did the

Scottish Aviation Pioneer in liaison work, while Austers marked targets and carried out reconnaissance. The terrorists began to surrender in 1956, but the emergency did not end until July 1960, almost a year after Malaya achieved independence within the Commonwealth.

Although some of the squadrons were then withdrawn or disbanded, many were retained under the South East Asia Treaty Organization, based in Malaya. When in December 1962 a new emergency arose in the Sultanate of Brunei and the colony of Sarawak in Borneo, these squadrons were well placed to deal with the jungle warfare, although the terrain was even more difficult and the climate far wetter and more humid. Using tactics similar to those learned in Malaya, the rebellions were suppressed. Then Britain came into conflict with Indonesian guerrillas who infiltrated across the borders of these countries and even made a few landings on the west coast of Malaya itself. These conflicts ended in August 1966, after modern aircraft such as Hunters and Belvedere helicopters had arrived in the area. By then, a rapid run down of FEAF was possible, and by October 1971 the last RAF squadron had left the Far East.

In the Mediterranean and Middle East, the RAF had been whittled down to fifteen squadrons by 1947, but still covered an area which included Malta, Cyprus, Palestine, Iraq, the canal zone of Egypt, Bahrain, Sharjah, Oman, Aden, Kenya and Somaliland. By 1949, the command was split in two, the Middle East Air Force and the air component of the British Forces Arabian Peninsula.

Below: *The de Havilland Hornet was designed as a successor to the Mosquito fighter, faster and with a longer range. Originally intended for the war in the Pacific, the first batch was slightly too late for the Second World War. However, Hornets flew operationally in rocket attacks against terrorists in the Malayan jungle during 1951. The last as well as the fastest piston-engined fighters in front-line service in the RAF, they were finally withdrawn in 1955. This Hornet, of 33 Squadron, was being serviced at Tengah in Singapore on 6 October 1951.*

Source: Keystone Collection

Once again, the RAF faced many problems as these countries progressed to independence, in an area which included vital air links as well as major oil fields. One of its first tasks immediately after the war was patrolling with Wellingtons, Warwicks and Spitfires, hunting ships bringing illegal immigrants into Palestine, while the RAF Regiment was involved with the internal security in that country. Some aircraft were destroyed in attacks on airfields. When the British forces pulled out of Palestine in May 1948, the general reconnaissance Lancasters were sent to Malta and the Spitfires to Cyprus.

Unrest in Kenya had been simmering for several years among the Kikuyu tribe, but it flared up into widespread violence in 1952 and by October a state of emergency was declared against the Mau Mau, as they called themselves. Army reinforcements were flown in by Hastings transports, while Harvards of the Rhodesian Air Training Group operated over the terrain, after being fitted with guns and bomb racks. Lincolns and Meteors were brought down from the Canal Zone. In 1955 many of the terrorists surrendered and the RAF was able to withdraw in June of that year.

Trouble arose in the Arabian Gulf during 1952, with an incursion by Saudi Arabians into an Omani village on the border with Abu Dhabi, threatening the important Buraimi Oasis. The RAF regiment, together with Vampires, Lancaster G.R.3s, Valettas and Ansons, blockaded the Saudi positions until they withdrew. However, the Saudis gave support to an 'Omani Liberation Army' formed in 1957 in the rocky interior of Oman, and the RAF gave support to the Sultan's forces and the British SAS by attacking these positions with bombing from Shackletons and rockets from Venoms. The conflict continued until ground forces overcame the rebels' positions in January 1959.

From 1952 onwards, the British withdrew from the Canal Zone, and by December 1954 the Middle East Air Force was established in Cyprus. On that island, however, Britain faced open hostility from April 1955 onwards, when elements of the Greek population began a guerrilla campaign with the objective of union with Greece. Shackletons from Malta were engaged on surveillance patrols to prevent smuggling of arms, while Sycamore helicopters worked with the army in trying to drive the terrorists from their mountain hideouts.

Above: *The first helicopter built in Britain to enter service with the RAF was the Westland Dragonfly, in 1950. It was, however, designed by Sikorsky in the U.S.A. In February 1953, Dragonflies were supplied to 194 Squadron at Sembawang in Malaya and employed on casevac and communications work in the jungle during anti-terrorist operations. 194 Squadron was the RAF's first to be equipped entirely with helicopters, and it continued to use Dragonflies until February 1956. This photograph, of Dragonfly serial WF321, was taken in February 1950.*

Source: RAF Museum P6121

Left: *The Scottish Aviation Pioneer C.C.1 was a high-wing monoplane with seating for the pilot and four passengers, first delivered to the RAF in August 1953. With a short take-off run of only seventy-five yards and even shorter landing run, it proved ideal for liaison work in rough or jungle territories. Forty Pioneers were delivered to seven RAF squadrons, based at home, in Libya, Aden, Cyprus, Malaya and Borneo. It was finally withdrawn in January 1970.*

Source: RAF Museum P9823

While these operations were continuing, the RAF participated in the Anglo-French venture code-named operation 'Musketeer', intended to prevent Egypt taking over control of the Suez Canal. Seven squadrons of Canberra bombers and two of Hunters flew from the U.K. to Cyprus, where three squadrons of Venoms were available, while four squadrons of Valiants and four of Canberras flew to Malta. From the end of October, numerous attacks were made against Egyptian airfields and many aircraft were destroyed on the ground. These were followed by attacks on tanks and communications, and on 4 November Valettas and Hastings dropped 600 paratroops near Port Said. The paratroops were reinforced by a seaborne landing, while Sycamores and Whirlwinds ferried Commandos ashore. A ceasefire was arranged for 6 November, and the last base of the troops was handed over to a United Nations force on 20 December.

In Iraq, unrest continued intermittently after the end of the Second World War and the remaining RAF squadrons were withdrawn to Cyprus from May 1955, closing down finally at Habbaniya in May 1959. In Jordan there was also hostility to the remaining British forces, and the RAF elements withdrew in May 1957. However, Jordan called for help in the following year, when stability was threatened following violence in neighbouring Lebanon. In July 1958 U.S. Marines landed in Lebanon, while Beverleys, Hastings and Valettas ferried British paratroops to Jordan, where they remained until the following month. Yet another problem arose in 1961 when Iraq threatened to annex Kuwait and the RAF flew Commandos to the State in July, discouraging these intentions. In Aden, violent unrest intensified in 1963. In January of the following year the rebels were attacked by Hunters and Shackletons, while Belvederes and Twin Pioneers supplied the ground troops. The rebellion continued until 1968, however, when Britain left Aden.

Air Forces Gulf was then based at Bahrain and a fairly quiet period followed while the Gulf States developed their own air forces, enabling the RAF to withdraw completely from the Gulf at the end of 1971. The last RAF units left Malta in 1979. The Near East Air Force was disbanded in 1976, leaving airfields in Cyprus under the RAF's Strike Command, which at present house a squadron of the RAF Regiment and a squadron of Wessex helicopters.

Right: *The Westland Wessex began service with the RAF in January 1964 as a troop carrier and for casevac operations, but from May 1976 also began search and rescue operations overland and in coastal waters. It is also employed in Northern Ireland on anti-terrorist work. This photograph shows Wessex H.C.2, serial XS675, of 22 Squadron at Finningley in Yorkshire in September 1986.*
Source: RAF Museum colour slide PO51770

Below: *The Westland Sea King H.A.R.3 helicopter was introduced into 202 Squadron in December 1977 for search and rescue operations. It has a longer range and a greater carrying capacity than the Westland Wessex, and many dramatic rescues have been achieved by the crews of this squadron, which is still equipped with the Sea Kings. In the Falklands, 86 Squadron has also been equipped with Sea Kings since April 1986.*
Source: RAF Museum colour slide PO51757

Below right: *Boeing Vertol Chinooks were introduced into 18 Squadron in August 1981, in response to the RAF's need for heavy-lift helicopters. Three squadrons and one flight are now equipped with these helicopters. Fitted with twin rotors, the Chinook is capable of lifting a huge payload of about 22,000 lb. This photograph of serial ZA707, 7 Squadron, was taken at Finningley in Yorkshire on 29 August 1986.*
Source: RAF Museum colour slide PO51803

Below: *The Westland Whirlwind H.A.R.4 was first delivered to the RAF in September 1954, a "tropicalised" version being employed in Malaya during the anti-terrorist campaign. The following February, H.A.R.2s were delivered to Coastal Command for search and rescue operations. These were followed in November 1961 by the H.A.R.10, fitted with a turbine engine instead of a piston engine; these also operated in Borneo, Cyprus and Germany. This photograph shows Whirlwind H.A.R.10, serial XP353, of 22 Squadron at Manston, which was equipped with these machines until November 1981.*

Source: RAF Museum PO13203

Left: *The first helicopter with twin engines and twin rotors to enter RAF service was the Westland Belvedere H.C.1, in September 1961. It was employed as a troop and freight carrier, and on casevac operations. Belvederes operated in Tanzania, in South Arabia and in Borneo, before being retired in 1969. This photograph, of Belvedere serial XG455 in service with 72 Squadron at Odiham in Hampshire, was taken in February 1967.*

Source: RAF Museum P2075

Left: *This Bristol Sycamore H.R.12, serial WV781, was first delivered to the RAF at St Mawgan in Cornwall on 19 February 1952, being the first British-designed helicopter to enter service in the RAF. At home, Sycamores were employed on search-and-rescue operations, but overseas they operated in Malaya, Borneo and Cyprus. They continued in RAF service until August 1972.*

Source: RAF Museum P8870

Right: *The Westland/Aérospatiale Puma was built both in France and in Britain for the RAF, first entering service in June 1971. Pumas are used for troop carrying, transport duties, casevac and as gunships, and have served in Germany, Northern Ireland and Cyprus, as well as in Rhodesia during the 1980 general election after the end of the guerilla war. They remain in service with two RAF squadrons. This photograph is of Puma serial XW220, 230 Squadron.*

Source: RAF Museum P721

Below: *The Hunting Percival Pembroke, derived from a civil feeder-liner, began to replace the venerable Avro Anson as a communications aircraft at the end of 1953. The capacious cabin included eight passenger seats, while reversible pitch airscrews shortened the landing run. Of the fifty-six ordered, six were modified for photo-reconnaissance with 81 Squadron in Malaya, arriving in January 1956. Pembrokes continued in RAF service until 1988.*

Source: RAF Museum PO19515

CHAPTER 16

THE FALKLANDS WAR

When the conflict with the Argentine began in April 1982, Britain's overseas commitments were largely concentrated in Europe, organized as part of NATO to meet any aggression from the Soviet Union. Indeed, it is probably true to say that the majority of British people were barely aware of the existence of the Falkland Islands and their dependency of South Georgia before they became headline news when seized by armed forces of the Argentine.

The decision to form a South Atlantic Task force with the objective of returning the islands to British rule, which the inhabitants had enjoyed for over 200 years, created unusual problems in logistics. The islands were about 8,000 miles from Britain, whereas the Argentine possessed three air bases (with runways of over 7,000 feet) within 600 miles of the combat area.

The first vessels of the Task Force left Portsmouth on 5 April, and the burden of recapturing the islands rested with the Royal Navy, the Royal Marines and the British Army, as well as the RAF. For air support, the Fleet Air Arm provided its Sea Harriers together with its helicopters, which included Sea Kings, Lynxes, Wasps and Wessexes. The Royal Marines Commando Brigade and the Army Air Corps provided Scout and Gazelle helicopters. The contribution of the RAF was numerically smaller but consisted of Vulcans, Nimrods, Hercules, VC10s, Victors, Harriers and Chinook helicopters. The RAF's Chief of Staff was Air Chief Marshal Sir Michael Beetham, who had taken over from Marshal of the Royal Air Force Sir Neil Cameron in March 1977. The ultimate success of the enterprise, which was named operation 'Corporate', depended on the skilful co-operation of all these branches of the armed services as well as the courage of those involved.

Fortunately, the RAF was able to use as a staging post the U.S. air base of Wideawake on the British colonial possession of Ascension Island. This island is situated about half-way to the Falklands, leaving a distance of about 3,900 miles to the targets. The tasks of the RAF included the establishment of an air bridge to Ascension Island and the protection of that tiny island from a possible landing by forces of the Argentine. Its other duties were the provision of anti-submarine and air cover for the Task Force, search and rescue operations, and the maintenance of a threat against airfields on the Argentine mainland in order to tie up enemy aircraft in defence. However, the only aircraft the RAF could use in close support of the navy and army during the reoccupation of the Falklands were its Harriers and helicopters, which could be accommodated in aircraft carriers or container ships. There was, moreover, a worrying defect with the lack of any 'Airborne Early Warning' aircraft such as the U.S. Boeing Sentry.

By comparison with the RAF, nevertheless, the equipment of the Argentine Air Force was not well-balanced, even though it was one of the most powerful in South America. There were only seven transport aircraft, C-130 Hercules, with two more in the tanker role. The long-range bomber fleet contained only six Canberra B.62s, with two Canberra trainers. The shorter-range bomber fleet consisted of about sixty Douglas A-4P Skyhawks, small but powerful single-engined jets which could be effective in anti-shipping strikes in spite of their age. There were about sixty IA.58 Pucarás, twin-

engined turboprop aircraft which were designed primarily for ground attack and were intended for counter-insurgency in their homeland. The jet fighter element, which could also carry out ground attack and anti-shipping operations, consisted of about twenty Dassault-Breguet Mirage IIIEAs, capable of flying at Mach 2, as well as twenty-six Daggers (the Israeli version of the Mirage 5). Among the helicopters, there were three Boeing-Vertol Chinooks, six Bell Hueys and three Aérospatiale Pumas.

The Argentine Navy also had an air arm, based partly on its aircraft carrier *Veinticinco de Mayo*. The aircraft carried included twelve Douglas A-4Q Skyhawks, six piston-engined Grumman S-2Es, several Sikorsky Sea King and three Puma helicopters, three Lockheed Neptunes for maritime reconnaissance, and ten Aermacchi MB.339s used as jet trainers or for attack. Perhaps most threatening of all, there were five Dassault-Breguet Super Etendard supersonic jets, armed with the deadly Exocet sea-skimming missiles. However, the aircraft carrier could not venture out of home waters, since the Royal Navy's nuclear-powered submarines would have soon made short work of it.

The Argentine Army possessed three Aeritalia G.222s, twin-engined turboprop transports which performed a similar role to that of the Hercules. Its helicopter force included two Boeing Vertol Chinooks, nine Agusta A.109s, seven Bell Jet Rangers, twenty Hueys and twelve Pumas.

Other than grass airstrips, there was only one airfield on the Falkland Islands, the

Below: *The aircraft carrier HMS* Hermes, *23,900 tons, approaching the Falkland Islands, with Harrier G.R.3s of 1 Squadron (RAF) and Sea Harrier F.R.S.1s of the Fleet Air Arm on her deck.*

Source: RAF Museum PO21362

4,200 ft strip at Port Stanley, built on rock with a tarmac surface. This could take the transports, the Pucarás and the Aermacchi MB.339s, but it was too short for the Mirages, Daggers, Super Etendards and Skyhawks, unless hydraulic arrester gears could be installed. The Argentine air forces thus faced their own problems in trying to establish superiority when the British attempted their landings.

The RAF had to overcome several difficulties in preparing its aircraft for sea transport. Its Harrier G.R.3 was fitted with the Ferranti FE541 inertial navigation system (in which instruments control the flight path by comparison with stored data), but this equipment was upset by the moving deck of a ship. Ferranti produced a inertial platform which enabled the equipment to be levelled and checked against true north before each Harrier took off, and this was installed on the aircraft carrier HMS *Hermes*. Also, special sealing used by Sea Harriers against salt water corrosion had to be applied to the Harrier G.R.3s.

On 3 May, ten RAF Harriers took off from St Mawgan in Cornwall for Ascension, refuelled en route by Victor K.2 tankers. One of these, probably a spare, turned back to St Mawgan, while another was diverted to West Africa. The other eight arrived safely. Six of these took off to land on the container ship *Atlantic Conveyor*. The other two RAF Harriers remained behind to defend Ascension, where they were joined by the diverted aircraft; these were eventually replaced by the RAF's Phantom F.G.Rs on 24 May. Five more RAF Harriers flew to Ascension at the end of May, and two of these eight Harriers reached HMS *Hermes* off the Falklands before the end of the conflict.

The RAF still possessed three squadrons of Vulcans, including S.R.2s (strategic reconnaissance), B.2s (bombers) and K.2s (tankers). These veteran aircraft were due for retirement, but a Vulcan bomber could still carry twenty-one 1,000 lb 'iron' bombs. Some of the B.2s were refitted with refuelling probes while one was fitted with extra fuel tanks in the bomb bay and equipped with Shrike anti-radar missiles. These B.2s already carried electronic counter-measures which could jam enemy radar. In addition, some of the RAF's Nimrods were fitted with Sidewinder missiles as well as Stingray or Harpoon torpedoes, while some Hercules were converted to the tanker role.

The RAF's operations began when eight Hercules flew to Ascension on 3 April, the day after the Argentine seized the Falklands and two days before the Task Force left Portsmouth. These were followed by streams of other aircraft, until Wideawake air base was dealing with as many as 400 aircraft movements a day, compared with the normal forty per month. Apart from the Hercules, which carried troops, equipment and helicopters, there were Nimrods, Vulcans, VC10s, Sea Kings, Harriers and Phantoms. In the midst of this congestion, priority was given to the RAF's Victor tankers, which played a vital part in enabling attacks to be carried out.

Below: *A British Aerospace Harrier G.R.3 of 1 Squadron landing on the deck of HMS* Hermes.

Source: RAF Museum PO21361

The Task Force arrived at Ascension and then sailed on 16 April for the Falklands, supported by air drops from RAF Hercules while FAA Sea Kings flew anti-submarine patrols from the vessels *Olmeda, Fort Grange* and *Fort Austin*. On the evening of 30 April, two Vulcan bombers left Ascension for an attack on Port Stanley airfield. The main purpose of this operation was to ensure that the Mirages, Daggers, Skyhawks and Super Etendards could not use the runway and would thus be forced to operate at the limits of their ranges from bases on the mainland. One Vulcan turned back with technical trouble but the other was refuelled en route by a series of Victor tankers. Before dawn on the next day it dropped its stick of twenty-one bombs at an angle of about thirty degrees over the runway at Port Stanley. One bomb hit the centre line of the runway, while others damaged parked aircraft and airport buildings. There seemed to be no defensive fire. The attack must have been a very unpleasant shock to the Argentinians, who had optimistically renamed the airfield 'Aeroporto Malvinas'. They were never able to land their fast jets there.

This high-level attack was followed up by a low-level strike at dawn by Sea Harriers of the Task Force, armed with 30 mm Aden cannons and 3,000 lb of bombs, escorted by other Harriers armed with Sidewinder missiles. These met intense ground fire but were not intercepted by enemy aircraft, and all returned safely. The airfield was then bombarded in the afternoon by warships of the Task Force. The Argentine Air Force was stung into action and sent over a number of Mirages. Britain's Harriers had never been involved in air-to-air combat, but on this occasion one of these subsonic aircraft (flown by an RAF pilot, one of seven seconded to the FAA's Sea Harrier force) brought down a supersonic Mirage with an AIM-9L air-to-air missile, while a second Sea Harrier probably destroyed another Mirage. A flight of Canberras then appeared near the Task Force, and one was shot down by a Sea Harrier before the remainder turned back. An Argentine patrol craft was sunk and another badly damaged during the next night by missiles fired by FAA Sea Kings and Lynxes. However, the destroyer HMS *Sheffield* was herself destroyed on the following afternoon by an Exocet missile fired by one of three Super Etendards, which attacked the Task Force from a range of over five miles.

On 4 May, another Vulcan raid was delivered on Stanley airfield, and a Sea Harrier was shot down by ground fire during an attack on Goose Green airfield. Two days later, two more Sea Harriers were lost, it is believed, in a collision in the fog which interrupted air operations for three weeks. On 12 May, several Skyhawks attempted to attack the Task Force; two were shot down and the remainder achieved nothing. Three days later, several Pucarás were destroyed on the ground by FAA Sea Kings, during a landing by SAS troops on Pebble Island, but a Sea King ditched as a result of a bird strike the following day, with the loss of twenty-one men. On 16 May, Sea Harriers destroyed the Argentine support vessel *Rio Carcarania*.

On 18 and 19 May, reinforcements of FAA Sea Harriers as well as the six RAF Harrier G.R.3s were transferred from *Atlantic Conveyor* to the two aircraft carriers HMS *Hermes* and HMS *Invincible*. On 20 May, the RAF Harriers flew from *Hermes* in a devastating attack against fuel dumps near Fox Bay. One of their number was lost the following day to a hand-held Blowpipe ground-to-air missile, during the landings of the ground forces at San Carlos Bay. Two Royal Marine Gazelles were also shot down on that day.

At this point, the Argentine air attacks intensified, the pilots exhibiting determination and courage. They came in low to keep below radar coverage but many were destroyed by Harriers or surface-to-air missiles. Some Aermacchi MB.339s managed to get through and sank the frigate HMS *Ardent* with bombs and rockets, but the British claimed the destruction of nine Mirages or Daggers, five Skyhawks and three Pucarás, without losing any aircraft. However, two Sea Harriers were lost in accidents within the next few days and a third was brought down by a Blowpipe missile. For the most part, the RAF's Harriers were engaged in close support of the advancing ground forces; they carried out this task very effectively, although two more were shot down by ground fire.

On 1 June, a Sea Harrier shot down an Argentine Hercules, probably one of several which were attempting to sink British supply vessels by pushing bombs out of their rear loading ramps. On 8 June, two Sea Harriers accounted for three of a formation of four Skyhawks which approached the Task Force. While these sorties were carried out, the Vulcan B.2 fitted with Shrike missiles operated from Ascension, refuelled by Victor tankers, and attacked enemy radar stations with some success. Other Victors and Nimrods provided photographic reconnaissance of enemy positions, and Nimrods also carried out search-and-rescue missions. The RAF's Hercules transports made parachute supply drops to the fighting troops in the battle zone, while a squadron of the RAF Regiment deployed its surface-to-air Rapier missiles around the beachhead at San Carlos and carried out numerous other tasks such as bomb disposal. On 9 June, an 800 ft airstrip was opened near this beachhead.

The container ship *Atlantic Conveyer* was hit by an Exocet missile. Although the vessel did not sink immediately, three RAF Chinook helicopters were destroyed in the explosion, leaving just one which carried out sterling work for the remainder of the campaign. A final Vulcan raid was made on 11 June. Three days later, the Argentine soldiers were seen to be waving white flags and the fierce campaign was over.

The Ministry of Defence listed the number of Argentine aircraft 'destroyed' or 'probably destroyed' as 117, including twenty-seven Mirages or Daggers, forty-five Skyhawks, twenty-one Pucarás, three Canberras, three MB.339s and one Hercules. The remainder were mostly helicopters. In addition, about thirty other Argentine aircraft were captured. The British lost ten Sea Harriers or RAF Harriers, of which five were in accidents, together with twenty-three helicopters, of which nineteen were in accidents or on board destroyed or damaged ships. No RAF pilots lost their lives. Without doubt, the FAA and the RAF played a major part in securing the British victory in the Falklands.

Above: *Lockheed Hercules C.1s of 30 Squadron, which were employed in the Falklands campaign on supply missions.*
Source: T. Malcolm English

Below: *Avro Vulcan K.2s of 50 Squadron, which operated with these aircraft in their tanker role during the Falklands campaign.*
Source: T. Malcolm English

Above: *British Aerospace Harrier G.R.3s of 1453 Flight at Stanley, formed from a detachment from 1 Squadron in August 1983. They were fitted with Sidewinder air-to-air missiles, with a range of eleven miles at a speed of Mach 3.*

Source: RAF Museum colour slide PO18407

Right: *An Avro Vulcan B.2, similar to those which carried out bombing attacks against Argentine positions at Port Stanley.*

Source: T. Malcolm English

Left: *The Westland/Aérospatiale Gazelle entered service with the RAF in October 1976 and has been employed mainly as a trainer helicopter, although a few serve as communications aircraft with 32 Squadron at Northolt. Most Gazelles were supplied to the Army Air Corps, the Fleet Air Arm, and the Royal Marines. This photograph shows a Gazelle A.H.1 of the Royal Marines in the Falklands during 1982, with a Westland Wessex in the background.*

Source: RAF Museum PO21370

Below: *On 12 October 1982, 1,050 members of the Falklands task force marched through the City of London in a victory parade. These Hawker Siddeley Nimrod M.R.1s, serials XV260, XV247 and XV230, took part in the flypast.*

Source: RAF Museum PO15210

Above: *A British Aerospace Harrier G.R.3 of 1 Squadron, armed with Sidewinder air-to-air missiles, hovering over Stanley aerodrome. Six Pucarás of the Argentine Air Force, all damaged, can be seen in the background.*
Source: RAF Museum PO15209

Left: *Boeing Vertol Chinook H.C.1, serial ZA713, of 18 Squadron, lifting the badly damaged FMA IA 58A Pucará, serial A509, from Stanley aerodrome.*
Source: RAF Museum PO15205

CHAPTER 17

TRAINING
AND SUPPORT

After the Second World War, the two train-ing commands, Flying and Technical, were reduced in size even more rapidly than Bomber, Fighter, Coastal and Transport Commands. Meanwhile, Maintenance Command was presented with the formidable task of salvaging immense stocks of equipment and thousands of aircraft which had suddenly become surplus when Japan was forced to surrender, and then disposing of these where possible to industry. Other aircraft, supplied on Lend-Lease, were returned to the U.S.A.

Most of the flying training during the war had taken place with Volunteer Reserve pupils under the Empire Air Training Scheme, which was rapidly wound down while the aircrew members were being steadily demobilised. The remaining provision for training either flying or ground crews was inadequate. Many officers with short-service commissions had served their time during the war and achieved senior ranks, but most of these could be offered regular commissions only at junior ranks. In any event, the RAF required a small but steady flow of younger entrants into the service.

The Royal Air Force College at Cranwell was reopened to provide basic flying training for suitable young men, as well as training entrants into the Administrative Branch and the RAF Regiment. Of course, one of the principal requirements was flying training in jets and very few wartime RAF pilots had experience in these machines of the future. The Gloster Meteor T.7 was introduced in 1948 and remained the only jet trainer for several years.

By 1950, the pattern of pilot training was established with Flying Training School (FTS), Advanced Flying School (AFS) and Operational Conversion Unit (OCU), with the Cranwell cadets joining at the AFS stage after about thirty months of training. Flying instructors were trained at the Central Flying School (CFS) and there was a Central Fighter Establishment (CFE) with flight or squadron commanders. There was also the Empire Air Navigation School and the Empire Test Pilots' School. In 1957 the training of aircrew on fast jets had become so advanced and costly that the Royal Auxiliary Air Force and the Royal Air Force Volunteer Reserve were closed down after a defence review with the object of limiting public expenditure.

As aircraft became more advanced, the RAF's maintenance units were faced with dealing with far more complex technical matters, and it became common for aircraft to be returned to manufacturers for repair. This led to the introduction of specialist working parties from civilian contractors on RAF stations, and a closer liaison grew up between manufacturers and the service. However, the RAF's maintenance units continue to carry out repairs and modifications, and are responsible for the storage of parts and reserves. In September 1973, Maintenance Command was combined with Training Command to form Support Command.

Recruitment into the RAF today is encouraged by sixty-three Careers Information Offices in the U.K. with headquarters at Stanmore in Middlesex. Publicity is provided by organising school and other visits to RAF stations, while recruitment is encouraged by the displays of the Red Arrows aerobatic team, the Falcons free-fall parachute team, the RAF Police Dog display team, the Queen's Colour Squadron of the RAF Regiment,

Left: *The Percival Prentice was introduced into Training Command in November 1947 as one of the successors to the de Havilland Tiger Moth biplane. Unlike its predecessor, the seats were side by side instead of in tandem. It continued as a basic trainer for pilots until 1953, and was also used as a radio trainer and for communications. This photograph of the prototype, serial TV163, was taken on 27 May 1946.*

Source: RAF Museum colour slide P100499

Below: *The Vickers Varsity was produced as a trainer of all RAF crew members, replacing the Wellington T.10 which was used during the war. It entered service in October 1951 and continued until May 1976. This photograph of the prototype Varsity, serial VX828, was taken on 10 September 1949.*

Source: RAF Museum colour slide P100640

and the RAF bands. There are 925 Air Training Corps Squadrons in the U.K., with a membership of about 39,000 cadets, and some thirty per cent of the RAF's entrants originate from that source. The recruitment organisation also arranges presentation teams for the RAF's Engineering, Medical and Nursing Services, which visit schools and universities.

It has always been expensive to train RAF aircrews, but a Harrier pilot now costs about £3 million and a helicopter pilot about £1.6 million. Students arrive in the RAF either from university or by direct entry. The University Air Squadrons (UASs) were threatened with disbandment in the 1960s but sixteen hung on until 1968 when the RAF introduced its university cadet scheme. Nowadays there are seventeen UASs, with the membership standing at about 900. Women have been admitted since 1985. In addition to attracting pilots, they cater for air navigators and the various ground specializations. The entrants are either cadets, bursars or volunteer reservists. Cadets are commissioned as acting pilot officers, while bursars are given the status of officer cadet. The reservists have no commitment to the RAF and are usually young people who simply want to fly but may later apply for a cadetship or a bursarship. The flying members usually spend up to a day each week in flying and one evening a week in ground studies, as well as four weeks a year of flying at an RAF station. The cadets sometimes spend these four weeks at an overseas base. This system is also beneficial to the RAF since it weeds out students who would be unlikely to achieve success in the advanced courses. About forty per cent of fast jet pilots in the RAF today began their service in a University Air Squadron.

The officer training course at RAF College Cranwell admits eight intakes a year. The entrants from university, civilian life, senior NCOs, and Commonwealth or foreign countries number about 1,200 a year, of both sexes. There is quite a tough initial training of eighteen weeks, designed to make each entrant develop his or her identity and qualities of leadership. From this, the entrants go on to basic flying training.

The basic flying training schools, including Cranwell, are being equipped with the new Shorts Tucano, a turboprop trainer which replaces the Jet Provost. Although slower than the aircraft it is replacing, it gives better value for money, since a top speed of about 310 m.p.h. is the maximum required during basic training while an altitude of no more than 20,000 feet is needed at this stage. The aircraft handles like a jet, however, and leads on to the Hawk T.1, the standard jet trainer at Advanced Flying School.

Pilots are 'streamed' according to aptitude. Group 1 includes those suitable for fast jet aircraft, while Group 2 includes multi-engined pilots and Group 3 those who become helicopter pilots. From FTS, the pilots move on to Advanced Flying School and then, if they are destined for fast jets, to a Tactical Weapons Unit (TTU). From there, the next move is to an Operational Conversion Unit, and at last to a squadron. For those pilots (and navigators) who are to join the Tornado G.R.1 squadrons, however, the move from FTS is to the Tri-National Tornado Training Establishment at Cottesmore in Rutland, which includes German and Italian pilots, and thence to the Tornado Weapons Conversion Unit at Honington, before joining a squadron.

The Central Flying School (CFS) trains experienced pilots, at three bases, in the procedures of teaching students how to fly. Graduates from the CFS move on to the other schools and become key members of the RAF's training system. The world-famous Red Arrows aerobatic team is based at CFS at Scampton in Lincolnshire.

All navigators are trained at the Air Navigation School at RAF Finningley, passing through basic navigation training and then moving on to the Tactical Air Navigation System (TANS), a digital computer which takes input from other equipment and displays the aircraft's position. The students practice in a radar navigation ground trainer before air training begins in the Hawker Siddeley Dominie. As with the pilots, the navigators are 'streamed', since they are required in a variety of aircraft such as Tornados, Buccaneers, Phantoms, Nimrods, Hercules, VC.10s and helicopters. Those who are destined for fast jets then train on Jet Provosts at Finningley, while those who are moving on to other groups go back to the Dominie for Advanced Navigation Training. Nowadays, navigators enjoy equal status with pilots on the RAF's ladder of promotion; they can become captains of aircraft and commanding officers of squadrons, stations and groups, although a navigator has yet to occupy the position of Chief of Air Staff. Air Electronics officers and Air Engineers are also trained on Dominies at Finningley.

Helicopter crewmen, including the winchmen, are trained on Gazelles and Wessexes at FTS at Shawbury in Shropshire, and on Chinooks and Pumas at Odiham in Hampshire. The Central Air Traffic Control School is also at Shawbury.

In 1940, the RAF established a Parachute Training School, at Manchester's Ringway airport under the joint direction of the RAF and the army. After various moves, the RAF's school arrived at Brize Norton in Oxfordshire during 1975 and remains at this base today. In 1982, it provided a valuable detachment to the Special Forces which supported the SAS in the Falklands. Training is provided by Hercules transports, which can carry up to ninety fully-laden paratroops of the airborne forces of the Army, Royal Marines or

Above: *The de Havilland Chipmunk was built as a tandem two-seat successor to the Tiger Moth biplane. It first flew in May 1946 and was adopted by the RAF in 1949. Easy to handle and with good aerobatic qualities, it provided* ab initio *training for many RAFVR, National Service and direct-entry pilots until finally withdrawn in 1973. This photograph shows the first production Chipmunk which entered service in the RAF, serial WB549.*

Source: RAF Museum P6589

Right: *The Handley Page Marathon T.11 was a navigation trainer adapted from the civil medium-range airliner, first delivered in December 1953 to the Air Navigation School at Hullavington in Wiltshire. It carried a crew of three and two pupil navigators. Twenty-eight Marathons served in the RAF, the last being retired in June 1958.*

Source: RAF Museum P820

the RAF regiment. Drops sometimes take place at night, from heights of up to 25,000 feet.

Ground subjects are taught at various stations, notably the Schools of Technical Training at Halton and Cosford, expected to combine at Cosford in the near future. Students from these schools can rise to high rank, and some enter the flying branches. In addition there is the Airman's Command School at RAF Hereford which began in September 1980 for potential sergeants and now runs two courses, one for senior and the other for junior NCOs. Over 3,000 students pass through the school each year, which gives three weeks of instruction to the senior students and two weeks to the junior students.

The RAF runs a small school at Mount Batten in Devonshire, which provides an aircrew survival course, a combat survival and rescue officers' course, a survival rescue course for instructors, and a non-temperate climate course which is held in Brunei. The students number about 2,000 a year. Most are from the aircrew branches but others are from the physical education and medical branches or from the RAF Regiment. Apart from this school, instructors from the RAF Regiment itself provide courses to RAF personnel of all grades, covering the subjects of ground operations, ground defence and combat.

Lastly, the RAF reserve forces provide important training facilities. In the mid 1970s, the value of the Royal Auxiliary Air Force and the Royal Air Force Volunteer Reserve was again recognised, so that nowadays there are sixteen R Aux AF and four RAFVR units. These forces carry out regular training exercises and are fully capable of backing up the RAF immediately in critical times. The R Aux AF maintains three maritime headquarters units, seven regiment squadrons, one movements squadron, one aeromedical evacuation squadron and four support forces, numbering over 2,000 men and women. The RAFVR consists of about 180 men and women, providing two intelligence flights, a photographic interpretation flight and a public relations flight. These groups of enthusiastic volunteers are both highly dedicated and cost-effective.

Left: *The second production Chipmunk, serial WB550, delivered to Oxford University Air Squadron at Kidlington, near Oxford, photographed on 29 September 1949. The type was designated T.10 and the total delivered to the RAF was 735, the last being XZ884 on 1 October 1953.*

Source: RAF Museum colour slide P100141

Below: *The Hunting Percival Jet Provost T.1 began to replace the piston-engined Provost in 1955. In this machine, the pupil pilot began basic training on jets, often after only a few hours air experience on piston-engined trainers. This photograph of the prototype Jet Provost, serial XD674, was taken on 25 August 1954.*

Source: RAF Museum colour slide P100113

Above: *The Air Training Corps, founded in 1941, has always been highly regarded by the RAF. This poster appeared in about 1959. Nowadays, 925 ATC squadrons encourage boys and girls to take an interest in aviation, their activities including evening lectures, visits to RAF stations and air museums, sports and even gliding.*

Source: RAF Museum (Crown copyright) P00356

Far right: *The British Aircraft Corporation Jet Provosts T.3, T.4 and T.5 followed the T.1 in succession, each with various improvements and developments. Provosts remain in service in the RAF's Flying Training Schools. This photograph is of T.5 serial XW319, 3 F.T.S.*

Source: RAF Museum colour slide PO18685

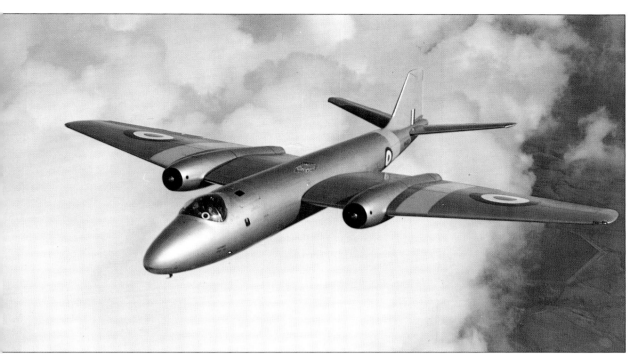

Left: *The dual-control English Electric Canberra T.4 entered service in 1954. This photograph, taken in September 1952, is of the prototype WN467.*

Source: RAF Museum colour slide P100254

Below: *In 1953, the Hunting Percival Provost began to replace the Percival Prentice as a basic trainer for pilots. It had a higher performance than its predecessor and four Provosts of the Central Flying School, known as The Sparrows, gave displays of formation aerobatics. The last machine continued in service until 1969. This photograph of the prototype, serial WE522, was taken on 21 May 1952.*

Source: RAF Museum colour slide P100515

Above: *Gloster Meteor F.7 trainers, photographed at Driffield in Yorkshire in October 1949. The last Gloster Meteor of the RAF was taken out of service in July 1961.*

Source: Keystone Collection

Left: *The Boulton Paul Balliol was originally designed as an advanced trainer with a turboprop engine, as shown in this photograph of the third prototype, serial VL935. However, a decision was made to revert to a piston-engined trainer as a successor to the North American Harvard. In 1952, piston-engined Balliols entered service at 7 Flying Training School at Cottesmore in Rutland. Soon afterwards, another decision was made to concentrate on jet trainers and the Balliol was phased out, until the last flew with the RAF in 1957.*

Source: RAF Museum PO18347

Above: *The Hawker Hunter T.7 was a modified version for dual-control training, entering service with the RAF's Operational Conversion Units from August 1958. Hunters* continued in service until June 1976. This photograph is of one of the first T.7s, serial XL586.

Source: Aviation Bookshop

Below: *A British Aircraft Corporation Lightning T.5, serial XS417, of the Lightning Training Flight.*

Source: RAF Museum PO18669

Above: *A British Aerospace Hawk T.1A of Central Flying School. Although it carries out the role of the RAF's standard advanced trainer, the T.1A is also a back-up aircraft in the U.K. defence system.*

Source: T. Malcolm English

Below: *The Hawker Siddeley Dominie T.1, a military version of the HS.125 executive jet, was the first jet aircraft employed by the RAF as a navigation trainer. It entered service in December 1965 and continues today at Finningley in Yorkshire. This photograph, of Dominie T.1 serial XS735 of 6 Flying Training School, was taken in August 1986 at Fairford in Gloucestershire.*

Source: RAF Museum colour slide PO51344

Left: *The Hawker Siddeley Gnat T.1 replaced de Havilland Vampire T.11s from February 1962 as the RAF's standard advanced trainer for jet fighters and bombers. It had two seats in tandem and was fully aerobatic with drop tanks. In 1964, Gnats of 4 Flying Training School at Valley in Anglesey formed an aerobatic team named the Yellowjacks, which was replaced by the Red Arrows during the following year. This photograph shows the third production Gnat, serial XM693.*

Source: RAF Museum colour slide P36009

Above: *The Scottish Aviation Bulldog began to replace the de Havilland Chipmunk as the RAF's standard ab initio trainer for pilots in April 1973. It is a sturdy piston-engined aircraft with two seats, used for teaching the full range of aerobatics, instrument flying and cross-country navigation. The trainer remains in RAF service. This photograph shows Bulldog T.1 serial XX515 of Central Flying School at Scampton in Lincolnshire.*

Source: RAF Museum colour slide PO18658

Below: *The two-seater trainer British Aerospace Harriers T.2 and T.4 entered service in July 1970.*

Source: RAF Museum colour slide PO18656

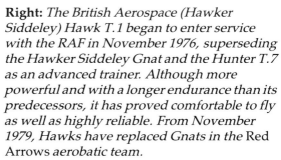

Above: *The Hawker Siddeley Gnat continued as the RAF's standard advanced trainer until replaced by the British Aerospace Hawk in 1978.*

Source: RAF Museum PO19098

Right: *The British Aerospace (Hawker Siddeley) Hawk T.1 began to enter service with the RAF in November 1976, superseding the Hawker Siddeley Gnat and the Hunter T.7 as an advanced trainer. Although more powerful and with a longer endurance than its predecessors, it has proved comfortable to fly as well as highly reliable. From November 1979, Hawks have replaced Gnats in the Red Arrows aerobatic team.*

Source: RAF Museum P3473

Above: *The Shorts Tucano turboprop trainer was selected as the RAF's successor to the Jet Provost, the decision being based partly on lower operating costs. Unlike its predecessor, it had tandem seating instead of the side-by-side seating employed for many years. The Tucano is now being introduced into the RAF training units.*

Source: RAF Museum PO22149

Below: *The Scottish Aviation Jetstream T.1 replaced the Vickers Varsity and entered Training Command in June 1973 for training pilots in twin-engined turboprops. Jetstreams continue in service at 6 Flying Training School at Finningley in Yorkshire. This photograph, of serial XX499, was taken at Upper Heyford in Oxfordshire.*

Source: RAF Museum PO51596

CHAPTER 18

RAF IN THE NINETIES

Below: *The Sepecat Jaguar, produced from an Anglo-French venture between British Aircraft Corporation and Dassault/Breguet, began to enter squadron service in March 1974. It is a single-seat aircraft, designed primarily for high speed and low-level ground attack, but it is also capable of classic air-to-air combat. Jaguars are now being replaced by Panavia Tornados. This photograph, of Jaguar G.R.1, serial XX119, of 226 Operational Conversion Unit, was taken at Upper Heyford in Oxfordshire in August 1986.*
Source: RAF Museum colour slide PO51609

Although the RAF of today is numerically small, it is equipped with some of the most advanced and costly machines yet devised for the purpose of defence or waging war. By comparison with the RAF at the end of the Second World War in Europe, which possessed an operational strength of 9,200 aircraft and over a million officers and airmen, the RAF in 1990 consisted of only fifty-two squadrons and seven flights equipped with front-line aircraft, with a total force of about 83,200 officers, airmen and airwomen. It shared in a defence budget which formed less than twelve per cent of the U.K.'s public expenditure. Air Chief Marshal Sir Peter Harding took over as Chief of Air Staff in February 1988, while Marshal of the Royal Air Force Sir David Craig was appointed as Chief of the Defence Staff.

Other than in Germany, the RAF's commitments overseas are not normally extensive. There are four flights in the Falklands, consisting of one of Phantoms for air defence, one of Hercules for tanker and reconnaissance, one of Chinook helicopters for air transport, and one of Sea King helicopters for search and rescue. These are supported by a squadron of the RAF Regiment equipped with Rapier missiles. In Belize, a flight of Harriers, a flight of Puma helicopters and half a squadron of the RAF Regiment discourage any territorial ambitions of the country's neighbours. Hong Kong is the home for a squadron of Wessex helicopters which work in close liaison with the army and police, in such tasks as search and rescue, troop lifting, disaster relief, prevention of smuggling and operations concerning illegal immigrants. Another squadron of Wessex helicopters is based at Cyprus, together with a squadron of the RAF Regiment equipped with light armour. Here, the RAF base of Akrotiri remains an important staging post for aircraft flying between Britain and Africa, the Middle East and Far East, while the island is frequently used by the RAF for training exercises.

In Germany, the RAF maintains seven squadrons of Tornado G.R.1s for strike/attack and one of G.R.1As for reconnaissance, together with two squadrons of Harrier G.R.3s for offensive support. The supersonic, two-seat Tornado G.R.1A is one of the RAF's most successful weapons in the constant need for tactical intelligence. It is fitted with the Infra-red Line Scanner (IRLS), with one sensor mounted in a blister under the fuselage and two more mounted sideways. These sensors measure the relative levels of thermal radiation, by both day and night, from horizon to horizon. The system is controlled by a computer and recorded with high resolution on video tapes. Although its two 27 mm cannons have been removed to make way for this equipment, the Tornado retains its offensive capability with a warload of 18,000 lb, which can include a nuclear weapon or laser-guided bombs. Pilots of these aircraft are required to fly at an altitude of about 100 feet at speeds in excess of 700 m.p.h., in all weathers, to avoid radar detection. For air transport in Germany, there is a squadron of Andovers as well as one of Pumas and one of Chinooks. For air defence, there are two squadrons of Phantoms supported by four squadrons of the RAF Regiment with Rapier missiles and one squadron with light armour.

At home, the RAF's Strike Command at High Wycombe in Buckinghamshire consists of three groups. With headquarters at Upavon in Wiltshire, No. 1 Group has

Left: *A Sepecat Jaguar G.R.1 of 54 Squadron, based at Coltishall in Norfolk, with two BAC Lightnings in the background.*
Source: T. Malcolm English

two squadrons of Tornado G.R.1s, three of Jaguar G.R.1s and one of Harriers, for strike/attack, reconnaissance and offensive support. The single-seat Jaguar is equipped with two 30 mm Aden cannons and five weapon stations which can carry up to 1,000 lb of bombs; these can be free-fall, cluster or laser-guided. It also has the Ferranti inertial navigation and attack system, which enables the pilot to navigate and deliver his weapons accurately, even at low level, and displays the aircraft's position to him on a moving map. The single-seat Harrier G.R.5 is coming into service, with a larger wing than its predecessor and capable of carrying double the payload for twice the distance. No. 1 Group also has twelve tanker and transport squadrons, equipped with Hercules, Tristars, VC10s, Victors and Andovers, as well as Chinook, Puma and Wessex helicopters. This air transport force maintains a twenty-four-hour-a-day service on a world basis, like a huge charter company working in constantly changing conditions. For ground defence, the RAF Regiment provides four squadrons with light armour and one field squadron. Three more field squadrons are manned by the R Aux AF.

With headquarters at Bentley Priory in Middlesex, No. 11 Group controls the air defence of the U.K., with five squadrons of Tornado F.3s and two of Phantoms, as well as a squadron of Shackletons for airborne early warning. The group also controls the ballistic early warning system and the aircraft early warning network. Its area extends from the coastal approaches to Norway and Iceland to the south-west approaches and the Scilly Islands. In this region, aircraft of the group sometimes provide a close 'escort service' for uninvited guests in the forms of the Russian Tupolev Tu-20 'Bear' or Tu-16 'Badger', although this type of intrusion has become less threatening with the détente between East and West. For ground defence in the group, the RAF Regiment mans two squadrons with Bloodhound missiles and two with Rapier missiles, while the R Aux AF element of the RAF Regiment provides a field squadron as well as another squadron armed with 35 mm twin-barrelled A.A. guns served by the Skyguard fire control equipment.

No. 18 Group, with headquarters at Northwood in Greater London, provides maritime patrols with four squadrons of Nimrods. Regrettably, the cost of maintaining this elegant aircraft are now so high that the remaining machines are likely to be run down and will disappear within a few years. There is as yet no arrangement for replacements for their role as maritime patrol and air-sea rescue aircraft. Until 1990, this group also maintained a squadron of Canberras for reconnaissance. This aircraft, dubbed the 'Cranberry' by the RAF, still continues its long service which began with its maiden flight in May 1949, but solely with Support Command. Canberra pilots point out that the machine can out-turn the Tornado at 50,000 feet, and they believe that it still has many years of useful life ahead. For strike/attack in the maritime role, No. 18 Group operates two squadrons of Buccaneer S2Bs, armed with either laser-guided bombs or Sea Eagle 'sea-skimming' air-to-surface missiles. For search and rescue, there is a squadron of Sea King helicopters and another of Wessex helicopters. For ground defence, there is a field squadron of the R Aux AF. The group also controls the Queen's Flight at Benson in Oxfordshire, with three BAe 146s and two Wessex helicopters.

Strike Command is in the middle of a major re-equipment programme. The Boeing Sentry will become the RAF's standard 'airborne early warning' aircraft, replacing the faithful Shackleton A.E.W.s of No. 11 Group. It had been intended originally that an A.E.W. version of the Nimrod would perform this role, but after mounting costs and much debate this programme was cancelled in December 1986. The Sentry, which has been in service with the USAAF since 1977 and with NATO since 1983, has an enormous 'rotodome' radar antenna above the fuselage which can detect aircraft flying at low level as well as high level. It operates as a command post for other aircraft and can remain on station for six hours when 1,000 miles from base. The RAF's first Sentry arrived at Waddington in Lincolnshire on 4 July 1990. It is an E-3D version, capable of two methods of air-to-air refuelling. This machine can also be equipped for maritime reconnaissance, and it is possible that Sentries will also replace the Nimrods of No. 18 Group.

Strike Command's new helicopter will be the multi-role EH 101, manufactured by EH Industries, a company formed in 1980 by Westland Helicopters and Augusta. The Royal Navy has ordered fifty EH 101s, to be known as the Merlin, and will use them in all-weather operations from land bases, as well as from large and small vessels and oil rigs. This naval version will be fitted with the latest detection equipment and will also be able to carry four homing torpedoes. The RAF has ordered twenty-five EH 101s to replace its Pumas as support helicopters during the 1990s. The new helicopter will improve the capacity of the RAF in providing mobility for the army, since it is able to transport thirty combat-equipped troops for an estimated distance of over 600 miles with standard fuel tanks. It will doubtless be used for other roles in Strike Command, RAF Germany and bases overseas.

One of the most ambitious projects which will affect the RAF is the European Fighter Aircraft (EFA), being developed by CMM and Dornier in Germany, Aeritalia in Italy, CASA in Spain and British Aerospace in the United Kingdom. Managed by Eurofighter

GmbH in Munich, the outcome will be a supersonic and very agile single-seat fighter, capable of short take-offs and landings, with a combat radius of about 320 miles. It is being designed mainly for the air-to-air role but will be also capable of ground attack. It is expected that large-scale production will begin in 1993. Deliveries of nearly 800 aircraft are expected to begin in 1996, subject to any political rethinking. In the RAF, the EFA will serve with Strike Command, replacing the ageing Phantoms and Jaguars. It will also replace the Phantoms in Germany, where it is believed that it will be more than a match for the equivalent Russian fighters, and will serve in RAF bases around the world. Equipped with the latest developments in avionics and most up-to-date weapons systems, it is designed for a service life of twenty-five years.

The RAF is being equipped with even more sophisticated and specialist weaponry. One of the objectives is to reduce the enemy's ability to bring down RAF aircraft, by the use of such weapons as the Martel anti-radar missile with which the maritime Buccaneers of No. 18 Group are equipped. The RAF has also obtained the Alarm (air-launched anti-radar missile) for a similar use overland. This enables the Tornados to create a corridor in the enemy's defences through which attacking RAF aircraft can penetrate. A forthcoming weapon is the ARD (anti-radiation drone), a slow-speed drone launched from the ground which will suppress the air defence systems of enemy aircraft and enable them to be tackled by the RAF's interceptors. This is expected to be in service shortly.

A weapon which has recently come into service with the RAF's Tornado G.R.1s is the JP233 cluster bomb, a dispenser containing SG357 explosive devices, which produce craters in runways, together with HB876 explosives, which prevent the enemy from effecting repairs for a period. The RAF's anti-tank (or armoured vehicle) weapon is the BL755, which contains 147 bomblets delivered on the principle of shotgun pellets but at very high velocity. An even more effective version of this weapon, designed to penetrate any advanced armour of the future, will enter service in the mid 1990s.

For the purpose of destroying static targets such as bridges, power stations or oil refineries, the RAF has a so-called 'smart' bomb, the laser-guided Paveway. The laser enables the bomb, after the target has been pinpointed by the acquisition system of one aircraft, to be delivered with precise accuracy by another aircraft. A similar bomb, capable of being launched at low level further away from the target, is expected to enter service shortly. This new bomb will be developed further so that it incorporates a seeker capable of recognizing its target. Fitted in its bombs, the RAF has what is regarded as the most effective fuse in the world, the multi-function bomb fuse (MFBF).

The RAF will also procure 'stand-off' weapons, which can be delivered from outside the range of some of the enemy's defences. For fixed targets, the RAF is obtaining for its Tornados the modular stand-off weapon (MSOW), which is being developed by five NATO countries. Another version of this weapon, designed for mobile targets, is also being developed.

Above: *Sepecat Jaguar G.R.1 of 41 Squadron, based at Coltishall in Norfolk.*
Source: T. Malcolm English

Left: *The pilots and Hawk T.1s of the Red Arrows constitute the RAF's premier display team of today, performing precise and intricate manoeuvres with nine aircraft. First formed with Gnats in 1965, the Red Arrows received their Hawks in the winter of 1979/80. The team has become a symbol of both flying skill and high standard of engineering. It has made an enormous contribution to the prestige of the RAF throughout the world. This photograph was taken at Mildenhall in Suffolk on 24 May 1986.*
Source: RAF Museum colour slide PO50519

Although it was hoped that the RAF's formidable array of aircraft and weaponry would never be put to the test in war, world events were to determine otherwise, after Iraq invaded Kuwait on 2 August 1990 and then announced that it had annexed the country. The RAF began to make plans immediately, since Britain was one of the thirty coalition countries intent on implementing the resolutions of the United Nations and removing Iraq from this sovereign state.

The British code-named the entire enterprise operation 'Granby', while to the Americans it was at first operation 'Desert Shield'. A week after the invasion, the RAF sent five Mobile Air Movements Squadron teams to the area by transport aircraft, together with cargo handling equipment. Two of these handling teams were sent to Dhahran in Saudi Arabia, in order to receive a squadron of Tornados, while five were sent to Akrotiri in Cyprus in order to reinforce this staging post. Shortly afterwards, two more teams were sent to Thumrait in Oman, to receive a squadron of Jaguars. Equipment was loaded by these teams at the RAF stations of Coltishall in Norfolk, Wittering in Northamptonshire and Coningsby in Lincolnshire. The pressure on the transport squadrons at Lyneham in Wiltshire was immense, but the work of moving equipment and troops was carried out smoothly. The combat aircraft flew out to the area, together with Victor K2 refuelling tankers.

After international sanctions had been applied to Iraq and all diplomatic efforts had failed, the coalition forces began air operations in the early hours of 16 January 1991, under the American operation 'Desert Storm'. The air attacks had been preceded by intelligence provided by satellite photographs, decrypting of Iraqi communications signals, and reconnaissance by high-flying American TR-1s and Boeing Sentries. Although the RAF's contribution was numerically small by comparison with that of the USAF, the squadrons were allocated one of the most important and dangerous tasks of the campaign – the neutralisation of the enemy's airfields and aircraft. The Alarm anti-radar missiles, which had been undergoing evaluation trials, were almost certainly used by Tornado F-3s and Jaguars to blind enemy defences while the Tornado G.R.1s delivered attacks with JP233 cluster bombs on runways and Paveway 'smart' bombs against aircraft bunkers. Jaguars also joined in attacks with laser-guided bombs, dive-bombing from heights of 15,000 feet. Then Buccaneer S2Bs of No. 18 Group were also sent from Lossiemouth in Morayshire to the Gulf, partly to act as target designators for the Tornados and partly to carry out their own bombing attacks. By 12 February, the RAF had dropped 2,000 of their 1,000 lb bombs on various military targets such as bunkers and bridges, and further consignments of these weapons arrived by sea. Air refuelling for the fighter-bombers was carried out by Victor tankers. The technical superiority of the RAF and USAF over the equipment supplied to the Iraqis by the Russians became startlingly apparent.

The Lynx helicopters of Fleet Air Arm, operating from British destroyers, made a valuable contribution to the air war by destroying Iraqi naval vessels with their Sea Skua missiles. It is possible that Nimrod aircraft of No. 18 Group located and identified some of these enemy vessels.

Below: *the Panavia Tornado must be classed as the premier aircraft of today's RAF. First introduced as an operational aircraft in January 1982, it is a swing-wing tactical strike aircraft capable of operating just above ground level with a formidable range of weaponry. The guidance system on board the aircraft enables the crew to penetrate deep into enemy territory in all weathers and deliver their warload with precision. This photograph is of the second prototype Tornado F.2, ZA267, in April 1983.*
Source: RAF Museum colour slide PO15198

Above: *A Tornado F.3 of 11 Squadron, based at Leeming in Yorkshire.*
Source: T. Malcolm English

Below: *A Tornado F.2 of 229 Operational Conversion Unit, based at Coningsby in Lincolnshire.* Source: T. Malcolm English

Unfortunately, six Tornados were lost during these operations. However, coupled with intense bombing from medium and high level by US bombers, the attacks were so effective that many of the surviving Iraqi aircraft, such as the Su-24s, MiG-29s and Mirages, were forced to flee the country for internment in Iran. Iraq was then bereft of any air cover for her ground forces and was also without reliable intelligence as to the movement of coalition ground forces.

When the ground war began in the early morning of 24 February, under the American operation 'Desert Sabre', the air supremacy of the coalition forces proved a potent factor. Within three days, armoured columns had routed and surrounded the Iraqi forces in Kuwait and southern Iraq. As the enemy columns attempted to withdraw to Baghdad, they were subjected to an accurate and devastating bombardment from the air and the ground, on a scale which the world had never seen before. The RAF's combat aircraft joined in these attacks, with the Jaguars using CRV7 rockets. The Iraqi forces suffered enormous casualties and collapsed. Large numbers of their troops surrendered, while casualties among the coalition forces were amazingly light. With the enemy defeated, the offensive was suspended on 28 February. The Chief of the Defence Staff, Sir David Craig, sent a message to Strike Command at High Wycombe, which included these words:

"Today's suspension of hostilities after one of the most outstanding, successful and impressive campaigns in warfare is a moment for congratulation and thanksgiving. Under your leadership all the forces and staffs of Operation Granby have performed superbly."

Once again, the RAF has served its country with skill and courage, but there is some doubt about its future role. Since April 1975, Strike Command has been allocated to NATO's Supreme Allied Commander Europe (SACEUR), but the political and military developments during 1990 have resulted in a decrease in tension between East and West. It seems possible that this will result in large-scale cuts in military expenditure and the RAF will lose more of its squadrons. There is no doubt, however, that the RAF will continue to maintain and improve its technical superiority as well as to provide such a high mobility that it is able to strike any aggressor in the right place and at the same time, over land, sea and in the air. No matter what the twists and turns of world politics, the RAF, with its excellent standards and distinguished history, will always be ready to serve both NATO and its country.

Left: *The experience of the Falklands War brought into prominence the need for both air refuelling and long-range transport in the RAF. Nine Lockheed Tristar airliners were purchased, all for serveice with 216 Squadron, which was re-formed at Brize Norton in Oxfordshire. The Tristar K.1 is a tanker/ freighter, while the K.C.2 is a tanker/passenger aircraft. This photograph of serial ZD948 was taken in 1983, while still in the passenger role and before conversion to the K.1 configuration.*
Source: RAF Museum PO18299

Above: *A Hawker Siddeley Buccaneer S.2 of 208 Squadron, photographed at Lakenheath in Suffolk on 12 July 1986.*
Source: RAF Museum PO52159

Right: *Buccaneer S.2s of 12 Squadron, based at Lossiemouth in Morayshire, on 'escort duties' with a Tupolev Tu-20 (Bear), a Russian maritime and reconnaissance aircraft which had been picked up by RAF radar.*
Source: T. Malcolm English

Left: *The Boeing E.3A Sentry was ordered from the U.S.A. in 1986 as the RAF's new early-warning aircraft, following the Ministry of Defence's decision to cancel the Nimrod A.E.W., which had been under development for several years. It is expected to come into service in 1990, when it will replace the Avro Shackletons which are still performing this role. This photograph of LX-N90456 of NATO's early-warning force was taken at Mildenhall in Suffolk on 24 May 1986.*
Source: RAF Museum PO50719

Right: *A McDonnell Douglas Phantom F.4 of 29 Squadron. This squadron has since been equipped with Panavia Tornado F.3s.*
Source: T. Malcolm English

Below: *Hawker Siddeley Harrier G.R.3s of 3 and 4 Squadrons, in the engineering wing hangar at Gutersloh in West Germany during 1981.*
Source: T. Malcolm English

Above: *McDonnell Douglas Harpoon air-to-surface missile. This sea-skimming anti-shipping weapon has a range of seventy-five miles, and several are carried in the bomb-bays of the RAF's Nimrods.*
Source: Jeremy Flack/Aviation Photographs International

Above: *British Aircraft Corporation Rapier ground-to-air missile, photographed in the Falklands. Since 1972, these missiles have been used by the RAF Regiment in defence of airfields against low-flying attack.*
Source: Jeremy Flack/Aviation Photographs International

Left: *The RAF operators of a Rapier missile.*
Source: Jeremy Flack/Aviation Photographs International

Below: *A British Aerospace BAe 146 C.C.2 of the Queen's Flight. The Queen first flew in one of these VIP aircraft on 2 August 1986. A BAe 146 was employed on the internal flights during her visit to China the following October.*
Source: Jeremy Flack/Aviation Photographs International

Right: *Four sections of Phantoms flying over Buckingham Palace during the 50th anniversary celebrations of the Battle of Britain, on Saturday 15 September 1990.*
Source: Jeremy Flack/Aviation Photographs International

Below: *A mock-up of the European Fighter Aircraft, now being developed by Britain, West Germany, Italy and Spain.*
Source: Jeremy Flack/Aviation Photographs International

Above: *Troops deploying from a Puma HC1 helicopter of the RAF, on manoeuvres at Ras al Gar in Saudi Arabia. Pumas were camouflaged in 'desert sand'. The rotor blades were temporarily removed, and the helicopters were then flown out to the Gulf in transport aircraft.*
Source: Crown copyright (RAF), print from M.A.R.S. Lincs

Below: *A Chinook Mk I helicopter of the RAF, This is the RAF's heavy lift helicopter, of great value in combined operations.*
Source: Crown Copyright (RAF), print from M.A.R.S. Lincs

Above: *Lockheed Tristar multi-role transport/ tanker of 216 Squadron, at Palermo, painted in the washable camouflage colour 'desert sand'. These aircraft were used to carry troops and freight to the Gulf, as well as for air-to-air refuelling. By early Janurary 1991, the RAF and charter aircraft had airlifted about 30,000 British troops to the Gulf.*
Source: Jeremy Flack/Aviation Photographs International

Left: *The short version of the Lockheed Hercules, the C1, being camouflaged in 'desert sand' at Lyneham in Wiltshire. This aircraft has a refuelling probe. Hercules C1s, together with the 'stretched' version, the C3, bore much of the burden in transporting personnel and freight to the Gulf. A Hercules of 47 Squadron was the first RAF aircraft to land at Kuwait airport after the liberation of the country.*
Source: Jeremy Flack/ Aviation Photographs International

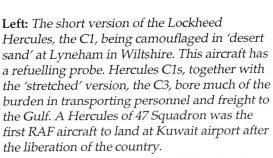

Left: *A Tornado F3 of the RAF, with standard European grey camouflage, flying from Dhahran over Saudi Arabia. It is fitted with Sidewinder air-to-air missiles beside the fuel tanks, as well as Sky Flash air-to-air missiles, for longer range, recessed under the fuselage. These fighter aircraft had little opportunity to engage in air-to-air combat, since many of the Iraqi fighters took refuge in Iran, where they were interned.*

Source: Crown Copyright (RAF), print from M.A.R.S. Lincs.

Below: *Two Tornado GR1s of the RAF, camouflaged in 'desert sand', flanked by two Tornado F3 fighters in standard grey camouflage. A laser target designator can be seen beneath the fuselage of each GR1, while the F3s are carrying air-to-air missiles. The photograph was taken from one of the F3s.*

Source: T. Malcolm English

Right: *A Nimrod MR1 of No. 18 Group, flying from Kinloss in Morayshire. A detachment of Nimrod MR2Ps, the version fitted with the more advanced 'Searchwater' electronic equipment, was sent to the Gulf to carry out maritime patrols as well as for the search and rescue of downed airmen. The Nimrod can also carry Sidewinder air-to-air missiles and Harpoon anti-shipping missiles.*
Source: Jeremy Flack/Aviation Photographs International

Below: *A Tornado F3 of the RAF, in standard camouflage, carrying Sidewinder and Sky Flash missiles, flying from Dhahran in Saudi Arabia. Detachments of several Tornado squadrons, both from the UK and from Germany, were sent to the Gulf.*
Source: Crown Copyright (RAF), print from M.A.R.S. Lincs.

Left: *A Jaguar GR1 deployed in the Gulf, with a laser target designator in the nose, 1,000 lb bombs in tandem under the wings, and overwing Sidewinder missiles mounted above the bomb pylons. The devices on the outboard pylons are intended to deceive enemy radar and missiles. These aircraft dived from 15,000 feet to bomb Iraqi positions during the Gulf War.*

Source: Crown Copyright (RAF), print from M.A.R.S. Lincs.

Below: *Two Jaguar GR1s refuelling from a VC10 tanker, with a Tornado GR1 in the foreground, flying near the Gulf war zone. The Tornado and the Jaguars are painted in 'desert sand'. The VC10 is painted in 'hemp', which is now the RAF's standard colour for this type of aircraft.*

Source: Crown Copyright (RAF), print from M.A.R.S. Lincs.

Above: *The Eurofighter will provide the backbone of the RAF interceptor force. It can carry a range of weaponry, including ASRAAM and Sidewinder air-to-air missiles.*
Source: Jeremy Flack/Aviation Photographs International

Left: *Replacement of the aging C-130K Hercules became an RAF priority and 25 of the much-improved C-130Js were ordered as the Hercules C.5 and stretched C.4 (shown).*
Source: Jeremy Flack/Aviation Photographs International

Below: *The Harrier GR.7 has replaced the GR.3 variant in RAF service. With a larger airframe and more powerful engine, it is capable of delivering an improved warload over a greater distance.*
Source: Jeremy Flack/Aviation Photographs International

THE RAF BENEVOLENT FUND'S BATTLE OF BRITAIN
50TH ANNIVERSARY APPEAL

In the summer of 1940, for four fateful months the future of Europe lay in the hands of a few courageous men.

They fought, and they succeeded, against all the odds.

One man in three failed to return.

Of the survivors, many are still alive today.

Between 1939-1945, some 1.75 million personnel served in the Royal Air Force, and the organisations associated with it.

Fifty years later the survivors of these, and their dependants, in need of support from the Royal Air Force Benevolent Fund are peaking in number.

World War II veterans now account for two-thirds of the claims upon the Fund. Their needs will increase over the next decade, placing a huge demand on our resources. That's why in 1990, we launched our *Reach for the Sky* Appeal, with a target of £20 million.

The Fund aims to ensure that no current or former RAF serviceman, or his family, suffers from need or distress as a result of accident, injury or illness. There is no time or monetary limit to the help that we give.

Why We Need £20 Million

We are at a point where we have a considerable and growing deficit of expenditure over income. It is imperative that we rectify the situation very swiftly.

By raising £20 million, we will help overcome the problem not just temporarily, but for the foreseeable future.

With our funds, as well as giving financial help for specific projects of equipment, we also commit ourselves to long-term help and care.

For example, we provide residential accommodation and convalescent homes for partially disabled and elderly former servicemen and their dependants, and serving RAF members and their families.

We provide block grants to institutions which assist us – over £500,000 was awarded to them in 1988;

Housing for widows with dependant children, an independent preparatory boarding school administered by the Fund, for RAF personnels' children, assistance with fees for further education and general welfare, from re-roofing a house to assisting with personal maintenance.

The Fund distributes all donations to the widows of RAF personnel, disabled RAF personnel and children and dependants of serving and former RAF personnel.

Of every £1 of total income, at least 85p goes to those in need. In supporting this Appeal, you'll be in very good company – helping to give an assured and dignified future to those who fought so courageously to give us our freedom.

"Reach for the Sky"
PO Box 1940
Fairford
Gloucestershire
GL7 4NA
England

RAF Benevolent Fund
67 Portland Place
London
W1N 4AR
England